dedicated
to my children -
and the
"wind beneath my wings"

Published by:
Champlin Fighter Museum Press
Falcon Field, Mesa, Arizona 85205

ISBN 0-942548-58-2
Printed in the United States of America

Library of Congress Cataloging in Publication Data:

Armstrong, Donald—1919 -

Bibliography: none
No index

LOC # 94-079810

INTRODUCTION

There's a saying that you're never too old to learn, and I want to say that this old fighter pilot certainly learned a lot from Don Armstrong's memoir. Those of us who were lucky enough to get out to the shooting end of the war in the Pacific just took it for granted that we'd have good airplanes for chasing Zeros. But I doubt if many of us gave a thought to all the hard work behind the scenes so that we'd have those terrific machines like the Vought F4U Corsair.

Any pilot will appreciate Don's sentiments about flying – the way it gets in your blood and becomes the center of your life. But beyond that, anyone who was ever a part of our nation's great aviation industry will appreciate the credit Don gives to thousands of anonymous folks – mechanics, manufacturers and designers who worked so long and hard to give us young bucks the weapons we needed to win the war in the air.

I know that the fighter pilots who flew the Corsair like I did with my boys in VMF-115 will find many surprises here. Without a doubt, the biggest was Don's work on contract approval flights of the Goodyear FG-1 version of the Corsair – months after we were flying those airplanes in combat! Not even WWII was enough to convince the paper shufflers in Washington, D. C., that if an airplane was good enough to go to combat, it was already pretty well proven – whatever the contract said!

Then, of course, there's Don's work on the F2G-1 "Super Corsair." His fine work as a factory test pilot brought him close to the edge more than once, but he got the job done just the same. That same kind of dedication is evident in this book, and I commend it to Americans of all ages.

Joe Foss
May 1994

CONTENTS

ACKNOWLEDGEMENTS

As you will read in the Preface, the primary impetus for writing this book came from a series of events related to (and while visiting) the Champlin Fighter Museum in Mesa, Arizona: the enthusiastic welcome that I received; the endless stream of excited questions everyone had; the unmasked surprise and awe on a young man's face - when he turned around and saw the person - THE TEST PILOT - whose picture/story he'd just seen on the "Test Pilots' Wall" (during one of my visits to the facility). All of these factors tipped the scale - convinced me that there were, in fact, people out there who might enjoy, be interested in, my story.

After making the commitment to myself and close family to "give it my best shot," I knew, right away, there would be many people to whom I'd want to say "Thanks" - and the number is legion. But, without a doubt, the one who should be acknowledged first is YOU - the reader. It is your interest in - and "love affair" with - aviation and its stories that prompted you to pick up this book, and I hope in the reading you will find yourself vicariously sharing some of my adventures with me. I appreciate that you want to know how it was "way-back-when." And I am deeply grateful that you are willing to accept this story as I tell it - the way that I remember it!

The first person I contacted at CFM was the shop and restoration manager, Dave Goss. I think that he already knows what an impact his sincere interest has made. Its owner, Doug Champlin, was the first non-family, professional person to agree that my story might make a book. He has offered encouragement throughout my writing, has agreed to be its publisher and, far more importantly, made me feel like a member of his extended family.

Doug's secretary Lynda Neves; winter-resident-author Barrett Tillman; and vintage aircraft restorer, Jim Appleby, also deserve a very special "Thanks." Without knowing anything about me, or my past, they invited me into their midst, and have continued to make me feel like a welcome member of the fraternity.

Barrett soon became much more than an interested by-stander and has been involved in editing the manuscript. He patiently answered the myriad of questions I had about punctuation, style and consistency. His timely suggestions have saved hours of work and reams of paper.

It was also at the Museum that I met Pat Bourque, whose beautiful drawing is on the dedication page.

Less than six months prior to my first visit to Mesa I, somewhat reluctantly, had agreed to go back to Patuxent Naval Air Station - just to see how much things had changed. It was while making the arrangements that I first "met" Pax Public Affairs Director John Romer. When circumstances kept John from being my guide, Fred Bradshaw ably filled in for him and gave me the red-carpet treatment: an introduction to Capt. Thom Bernsen and Lt. Col. Robert Price, U.S. Naval Test Pilot School; a tour of the Anechoic Chamber and Carrier Suitability Department; my first visit to the Tracking Station and Telemetry Data Center; lunch at the officers' club with Aleck Loker, NAS Executive Director, and several other wonderful experiences.

As a result of this visit, I was invited to return for the 50th Anniversary Gala (April 1993) and there was privileged to meet many other wonderful, supportive people: Capt. Roger Hill, Commanding Officer; Tom McCaughey, Chesapeake Test Range; Pat Hall and Aurora Moynihan, TID staff; Jack Nial, executive director of the Naval Air Test and Evaluation Museum; and David Seeman, historian. Although I didn't have an opportunity to be introduced to them, I am also grateful to Rear Admiral Barton Strong, Commander, Naval Air Warfare Center (Aircraft Division), and Capt. Joseph Dyer, Director, Flight Test and Engineering Group, for graciously giving permission for me to visit and interview the personnel in their departments.

Throughout all of the planning and coordinating, John Romer has proved to be not only an invaluable resource, but a wonderful friend - and I owe him a special "Thanks!" He and Aurora Moynihan also spent untold hours obtaining a copy of the carrier suitability report on the Grumman F9F-2.

In Chapters 17 and 18, I mention (in depth) the contributions of three others: John William "Bill" Rymer

(Telemetry Data Center) for his contribution, with text and pictures, to the "Then and Now" chapter and Joe Carbonaro and Joe Kleponis (Manned Flight Simulator) for teaching "an old dog one new trick!" These three gentlemen were sensitive, cooperative and extremely knowledgeable and articulate. It was a great privilege to be with them, and I am deeply indebted to them for sharing of their time, expertise and - most of all - themselves.

By now my ego had been inflated almost beyond my wildest imagination. And the reality of the research that would be necessary had begun to sink in. The F2G project had been, by far, my most significant "claim to fame." I would tell the story of my experiences with the Super Corsair, but I wanted to include some of the interesting facts about what had happened to these great fighters after the war. A very good friend and Lloyd Shaw Foundation associate, Henry "Hank" Caruso, spent hours at the Western Reserve Historical Society (the recipient of much of the memorabilia/information re: the National Air Races prior to 1950) and provided me with the early-racing facts and pictures that I have included in Appendix I. A visit to Chino, California, where I met Steve Hinton, helped me complete the data.

Nicholas "Nick" Hauprich wrote a "letter-to-the-editor" to *Aviation*, which by happenstance I saw, stating that he had done extensive collecting and research on the F2G project. (He was an aeronautical engineer at Goodyear at the same time I was there.) He, working together with Ken Olinger, had been able to salvage many drawings, manuals and reports to which he provided me access. Another researcher, Rodney Williams (whose father was a GAC engineer during the project), sent me some of the material that he has collected. Nick Veronico (he doing research for a book - *F4U Corsair)* and I shared research - and researchers. I also had been given the address of D. A. Beck, one of the key project personnel who had accompanied me to the Fighter Conference at the Naval Air Test Center in 1944. I had contacted him to see if he would share some of his memories with me. His son replied, in a letter dated January 12, 1993, "My father... was looking forward to talking with you... However, he passed away early on the morning of January 8, 1993."

Heading the "I-must-include" list was the story about Dr. William Frederick "Doc" Gerhardt - the person responsible for teaching me the procedures of flight-test. While I remembered him and the invaluable lessons that he taught me, I did not remember many of the details of his personal life. I had a copy of a letter he sent to Wright Field (USAAF), which indicated he had worked there, so I contacted David Menard, historian at the USAF Museum, Wright-Patterson AFB, Ohio, and he graciously put me in touch with Diane Cornelisse (History Office, Aeronautic System Center). Diane not only had material that would greatly benefit me - endowed to Wright-Patterson by Mrs. W. F. (Darlene Crist) Gerhardt - she had known and visited with Mrs. Gerhardt.

Now, with a general outline, as well as concise and thorough informa-tion on the two BIG periods of my career, it was time to start filling in the gaps.

Florence Haskins (Virginia Aviation Museum, Sandston, Virginia), John William "Jack" Ramsay (New England Aviation Museum, Windsor Locks, Connecticut), Joshua Stoss (Cradle of Aviation Museum, Garden City, New York) and the staff at the Marine Air/Ground Museum (Quantico, Virginia) and Planes of Fame (Chino, California) have earned a very special "Thanks" for taking time to provide courteous service, vital data - and some great pictures - to me and my research assistant.

In addition, Renald Fortier, researcher, at the National Aviation Museum (Ottawa, Ontario) and Ray Wagner, archivist, at the San Diego Aerospace Museum (San Diego, California) went at least one "extra mile" - especially in locating those seemingly "impossible-to-find" photos. And I am extremely grateful.

The source of all pictures (including those in my personal collection) will be identified in the captions, but I also want to publicly express my "Thanks" to the following for helping in the "great picture search": Lois Lovisolo (Grumman), Mrs. B. D. (June) Maule and Chester Boltz.

The initial research, and preliminary rough-draft, of Chapter 16 was done by my wife, Marie, and I am most grateful for this contribution.

Another long-time dance associate, Chip Stewart, and Ned Preston (FAA agency historian and public affairs, Washington, D. C.) provided the background on the history of the CAA/FAA used in Chapter 9. Helen Samuels, archivist at MIT, found information re: the Radiation Lab and Dr. T. W. Bonner. And Tom Smith, executive director of the Society for Experimental Test Pilots (Lancaster, California), took time to look up the particulars of Lloyd Child's life, and death. (Lloyd is one of the few of my peers who survived his career!)

This list can not be ended without mentioning several other aviation enthusiasts, whose help and support have meant so much: John Cournoyer, Kevin Grantham (Lightning Historical Research), David Plaunt (dosent, National Aviation Museum, Ottawa, Ontario) and Wayne Valey (aviation author).

There remains only one group of people to be acknowledged - by far the largest consortium to assist in any single phase of the research: those who have tried to piece together the puzzle of the Grumman story (Chapter 14). For months we have tried - sometimes hopefully, sometimes frustratingly - to locate further information re: the company and tests I did on the Grumman F9F-2 Panther in 1951-1952. It is with heart-felt gratitude that I thank "Schoney" Schonenberg, Dr. William Armstrong, Rene Francillon, Corwin "Corky" Meyer, Elizabeth Garges, Shirley Garrett, Rebecca Livingston, Rebecca Collier, Richard von Doenhoff and (mentioned previously) John Romer, Bill Rymer, Doug Champlin, Barrett Tillman, Lois Lovisolo, Aurora Moynihan, Jack Nials and David Seeman.

All of the persons listed above have been invaluable in their contributions to *I Flew Them First*. However, Rusty Wright is the man who made it technically possible: he took me by the hand and taught me how to use a computer. There is no way to adequately say "Thanks!"

One person, more than any other, created this book with me. She devoted over a year to painstakingly researching mountains of information; chronologically compiling dates, events, names, addresses; and tracking down long-forgotten reports and photos. Without question, it was she who inspired me to overcome my frustrations, accept the inevitable delays; encouraged me to continue and then, patiently and with great kindness, proofread my work. She has been a very close personal friend, not only to me but to all of my family, for more than thirty years. The fact that our friendship remains intact, after working with me on this project, is a tribute to her tact and understanding. Without her, it is doubtful that I would have found the strength and will to complete this book. Therefore, to my dear friend Elizabeth H. "Libba" Grey, I extend my deepest and most sincere thanks.

"Don, you must write a book about your flying career."

If I've heard that statement once, I've heard it two hundred times. But, for all of these years, I didn't want to write a book. I knew my career had been unique and, if I wanted to do so, I felt confident I could tell my story well. But I dreaded reliving the tragedies - the deaths of so many of my friends and peers. And I was reluctant to let "just anyone" penetrate my cultivated shell of privacy. I was more than willing to share my joys but, like most people, I was hesitant to reveal my moments of terror and tears. And I couldn't do one without the other.

To my family and friends who kept after me to document my story, I freely acknowledged that my flying career spanned one of the most exciting times in aviation history. World War II had inspired new ideas and designs and nurtured their growth by force-feeding them with deaths and dollars. From 1939 through 1946 more airplanes were built and flown than anyone could have ever imagined. And the world will never again duplicate this massive expansion, because advancing technology has made the unit cost totally prohibitive.

My career bracketed these years perfectly, giving me the opportunity to do things that very few others had been able to accomplish. Unlike most of my peers who flew primarily for one, or perhaps two, companies, I was a test pilot for the military, civil service and four different manufacturers. I flight tested everything from tiny target drones to C-54 Skymasters. I flew one-, two-, three- and four-engined aircraft: trainers, fighters, bombers, flying boats; planes on wheels, floats and skis; and a myriad of civilian aircraft. I flew planes designed and built years before I was born - and did my last flight tests on the famous Grumman jet fighter, the F9F-2. You could probably count on the fingers of one hand those few pilots who flew as many different designs and types of planes as I did - and have fingers left over. Moreover, it is extremely unlikely that any pilot will ever have the opportunity even to approach anything close to this in the future.

Even though I conceded my story had merit, it took a fortunate coincidence to get me started. Of the many airplanes I flew, my favorite fighter was the Goodyear F2G "Super Corsair." It was the most powerful single-engine, propeller-driven aircraft in the world, and I had been its test pilot throughout the entire project. The only existent, original-configuration F2G is in the Champlin Fighter Museum in Mesa, Arizona, and I went there to see it.

CFM really opened my eyes. I had visited many other aircraft museums, including this country's most famous ones, and none compared to this. Everything is beautifully and spaciously displayed in immaculate surroundings and combines about fifteen WW I and ten WW II fighters, four postwar jets and many unusual aircraft engines. It also houses the J. Curtis Earl Automatic Weapons Collection and, because it is the home of the American Fighter Aces Association, the walls of the hangars are adorned with over six hundred photos and biographies of aces. Oddly enough, Champlin's beautiful F2G turned out to be one of two manufactured that I had not flown (No. 88454), a true production model, flight-checked before delivery to the Navy by my friend Art Chapman.

The museum is owned by a truly fine gentleman, Doug Champlin, and it is evident that he is an inspiration to all of his staff. His restoration manager, Dave Goss, is a happy and meticulous young man who instantly reminded me of my most talented crew chiefs.

Serendipitously, I happened to be there on a Friday, the day Doug has lunch with Dave and many of the rest of the staff; and I was delighted to be invited to join the group along with another friend of theirs, Barrett Tillman. Barrett is the author of three military flying novels and a number of excellent nonfiction works dealing with aviation history.

For me this little, informal get-together was wonderful. I was surrounded by people, most of whom were immersed in the history of flying, who seemed to be sincerely interested in me and some of my stories about the planes I had flown and the people I had worked with. I can only compare what happened there to the sensation of "popping out" into the beautiful, clear, smooth air "on top" after climbing up through a dark, thick and turbulent overcast. I finally was convinced that people were, indeed, interested in what had happened fifty years ago and - because my career had been so widely varied and I had survived - I could weave a story and bring to life how it was being a test pilot before, during and after those explosive years. Doug, Dave and Barrett, each in his own way, gave me that final, caring push and jump-started what so many friends have wanted me to do for years - tell my story: the ups, the downs; the successes, the failures - as I lived it, as I remember it.

Immediately after committing myself to do so, I knew exactly how I would like to present my story. The key word was "my." It would be a first-person, anecdotal narrative - a memoir - not another aviation treatise. I would try to bring readers right into my living room, in front of a softly-burning fireplace, and just talk to them on paper. I'd tell it like it was: the good and bad, the happy and sad, the fears and tears, and not be afraid to admit my mistakes or take credit when due.

My story needed to be entertaining for the non-pilot, yet technically detailed enough to satisfy the aviation buff. Though I knew there would be some omissions and errors, I'd do my level best to keep things straight by researching, as much as possible, in support of what I remembered.

I was certain that I could convey to a reader what I did during my career and that I could make the "hows and whys" reasonably clear. But I needed to do far more than that - I sincerely wanted to permit the reader to peek into my heart and soul, to feel vicariously what it was like to "fly them first."

And finally, a word about the title. For over fifty years I was (and still am) frequently invited to speak to schools, church and civic groups, scout troops or flying clubs. The first few times I entitled my presentations "We Fly Them First" because I talked about my peers, civilian test pilots, who invariably tested most planes before a military pilot ever flew them. In 1943 I also used this subject and title in a magazine article. Because this is primarily my story, I merely changed it to *I Flew Them First*.

So, welcome to my hearth - and I fervently hope you enjoy my adventures!

PROLOGUE

My formative years were greatly influenced by both sides of my family and, although I have no memory of either grandfather, I was fortunate to have both grandmothers with me into my middle teens.

My maternal grandmother was born in the United States of German-American parents and she, together with my mother and her family, instilled in me social graces, determination and a deeply-rooted appreciation of music and the arts. We had season seats in the Family Circle at the New York Metropolitan Opera and regularly attended many classical and contemporary theater performances in New York City. On dozens of Saturdays I spent my mornings in the Museum of Natural History or the Metropolitan Museum of Art.

Since, when I was only eight or nine years old, unescorted children were welcome at the Natural History museum, I frequently went there before meeting my dad for lunch. Dad's office was in the Grand Central Station building; so I often rode the train alone into the city, went upstairs to let him know I had arrived and then went to the museum. Later he would meet me there and we would go to some wonderful place for lunch.

Dad felt that my education should include learning how to conduct myself at the Commodore or the Waldorf Astoria Hotels, at one of his Clubs or at any of the delightful ethnic restaurants. Many times we'd be joined by one of his business associates or aviation friends and, although the conversations were never keyed to me as a "child," I'm sure they chose to speak in terms I could understand. I never remember eating a hamburger. Instead, I was always encouraged to try the "different" entrees, and certainly you can imagine the great pleasure this practice has given me as an adult in my world-wide travels. Looking back at it all, I realize that these lunches were a very special part of our relationship and just how much I looked forward to them. Now, of course, I recognize that Dad's subtle grooming gave me a tremendous edge over my peers, especially in my early professional years.

Whereas the majority of Dad's reading tended to be focused on scientific, mechanical or business-related subjects, Mother whetted my appetite for a wide variety of literature that remains with me to this day. She had been a teacher when she married and, during the depression years, returned to teaching in order to supplement Dad's much-reduced income. A lifetime love affair with reading made her acutely aware of reading deficiencies and she was one of the earliest pioneers in New York State's remedial-reading program. We shared her pride when she received state-wide recognition for her assistance in developing both a program and a machine that assisted in improving reading and comprehension skills.

When I was away from home a great deal, Mother gave my daughter Terry a room in her home; and her love and guidance exerted a tremendous influence on Terry's future. Mother would have been very pleased to know that Terry has become a superb teacher and that Terry's daughter, Kadie, is following the same path.

My paternal grandmother epitomized her Scottish-English heritage and, with my father and his siblings, reinforced my social graces with English tradition, cultivated my inherent inquisitiveness and infused me with an almost tangible desire for adventure and an unwavering sense of self-confidence. Being around Dad's aviation friends and spending time together at the New York Yacht Club and sailing regattas were comfortable experiences, even for a young boy and, since leaving the nest, I have never been in a social situation in which I did not feel totally at ease.

Both my parents contributed to my zest for living and each gave me immeasurable help along the way. My life remains enriched from their love and guidance, and I will continue to draw upon the philosophical foundations they formulated within me. But, insofar as my flying career was concerned, it was my dad who had the greatest influence on me.

My father, Archer Armstrong, was born on the Island of Barbados in the British West Indies. His father, a pharmacist, had come to the island from an area near the border of England and Scotland and soon had very successfully established himself - well enough to support his wife and six children in a very comfortable fashion. As a young man Dad enjoyed sailing, even taking his boat as far as Martinique. Soon, however, his insatiable curiosity and voracious reading created a longing to travel farther afield and, after finishing school, he was the first of the children to emigrate to the United States.

He was fascinated by almost anything new - especially those things which called for a combination of skill and daring - and it was logical for him to become involved in two pursuits which were unavailable to him in his youth - flying and motorcycle racing. He was quickly accepted into both circles because many early flyers were also motorcyclists, some of whom were trying to incorporate modified motorcycle engines into their flying machines.

One of the early members of The Aeronautic Society, Dad joined the group on February 18, 1910, and less than a month later was one of the founding members and a director of The National Model Aero Club whose initial meeting was held during March 1910. At

Pla "Dad"; Archer Armstrong, ca. 1913; racing publicity photo. (D. Armstrong collection)

approximately the same time he (with his brother, Murrell) became one of the early high-bank, board-track motorcycle racers and earned enough money racing to finance his flying.

Dad's reputation soon spread to promoters and sponsors in Europe, and he spent almost a year abroad racing and demonstrating an early French monoplane at "speed and aeronautical events." (From old photographs I think it was a Bleriot.) I remember him telling me that he had done so, but I cannot remember the name of an Italian plane he flew.

A friend and fellow motorcycle racer and builder, Glenn Curtiss, influenced Dad's decision to return to the States. But soon thereafter Dad was severely injured in a racing accident which left him with permanent, although partial, loss of strength and articulation of his left arm. Much of the humerus bone between the elbow and his shoulder had been destroyed, so he was faced with the unpleasant choice between an amputation just below the shoulder or a venturesome, unpredictable attempt at a bone graft. True to character, he chose the graft - and it worked. It ended his racing but, until his death, he remained an ardent supporter of aviation and maintained long-lasting friendships with pilots and builders, many of whom became world-famous and the "giants" who later nurtured and cultivated my childhood dreams and aviation career.

Dad had fostered my belief that those who are unwilling to try to turn their visions into reality are unlikely ever to experience the true joy of living. There's no question in my mind

that this philosophy was manifest in my dad's willingness to help me explore the questioning, wishful-thinking dreams of my childhood. Consider the following imaginative and innovative experiences he shared with me even before I had reached my teens.

His business supplied the compressed air used in such construction projects as the George Washington Bridge, Radio City and some of the tunnels under the Hudson and East Rivers. So when I expressed a desire to see the riveters working on the bridge span, he took me by the hand and walked me out - on a plank about twelve-inches wide - high above the river to watch the men at work. In those days rivets were heated until red-hot by a couple of men situated between three or four pairs of riveters. When a riveter was ready the "heater," using a pair of tongs, threw a hot rivet up to the rivet-boss, who would catch it in what they all called a "hat" - not unlike a large tomato can with a coffee-mug handle. That day the rivet-boss let me catch several of the rivets - I thought it was great fun! And I took a couple that I had caught myself home with me to show the kids at school.

When I wondered aloud what it was like to be a "sand-hog," Dad took me down into a caisson - out into the muddy hole - and showed me how a tunnel was being built underneath the river bottom. He explained how compressed air kept the mud and water out until the men dug away enough material so that more side plates could be installed. It amazed me to think that two different crews, working from opposite sides of the river, could be accurate enough to meet in the middle. Throughout my subsequent travels, whenever I drive through a similar tunnel, I remember with pleasure and admiration the dirty, sweaty-but-smiling faces of the men who called themselves "sand-hogs."

One day I went with Dad to a skyscraper construction site and admired the Mohawk Indians

working the "high-steel" many stories above the city streets. The next week he took me up to the top and we ate a sandwich-lunch along with the steelworkers - perched on a girder with our feet dangling down, just like the crew!

Whenever he could, Dad responded to my desire to see for myself how other people worked and lived or what made things function. And no matter what we cooked up, Mother seemed to trust us and wish us well. I remember only once when she showed any outward sign of distress or reluctance about Dad indulging one of my dreams, and Dad and I chuckled about it many times over the years. I wanted to go under water in a diving suit, and Dad arranged for me to accompany a diver who was working on a dock in the Hudson River. True, I was only going down about twenty feet, in a sheltered area and with a highly-qualified diver right next to me, but Mother didn't like the idea at all. I recall that I couldn't see a darn thing and it was muddy and hard to move, and that I did not like it. I was frightened, but at the same time I was glad to have done it. I still don't know what about it was distressing to me since, years later, I did a lot of deep scuba diving in the Caribbean and thoroughly enjoyed that.

I recount these things in order to show what a supportive parent my father was and how he encouraged me to inquire, investigate and indulge in my dreams. When I said, at a very early age, that I wanted to be a test pilot, Dad's attitude was simply if I wanted to badly enough, I could be. He, with Mother's help and support, instilled in me an absolute confidence that any reasonable goal was within my reach, as long as I was willing to devote myself fully to the task. Throughout my flying career I never felt that I could not do my job. I did recognize that any external factor - a structural failure, for example - could easily kill me. But test flying was my dream; it was within my power to turn it into reality, and I did. Thanks to both my parents, but mainly to the man who was Dad, I have experienced the true joy of living!

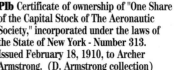

P1b Certificate of ownership of "One Share of the Capital Stock of The Aeronautic Society," incorporated under the laws of the State of New York - Number 313. Issued February 18, 1910, to Archer Armstrong. (D. Armstrong collection)

A man who has had good parents is twice blessed, first when they were alive and second for the memory of them.

Source unknown

CHAPTER 1

MY VERY EARLY YEARS
From Toddler to Travel Air

I was lucky. I grew up in the shadow of giants who held me in the palms of their hands! I was born (in New York City) at exactly the right time, and I couldn't have selected better parents. Born in 1919, I was fortunate to grow up being inspired by Eddie Rickenbacker and other air heroes of WW I, comic books like *Wings*, stories about the *Lafayette Escadrille*, "Lucky Lindy's" flight in the *Spirit of St. Louis*, and the presence of many famous pilots at our dinner table. Aviation literally surrounded me, and it would have seemed strange indeed had I chosen another career. By 1939, I had become an experienced commercial pilot and was exceptionally well suited to participate fully in the fantastic development and expansion of aviation created by World War II.

My dad, Archer Armstrong, completely understood my dreams because he'd been a pioneer aviator as early as 1910. My mother, Lillian Goldbacher Armstrong, was a loving, tolerant soul who was always there to support me in whatever direction I wanted to go. Imagine, if you can, growing up in the aura of aviation giants such as Jimmy

Collins, Clarence Chamberlin, Jimmy Doolittle, Wiley Post, Roscoe Turner, Amelia Earhart, Admiral Richard Byrd and others. They had befriended me because of my dad and now, more than six decades later, I fully realize that when Dad and I talked with them, they did not merely tolerate me, as "Archer's little boy," but instead went out of their way to encourage my ambitions. In retrospect, perhaps I was destined to become a test pilot.

In the depression years Dad and I stayed home a lot, building and flying special kites and rubber-band model airplanes. My preteen vocabulary included words like "dihedral, stability, stall," and I honestly understood such things as how lift and thrust overcome gravity and drag. We visited airports and I climbed in and out of all types of airplanes. Occasionally, I was given a ride (then we called it a "hop"), several times even sitting on the pilot's lap and holding the control stick with him.

Later I rode my bike to small private fields near our neighborhood and wiped the grease off any airplane I could get close to. In those days airplanes were always streaked with oil and grease

because the gaskets never seemed to overcome the expansion and contraction created by heat. At only eleven or twelve years old, I was swapping work (wiping, fueling, pumping tires, adding oil, cleaning cockpits) for a hop or, even better, some flight instruction.

One Friday evening I was delivering magazines on my bike and I saw an OX-5 Travel Air spiral down for a landing just a couple of miles from our home in Crestwood, New York. Early the next morning I set out to find where the plane might have landed. What I found was "Mr. Bill" (Walther) working on one of his two airplanes. Both were OX-5 Travel Air 2000s, one of which was a beautiful royal blue. The other was, as Mr. Bill put it, "a drab little lady with a crabby disposition." Each airplane, like a ship, has a distinct personality, but to me, because he let me work on them, they both were wonderful.

Mr. Bill had no family and seemed to enjoy having me around. I spent every available hour cleaning

---

1 Travel Air 2000, "Old Elephant Ears"; tandem, two-cockpit (open), biplane; Curtiss OX-5, 90-hp liquid-cooled. (Courtesy of Virginia Aviation Museum)

his planes, doing other odd jobs at his small, private strip and getting "shown how to fly." He even made a special seat and back cushion so that I wouldn't have to stretch to reach the controls and see over the cowling.

Then one day he said, "Take it around yourself, Kid." And I did! I was thirteen! I've often wondered about my reaction to my first solo flight. While many others have told me theirs were thrilling or frightening, I distinctly remember only two thoughts about mine. First, the plane was lighter, climbed faster and the front cockpit was empty. And second, I was disappointed that the flight was over so quickly. We kept this secret from Dad and Mom for almost three years.

Several years later, during the war, I visited Bill Walther for the last time. I was a flight lieutenant, the senior engineering test pilot for the Royal Canadian Air Force. Wearing my uniform, I was ever so proud to have been his "grease monkey" and now his friend. I brought him an official RCAF flag and a set of embroidered wings just like those on my own tunic. His "bluebird" was in the barn, lovingly covered with cotton sheets and, unlike Bill, still in good flying condition. I have always deeply regretted that I didn't have the time, that the strip had not been mowed and that Bill wasn't physically able to get into his plane. I would have liked to have been able to give him his last "hop." I hugged him, we both cried and I never saw him again. He died in 1942 and I never could find out what happened to his airplane. For sometime after my unofficial and illegal first solo flight I continued to work with Mr. Bill, flew whenever I could and did some speed skating, hockey playing, deer hunting and fishing. I earned enough money delivering *Ladies Home Companion*, *Country Gentleman* and *Liberty* magazines to buy, rebuild or repair and sell (at a profit, of course) several old Henderson and Indian motorcycles and a couple of Model T and Model A Fords. Mom put up with a dirty basement and garage and washed all the filthy clothes and rags; Dad helped me, as did Mr. Bill, by making me learn

by logic and by doing. I can remember how I rebuilt a motorcycle gearbox three times before getting it right!

Then I did what most teens did (and still do, I guess): I thought I knew more than my elders. Against the advice of Mr. Bill, and unbeknownst to Dad or Mom, I bought an airplane! A friend of mine who was also interested in flying, and had slightly more money than brains, heard about a man in upstate New York who had an old and "slightly damaged" OX Travel Air. George had a car that would make the trip so we went up and looked it over. The owner had dragged a wing, damaging the right, lower, rear spar; and the Curtiss OX-5 engine was (to put it kindly) very tired. But it was cheap, we had the cash, we let our enthusiasm overcome our intelligence and we bought it.

The spar was spruce, I think; the cracks were longitudinal and not too severe. We clamped and glued gussets - poplar, from an apple crate - on both sides, straightened the bow on the wing tip, patched and doped the fabric and agreed it was OK to fly. The radiator needed soldering in a couple of places but the engine ran smoothly when we fired it up. We got some fresh gasoline and I made my first "test flight."

Everything was ready. We drove home and the following weekend hitchhiked back. We inspected the repairs and did a preflight that would have made Mr. Bill proud. I was about to take off on my first cross-country flight! I did the flying and I guess George did the praying.

The engine was liquid-cooled and the individual cylinders were connected with water hoses about three inches long. The fittings were badly worn and the hoses kept popping loose, spraying our faces with hot water and forcing an immediate landing for repairs and more water. Let me leave it at this: the trip was 107 miles long and took us three and one-half days. We had seven unscheduled landings, but we made it. I'll always remember that trip, not only because we were very stupid and lucky, but for the totally incredulous expressions on the faces of the farmers in whose pastures we landed. One lady, who fed us some great chicken and

dumplings, simply couldn't believe that such young kids were flying an airplane!

As anyone can imagine, a friend of my father learned of the adventure and wisely informed my family. My flying came to a screeching (some of it mine) halt. I "gave" my share of the airplane to George, whose parents promptly arranged its disposal, and I was sent off to Cazenovia High School and Junior College in central New York state.

One of the Saturday night attractions for me was a nearby barn dance. It only cost a quarter to get in and the dancing was fun. The music was just one fiddler who sat on a stool and called out the dance figures as he played and clogged the rhythm with his feet. The dancers didn't need much calling because they knew most of the dances. We did old-time squares, contras and a few waltzes and polkas. One night the fiddler had a little too much brandy and called me up to the stage and said, "Hey, Kid, can you call the Barge Canal Reel?" When I said I thought I could, I called my first dance. From that day to this I have enjoyed calling and teaching dances all over the U.S., Canada and much of the rest of the world.

I told my parents many times, a few years later, just how much I appreciated and loved them for what they did next. Their understanding and insight was amazing. They must have known that my childhood talk of wanting to be a test pilot was serious. So, at a truly great financial sacrifice, they made arrangements to send me to the Dallas Aviation School and Air College in Texas.

During a phone conversation with Dad, I was invited to visit the Jimmy Doolittle family in St. Louis, Missouri, as a break in my bus trip to Texas. When we returned to their home following a performance of Gilbert and Sullivan's "Pirates of Penzance," Mr. Doolittle spoke to me very sternly, but sincerely. Since he had always been a hero to me, when he said, "You must do it right, or get yourself killed," I listened and I've always remembered.

They were holding me in the palms of their hands.

CHAPTER 2

DALLAS AVIATION SCHOOL & AIR COLLEGE
1938-1939

The bus trip from St. Louis to Dallas was geographically much shorter than from New York to St. Louis, but I can still remember feeling as though I'd never get to Texas. I was so eager to start my new adventure, to start flying every day, to do what I'd always wanted to do - become a pilot! And yet I was apprehensive as well. What would the Texans be like? How would I like the newer planes with the radial engines? Would they fly the same? Could I possibly remember all that I had been told by Dad and Mr. Bill? Yet, within fifteen minutes of my arrival at the Dallas bus station, my doubts evaporated. I was picked up by one of the ground-school instructors, a great guy named Johnny Barnes, who had a knack for making a

5 Waco YKS-7; five-seat, cabin, biplane; Jacobs L-4, 225-hp radial. (Courtesy of San Diego Aerospace Museum)

new kid feel welcome. When we arrived at Dallas Aviation School, I was almost overwhelmed. My previous flying had been off short, narrow one-way strips or bumpy pastures; the three airplanes I had flown were quite old; and I don't think that Mr. Bill ever had a license, although I know he had flown in WW I. Now, here I was on a huge airport (Love Field) with a control tower. There were bright yellow Fleet biplanes everywhere I looked. And I was certain that everyone had proper credentials and that everything would be "legal and by the book." What a transition! Johnny must have sensed my feelings and immediately gave me a quick tour of the hangars, shops and the flight line which had me full of anticipation in no time.

My roommate, Henry Oppenheim, was a young German Jew whose family had escaped from Germany. Even in 1938 he was firmly convinced that

Hitler was a mad man who would involve all of Europe in a terrible war and that the U.S. would have to be in it. We got along together really well and he turned out to be a fine pilot. Our room was in a corrugated iron, one-story building with no inner walls or ceilings. The room dividers weren't more than eight feet high so that air could circulate above them. There was no cooling system of any kind and, in the summer months, I truly understood the meaning of the phrase "hotter than hell!" On the other hand, in January when a Texas norther whipped down from the Panhandle and one of the guys said, "It's as cold as a well-digger's ass in Alaska," I believed it!

There were a couple of points that Jimmy Doolittle and Dad had attempted to impress upon me, and I took both of them to heart. The first was that I should not brag about having flown before, but not deny it if asked. The sec-

ond was to take every bit of instruction I could get, not only in flying but in everything related to it, in order to learn as much as I could. After a few hours in the air I began to realize how little I did know, so following the first suggestion was easy. Their second suggestion almost became an obsession. I don't remember making a nuisance of myself - at least nobody told me I did - but I was a real sponge, taking advantage of every opportunity to soak up anything that was new. This habit lasted throughout my flying career, and I never stopped learning. I'm sure it enabled me to become a more competent test pilot, and I'm absolutely positive it helped me to survive!

I flew every day that the weather permitted and, when not flying, I was either working on airplanes or attending ground-school classes. Since I never seemed to have any extra spending money I didn't hang around the air-port coffee shop very often. Instead, I used my free time to do extra work on aircraft and engines and I'd also clean the school's Bellanca cabin monoplane and the Wasp Junior Stearman. To use a Texas phrase, "I was in high cotton."

Ground school emphasized five subjects: airframes, engines, CAA regulations, meteorology and navigation. Airframes and engines basics were a breeze, so I had more time to study intricate technical details which would prove valuable in later years. The CAA regs simply required memorization. Meteorology fascinated me, and the knowledge I retained from these classes helped me innumerable times, especially when flying over water or northern Canada and when determining if certain test flights could be accomplished without interference from adverse weather. Navigation emphasized dead reckoning and map reading.

6 Curtiss JN-4, "Jenny," known in Canada as the Canuck; tandem, two-cockpit (open), biplane; Curtiss OX-5, 90-hp liquid-cooled. The only American mass-produced aircraft to have played a major role during WW I. Ninety-five percent of all American and Canadian aircrews were trained in the Jenny. (Courtesy of San Diego Aerospace Museum)

Both of these skills were to save the day for me those times when my sophisticated electronic equipment went "belly-up." I enjoyed the academic work and when it came time to take the commercial pilot's license written exams, I had no trouble at all.

The shop work (they called it "practical experience") included normal maintenance chores, plus the actual repairing and rebuilding of engines and aircraft. I couldn't possibly count the number of times this experience benefited me. One example immediately comes to mind: In the early 1970s the U.S. Coast Guard was unable to fly a severely-injured seaman off Swan Island in the Caribbean. I was asked to fly over from Grand Cayman Island in my Cessna 336 to try to make the pick up. Splashing mud and stones damaged my aircraft on landing and had I not been able to repair it myself, then and there, my litter patient probably would have died. As it was, I got him to the hospital in Kingston, Jamaica, with relatively little difficulty. His recovery took months but he was able to return to work.

Flying was the best part, of course. My flight instructor liked to be called "Cotton." He was a fine person and a very competent pilot and instructor. He sensed immediately that I had flown before, so I truthfully answered his questions about my experience and then requested that he keep this knowledge from the other students. As far as I know, he told no one except the other instructors and staff. I also kept my mouth shut and went about the business of learning the skills and finesse that make a good pilot. It was among the most wonderful times of my life! The main thing I remember is that, after flying about sixty or seventy hours, I realized how the act of flying was almost as natural to me as breathing. The controls seemed to be mere extensions of my hands and feet. It was a truly marvelous feeling; and, happily, one that I reveled in for thousands of hours of flight. The Kinner, or Warner, Fleet was a fine, open-cockpit biplane. It, like most trainers of that time, did not have brakes or a steerable tail wheel. This lack kept a pilot fairly busy on a cross-wind landing. I didn't have much trouble because I had flown similar aircraft off strips that had cross winds most of the time. But it gave a student named Van Lloyd a nickname that stayed with him for years. One day the aircraft got away from him on landing and ground-looped - dropped a wing and spun around, damaging the wing and a wheel. He was a strong young man, so he lifted the tail, put the skid on his shoulder and dragged his plane back to the flight line. From that day on we called him "Groundloop Van Lloyd."

Once every two months each of the students had to work for a week or so on the night shift, getting the aircraft ready for the pre-breakfast flights we termed the "Dawn Patrol." This, of

course, meant sleeping days and no classes or flying. Not flying was awful, but trying to sleep in the iron barracks during a hot, Texas summer day was absolute torture. About the only way I could do this was to take the sheets off the bunk, stand in the cold shower and get them soaking wet. Then I put one wet sheet on the bunk, covered myself with the second sheet and turned on a fan. As the sheets dried, I repeated the process until it was time to get up. Most of us did the same thing, but I don't remember anyone catching a cold.

Just before my nineteenth birthday Katherine LaVerne Crane and I

7 Swallow, a refined Laird Swallow; tandem, two-cockpit (open), three-seat, biplane; Curtiss OX-5, 90-hp liquid-cooled. (Courtesy of National Aviation Museum, Canada)

were married. We had met soon after my arrival in Texas and, with the confidence of youth, decided to take the big step. We kept our marriage a secret from everyone except my roommate and told our friends after I graduated and had my license.

In a welding class my ego suffered a real blow when I found that I was, kindly stated, a "lousy welder." It was a skill I simply could not acquire. I could "stick things together," but so poorly that Johnny finally had me make a solemn promise never to weld anything that would be a part of an airplane. I have kept that promise to this day, but my ego still resents my inability!

However, it wasn't long before my ego was reinflated by being given special permission to clean and rebuild some parts from a JN-4 owned by Mr. D. J. Brothers. In gratitude, Dee Jay gave me a flight in his Jenny and then let me fly it solo for about forty-five minutes, to the great envy of the other students. I also had the opportunity to fly both the 225-hp and the 330-hp Stearmans, the Waco cabin biplane, as well as the famous Bellanca.

One day, just after I had passed my commercial pilot flight test, Dee Jay flew into Love Field in a beautiful OX-5 Swallow. When Cotton told him about

my early Travel Air experiences, Dee Jay gave me a brief preflight talk-around and then told me to give it a whirl. It was almost like returning to the nest. I had someone take our picture standing beside the aircraft and sent copies to Dad and Mr. Bill.

Now I was a licensed pilot, married and looking for a job. Delta and Braniff airlines made some inquiries to the school about me, but I didn't want the routine of airline flying. I got wind of another job through one of the Braniff pilots, Doc Speegle. Doc's father was a physician on staff at the hospital in Palestine, Texas, and knew that there was no flight instructor at the local airport. I immediately hitch-hiked to Palestine for an interview and landed my first job as a licensed pilot.

[Historical note: Dallas Aviation School and Air College was established by Major Bill Long around 1926 and operated for thirty-five years. In May 1939, he was summoned to Washington for a secret meeting with General H. H. "Hap" Arnold to help establish a flight training program. By the end of WW II, Dallas Aviation School had trained 23,000 U.S. pilots and 1,500 additional pilots for the Royal Air Force.]

4 Bellanca Pacemaker; six-seat, cabin, high-wing, monoplane; Wright Whirlwind, 300-hp radial. (Courtesy of San Diego Aerospace Museum)

CHAPTER 3

FIRST JOB - EAST TEXAS
August 1939 - March 1940

Dr. A. Arthur Speegle was the chairman of the aviation committee supervising the Stephen E. Reed Airport at Palestine, Texas. I deeply appreciated his support and assistance in helping me get a job because I was married, a baby was on the way and I wanted to get to work as soon as possible.

Sessions' Aircraft Service was mainly a repair shop at the Palestine airport. When I first started working for Mr. Hubert Sessions he had a three-place OX-5 Robin, a Monocoupe, a Curtiss Junior (Szekely pusher), a Cub for a trainer and a four-place Challenger Robin for passenger hops, but no commercial licensed pilot or flight instructor. My job was to do all of the commercial flying and flight instruction; in exchange I was to have a one-room apartment which had been added to Mr. Sessions' house, groceries and the princely sum of $5 per week.

The airport consisted of 265 acres of fairly smooth grass, with no runways or boundary lights, and an old hangar and a shop that were both in fairly decent condition. There were two mechanics, Ralph Elliot and Hobby Miller, who helped the owner maintain the aircraft and engines and, of course, the usual "airport dog."

Before being hired I had discussed with my prospective employer the terms-of-hire policy that I had decided upon and would adhere to

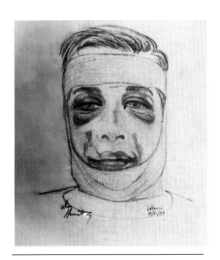

3a My face in bandages. "This is a very accurate photo of a sketch made of me in the hospital three days after the crackup. Oh, yes - LaVerne made the sketch." (D. Armstrong collection)

throughout my flying career. I made it clear that I would work for him to the utmost of my ability and with his best interests in mind but, when offered an opportunity to advance my career, I would do so. I also reassured him that I would give sufficient notice and make every effort to leave him with a suitable replacement. He understood and agreed. (I changed jobs very frequently during the following years, seldom simply because of "more money," but almost always to be able to learn something new, fly different aircraft or acquire additional skills. In doing so, I'm proud to say, I don't think I ever left a job that I couldn't return to.)

I quickly familiarized myself with all the aircraft at the field and began instructing several waiting students. In a few weeks we had almost fifty student pilots and I insisted that I should get paid by the hour. (I had received my "salary" only once anyway!) Articles I was submitting to *Southern Flight* magazine and the cooperation of *The Palestine Herald and Press* really promoted the newly formed flying club. Shortly thereafter we started having spot-landing contests, cookouts and other activities that brought in new pupils and, on weekends, lots of passengers for hops.

One Sunday we sponsored an aviation safety program which brought hundreds of people out to the airport. The repair shop was getting ready to re-cover a Cub with new fabric. After stripping the old fabric from the entire plane and removing all the engine cowling, we made a display so visitors could see all the insides of a plane. I also did several dead-stick landings to reassure people that aircraft maneuvered well without engine power. Almost a hundred people took rides that day, and a couple of new students signed up for lessons.

Occasionally, Mr. Sessions and I did some barnstorming, especially at cotton-picking time, in towns that had a cotton gin but no airport. One weekend we took the Cub, a Great Lakes and the four-place Robin and

went to an area that evidently no one had worked before. Every passenger paid us with tokens which we later exchanged for cash at the local bank. Residents used the tokens like money, and I guess the only time they had dollars was when they shopped out of town. We knew that people were more likely to go for a ride if they saw someone else go first, so I "primed the pump" - gave two of the couples a free ride - and that's all it took. Like getting olives out of a bottle - after the first few, the rest come easily. Our total take for three airplanes that weekend was $837 and, in 1939, that was "big bucks."

The Challenger Robin was the money maker, of course. It carried the pilot - me - plus three passengers (four, if they were small and if I kept the fuel tanks less than one-third full) and got off the ground with a surprisingly short run. The pasture from which we flew was fairly long, but with three shallow dips and terraces running across our path. My takeoff system was simple: get up speed going across the first terrace, gain more speed in the dip, lift off on top of the second terrace, bounce (if necessary) off the top of the third terrace, clear the fence and climb. My landings were made in the opposite direction (wind wasn't a factor at any time during the weekend), fully stalled in order to touch down without a bounce. I could then roll to the passenger-waiting area without having to turn around and taxi, making my turnaround time very short.

A Challenger six-cylinder engine developed about 170 hp and was, on paper, the smoothest engine of its time. It was actually two, three-cylinder radial sections, one behind the other, creating a "symmetrical" engine with each cylinder sixty degrees from the next. But, as so often happened, the designer forgot to tell the engine that it was supposed to be smooth, and I think it was the origin of "shake, rattle and roll!" However, in spite of the vibration, it was an extremely reliable engine that never let me down.

[Historical note: In July 1929, a Challenger Robin set a world endurance record, refueling in flight, staying aloft for over 420 hours. Again, in August 1930, another Challenger Robin set a new record by remaining in the air for over 647 hours.]

It was also about this time that I was to do my second "test flight." A local pilot, Harry Bevil, had obtained CAA permission to place a sound system and an oversized generator in a new Franklin 50-hp Cub and asked me to help work out the weight and balance problems. Following installation of the generator and sound system, including a huge speaker in place of the front seat, the CAA inspector checked it out and observed my test flight. The aircraft flew normally, just as we expected. If I remember correctly, the outfit was still being used for advertising flights over Texas towns and fairs long after I left the area. Harry also owned a beautiful Great Lakes biplane which had a checkerboard-painted fuselage. It was a fun aircraft to fly and, undoubtedly, influenced my future use of the checkerboard.

Soon there were mornings when I wanted to jump with joy. I had a newborn son and I was actually getting paid to fly! To be sure, my pay was minimal, but I could always trade a few hours of instruction for things we needed. On the regularly scheduled days when I instructed students in nearby Athens, Corsicana and Mexia, someone usually sent me home with fresh vegetables, a freshly killed chicken or, perhaps, some home-made jelly. During one trip I spotted a big watermelon field beside a wide dirt road between Athens and Palestine and several times afterward I just happened to land there "to check the oil." Quite amazingly, a ripe watermelon, or two, would manage to jump into the aircraft before I took off. Fortunately, the owner never took a shot at me, but maybe that's because I soon met the farmer and gave his son and him a ride over their farm. And it really is true: a swiped watermelon always tastes sweeter.

Somebody did take shots at me, though, several Monday mornings when I was flying to Mexia. We found six holes made by three bullets hitting the aircraft but, luckily, none had done any severe damage. After the local paper ran a story about it, the shooting stopped. I'll admit to flying

higher on that route from then on. Once in a while we'd even do some shooting of our own - at the jack rabbits and cottontails that plagued us on the airport. We would fly over the field in the Curtiss Junior and shoot at them with a .22 rifle. The plane had a Szekely pusher engine behind the pilot and passenger, and flew very slowly, making it great sport and quite safe. Sure it was "illegal," but one of the CAA inspectors tried it a couple of times on his visits to the field, and he had as much fun as we did. And those cottontails made mighty good stew.

There is also a dramatic charter flight that I've never forgotten - one in which I was to play the role of "attending physician." I was sent by a local mother to pick up her daughter from an oil-field rig on a ranch about fifty-five miles away. The girl and her husband were living in a trailer on the site where he worked as a driller. Since she was nearly nine months pregnant, her mother hired me to fly her home for the delivery.

9 Monocoupe; side-by-side, two-seat, cabin, high-wing, monoplane; Velie, 55-hp radial. (Courtesy of San Diego Aerospace Museum)

Upon arriving at the ranch I assisted Alice Ann (believe me, I'll never forget her name) into the rear seat of the Cub and took off. Midway on our trip she told me in no uncertain terms, "The baby's coming!" I was scared but realized I had no choice except to land on the closest, suitable dirt road: you could see the baby's head! I got the plane down as quickly as possible and lifted Alice Ann out, placing her on seat cushions I had pulled from the aircraft. The baby seemed to pop out within minutes. All I did was hold the head and keep the baby from dropping onto the ground.

I definitely wasn't sure what to do next, but I remembered having overheard my aunt talk about "tying-off-the-cord," so I took my knife and cut the umbilical cord in the middle. I tried to tie a knot next to the baby, but that didn't work because it was too slippery. While having Alice Ann hold both ends of the cord, I pulled a lace off the back of one of the seat cush-

ions and succeeded in getting the cord tied off. When it looked like the delivery of the afterbirth was over, I took some of the extra clothes Alice Ann had brought with her, cleaned up both of them, as best I could, and wrapped the baby to keep it warm.

After she had rested awhile, I

12 Curtiss Junior; tandem, two-cockpit (open), parasol-wing, monoplane; Szekely, pusher, 45-hp radial. (Courtesy of San Diego Aerospace Museum)

13 Ford Trimotor, "The Tin Goose"; multi-seat, cabin, high-wing, monoplane; two Wright J6, 300-hp (wings)/one Pratt and Whitney Wasp, 450-hp (nose) radials. Fuselage was corrugated metal. (Courtesy of National Aviation Museum, Canada)

settled mother and babe in the plane and completed our flight home. When we landed at the airport I phoned the doctor (the Cub had no radio) and drove them to the doctor's office. The doctor said all was well, that I'd done the right things. A happy Alice Ann, her mother and the baby were discharged home, and I suddenly realized I didn't know whether the baby was a boy or a girl. (It was a boy!)

To instruct student pilots can be very rewarding, but it certainly is not without risks. My first crash occurred when a student and I were doing touch-and-go landings and the student had a seizure while he was at the controls. Since we were at low altitude, I did not have the time or strength to prevent nosing into the airport. The Cub was destroyed! My injuries were

facial, quite extensive, and it was a month or so before I learned to enunciate clearly again. Throughout my recovery, my friend Dr. Speegle tried to keep me as comfortable as he could.

By the time I was released to fly again (my face still in a cast) our friend Harry Bevil had acquired two Cubs and taken over the operation of the flying service at both Palestine and Mexia. Mr. Sessions retained the repair shop and refueling service. To top it all off, the Mexia Flying Club had acquired a red and white Spartan biplane powered by a Wright J6-5 engine. This was an especially nice airplane to fly, and I really enjoyed getting back into an open-cockpit aircraft again - except for the cold! It was February (1940) and so cold in Texas that winter that stock ponds and small lakes froze over. We had recently moved to Mexia, and I became quite a celebrity when the

local newspaper printed a story about me - ice-skating in east Texas!

Whenever I think of the Mexia Flying Club, I have many fond memories of Louis Stathis. He was the club's organizer, one of the owners of the Spartan and the driving force in enrolling over forty students into the group. Although he could only walk with the aid of crutches and it took him at least five minutes to crawl up on the lower wing and pull himself into the cockpit, Louis frequently reminded us that he wasn't handicapped, he just had four legs instead of two. He was an enduring inspiration to us all.

In 1939-1940 things were vastly different from what they are today. Many flyers were unlicensed, the regulations were fewer and simpler and, in rural areas, frequently not

154 Arrow F (Sport); single-seat, open-cockpit, monoplane; converted Ford engine. Designed to use cheap, mass-produced motorcar engines, the high weight-to-power ratio, in my opinion, made this "female dog" miserable to fly. (Courtesy of San Diego Aerospace Museum)

10 Curtiss Robin; three-seat, cabin, high-wing, monoplane; Curtiss OX-5, 90-hp liquid-cooled. (Courtesy of National Aviation Museum, Canada)

strictly adhered to. The following two stories are perfect examples.

A student in Mexia broke off about four inches of one of the wooden propeller blades while taxiing. We removed the prop and, suspending it on a fence, balanced it by adding the weight of brads and roofing copper to the shorter blade. We put it back on and ran up the engine. When it displayed no significant vibration, I babied it back to Palestine (less than fifty miles) without incident.

The second episode illustrates another aspect altogether. One day two Ford Trimotor airplanes landed at the field because one of the pilots was having a kidney-stone attack. He had to be hospitalized and I was asked if I could fly his plane. With the optimism of youth I replied I thought I could, if given a decent check flight. (Actually, it flew just like most other aircraft except that it was heavier on the controls, far noisier and had three engines to manage.) The check flight went well and I was hired on the spot to accompany the other aircraft to Vera Cruz, Mexico, with the oil-field supplies that were already on board.

While on the round-trip flight I used the sick pilot's name so he wouldn't lose his job. I enjoyed every minute of the experience, had no problems and pocketed a nice bit of cash in the process. Can you imagine things like this happening now?

Giving dual instruction in the side-by-side Monocoupe was also quite different, since the only control I (the instructor) had was a device resembling an automobile-engine crank handle stuck into the top of the student's stick. To say the least, it was a primitive method, but it worked. And the night landing system in Palestine was just as peculiar: I'd locate the airport (it was the only dark, rectangular spot in the midst of the gas flares of the oil field) and I'd fly over to alert Ralph or Hobby. One of them would then check the wind direction and place a car in the correct position so that I could safely land just to the right of the headlights. Simple and effective, even though not quite according to regulations.

One of the last jobs I had in Texas was crop dusting in a beat-up Stearman biplane. It lasted fourteen days - thirteen days too long. The flying was great, but the equipment was terrible; everything was dirty and breathing in the same stuff that was

killing bugs was certainly not for me. It did me the favor, however, of making me realize that it was time to move on.

I knew, from talking with Dad, that there was a shortage of flight instructors around Long Island and New York City and felt this would be as good a time as any to return to the northeast. I hoped that I could find a job involving aircraft I had not flown before or in different circumstances. My aunt had a beach house in Roxbury that was close to several airports and Dad had assured me we could stay there as long as we needed to.

Everything fell into place when LaVerne's father gave us a 1934 Chevy coupe for the trip. I removed the rumble seat and installed a fifty-five gallon drum for "drip gas," enabling us to start our journey with

about seventy gallons of fuel.

[Author's note: Drip gas is a byproduct we "found" and drained from condensation chambers in natural-gas pipelines near the airport. When mixed half-and-half with regular gasoline, it "burned" quite well in low-compression automobile engines.]

After traveling for five days we found ourselves at the bridge that crosses Jamaica Bay, from Floyd Bennett Field to Roxbury, with the exact change for the toll - plus ten cents.

When I left New York for Texas I was a youngster filled with equal parts anticipation and apprehension. I returned a licensed commercial pilot and flight instructor with a wife and son. The apprehension was gone but the anticipation of what might be in store was greater than ever.

[Author's note: I had the opportunity to visit the airport at Palestine fifty years later and found it to be not much different from when I had last seen it. The house and shop were gone but the old hangar was well maintained and appeared relatively unchanged.]

15 Spartan C-3; tandem, two-cockpit (open), bi-plane; Wright J6-5, 175-hp radial. (Courtesy of San Diego Aerospace Museum)

151 Aeronca C-3, "Flying Bathtub"; two-seat, high-wing, monoplane; Aeronca E-113C, two-cylinder, 40-hp opposed. (Courtesy of San Diego Aerospace Museum)

CHAPTER 4

SEAPLANES AND STUFF
March 1940 - September 1940

The first day after we arrived in Roxbury, while LaVerne was getting our things arranged in my aunt's place, I went across Jamaica Bay to Floyd Bennett Field to see if I could get a job. This airport had many special memories associated with it, because when I was a kid Dad and I had gone there frequently and talked with many of my "giants." The last time I had been there was July 14, 1938, just before I left for Texas. We had gone to see Howard Hughes land the *Miss World's Fair* at the end of his record-breaking, around-the-world trip. I still have five snapshots I took that day. I can remember telling Dad I thought Mr. Hughes was rather peculiar because, unlike Roscoe Turner and some of the other famous pilots, he didn't appear to enjoy being around people. He even seemed reluctant to be photographed shaking hands with Mayor Fiorello La Guardia. (At that time I certainly never dreamed I would one day be talking to Howard Hughes about testing one of his planes.)

Within a couple of hours, after visiting with some of the people whose faces I recognized, I was offered a job. In spite of having less than a dollar in my pocket, I turned it down! The owner of a small airshow needed a pilot to ferry one of his planes around New England during the spring and summer. The "zinger" was that he expected me to do parachute jumps at each of the stops. I

didn't think much of that idea, and when he informed me that I'd only get $50 a month, room and board plus $10 for each jump, I said, "Thanks, but no thanks." I knew I'd made a wise decision when, later the same day, I heard about a man in Jersey who needed a seaplane instructor and pilot.

I immediately called Harold J. Lentz, owner of the Marine Air Transport Company, in Carlstadt, New Jersey, and arranged to meet him the next morning. He picked me up in a Luscombe on floats and took me to his Sky Harbor Seaplane Terminal on the Hackensack River. These were rather pretentious names for an outfit that operated only two planes - the Luscombe and a Fairchild 24 - but it was a potential job, and what's more important, it would give me seaplane experience and a chance to fly under completely different circumstances.

Mr. Lentz reviewed my logbook and references, and had me fly him around and shoot a few landings. Even though I didn't have a seaplane rating he hired me. Both of us felt that it would be fairly easy for me to fly his float planes and get my rating since I had done a considerable amount of sailing while growing up.

Handling an aircraft on water was actually a lot of fun for me. I was a good sailor, knew how to read the water and tide, could pull up to a dock under sail or pick up a buoy. Water taxiing, drifting, backing, docking and beaching a floatplane were just adaptations of my sailing skills. The takeoff techniques varied according to water conditions, and the concepts such as lifting one float before the other, to reduce drag and shorten take-off distance, were logical. I don't remember how many hours of seaplane experience the CAA required in 1940, but as soon as

I had accumulated the necessary time, I obtained my rating and confidently went to work.

The day-to-day work at Sky Harbor surprised me in a number of ways. First, our lifestyle had completely changed. Second, my job was more "charter" work than instruction. Third, the flying was all in seaplanes. And last, but not least, the visibility and weather were vastly different from Texas.

Instead of living on a dusty airport and my walking to work, we now lived in a summer cottage built on pilings in the river and I went to work in a boat powered by a cranky outboard motor. It was early spring and the weather was still cold, so the rent on the cottage was practically nothing. It was close enough to the seaplane base that LaVerne could watch the flying and still keep an eye on our young son, and I could go back and forth across the river for coffee or lunch.

The charter flying was a big surprise, too - I was astonished at how many flights I made each week. (In Texas I had averaged fewer than one per month.) The Wall Street Seaplane Terminal on the East River served the financial district of Manhattan, and we had businessmen who commuted from as far away as Toms River in South Jersey. On Fridays, in the Fairchild, I crossed the Hudson River, made my approach between the skyscrapers and landed. The passengers would board the aircraft to be flown to their cottages and clubs. On

17 Fairchild 24; four-seat, cabin, high-wing, monoplane, Edo floats; Warner Super Scarab, 145-hp radial. (Courtesy of National Aviation Museum, Canada)

Mondays I'd pick them up and fly them back to the city to work. Some weekends I made as many as three Toms River flights, plus a couple to a lakeside resort. In addition, two or three times a week, I'd take the Luscombe and fly a broker who intensely disliked city driving (who can blame him?) from Sky Harbor to Wall Street to work. This trip took about fifteen minutes each way; but adding the taxi and load/unload time meant that he paid for one hour of fly-ing, twice a day. He must have felt it was worth it, as well as fun, because he took a few flying lessons from me that summer.

Instructing here was different for me as well. Previously the major-ity of my flight instruction had been with new pilots, most of whom had not yet soloed. In contrast, at Sky Harbor most of my students already had their private or commercial license and either were interested in getting a seaplane rating or simply curious to know how it felt to fly a floatplane. In order to have plenty of space, especially for water-handling practice, I used a lake northeast of us. I was amazed at how many prob-lems some of the pilots had when they tried to approach a dock or anticipate wind drift while taxiing. It was quickly apparent how much Dad's devotion to detail and perfec-tion, during the years he was teach-ing me to sail, enabled me to under-stand and help many of my students.

A unique aspect of flying with floats is that takeoffs are sometimes difficult, or even impossible, when the plane is heavily loaded, the wind velocity low or the water exceptional-ly smooth. When taking off was trou-blesome at Sky Harbor I felt very for-tunate to have the Jacoby Outboard Racing Team's shop next to us on the river. The Jacobys liked to fly and thoroughly understood my dilemma. If they saw me having difficulty get-ting the aircraft up "on the step" (when the floats "planed," permitting the aircraft to gain sufficient flying speed), someone would jump into one of their boats and run around in front of me to create waves and make it easier for me to take off. In return, I was always available to deliver parts to the team when they were racing close enough to make the flight practical.

Poor weather and pollution-restricted visibility were two conditions that differed unbelievably from what I'd known in Texas. These, combined with towers and high buildings and bridges, created a multitude of problems that were further compounded by the proximity of Newark and La Guardia airports. Radar control zones hadn't been established and many of the small aircraft lacked radios. Pilots usually wished they had ten pairs of eyes so they could watch everywhere at once. Often at the end of a busy day I'd have an eye-strain headache I never would have had in the wonderful wide-open spaces of the great southwest. Without a doubt, it was another learning experience!

The developing war was responsible for the Civilian Pilot Training Program which taught basic flying skills to hundreds of men and women throughout the country. This sudden influx of new students into the CPTP mandated a standardized curriculum and led to the need for more secondary (advanced) training centers. In view of the paucity of capable instructors, and to assure the implementation of the new curriculum, an official instructor re-rating program

was instituted. I was one of the first to requalify and subsequently was asked to teach in a secondary program at Roosevelt Field on Long Island. A pilot I had been training in seaplanes already had his commercial license and, with the approval of Mr. Lentz, took over my job. I was free to move... again.

Every flying buff is familiar with Roosevelt Field: it was from this airport that most of the early trans-Atlantic flights, including Lindbergh's and Corrigan's, had departed. I had been there dozens of times, with and without Dad, and when I arrived to start my new job I felt right at home. The boss was a fine gentleman, Max Rappaport, who ran a well-organized flight school. His pilots were good, his shop excellent, his ground instructors conscientious, his discipline strict and his disposition pleasant.

My job was to do secondary and aerobatic instruction in Stearman biplanes, and I thoroughly enjoyed the short time I spent there. Two particular situations made me realize how much I was maturing and learning through my teaching. One had to do with the fear that some of the students felt about doing aerobatics, and the realization that I could help alleviate it by face-to-face, honest, sensitive conversations. The other was regard-

ing the shabby treatment a young woman received from the other students. She had been assigned to me for instruction and I found her to be an excellent pupil and, much to my delight, an above-average pilot. (She later became a military ferry pilot and did a fine job.) This was my first, but not my last, experience with discrimination.

In August 1940 the war was going disastrously for England, and it was increasingly obvious that it was only a matter of time before the United States would be involved, as Henry Oppenheim had predicted while we were at Dallas. The Royal Air Force (RAF) and the Royal Canadian Air Force (RCAF) desperately needed pilots and both had established the mechanism whereby U.S. airmen could become commissioned officers without losing their citizenship. I analyzed the benefits of each, listened to Dad's comments and chose the RCAF, because I felt that in Canada I would have more opportunity to fly a larger selection of military aircraft and, thereby, broaden my experience. Max gave his enthusiastic approval, I talked to Mr. Bill, said goodbye to Mother and Dad and left for Ottawa.

14 Great Lakes 2T-1A; sport trainer;
tandem, two-cockpit (open), biplane.
(Courtesy of Aerofax, Inc.)

CHAPTER 5

ROYAL CANADIAN AIR FORCE
September 1940 - October 1941

The following words are taken from a 550-year-old tombstone in the Church of Kirby Cemetery:

When pictures look alive with movements free -
When ships like fishes swim beneath the sea
When men outstripping birds shall scan the sky
Then half the world - deep drenched in blood shall lie

It would be fifteen months before the United States was attacked and at war but, in September 1940, most realistic Americans knew that full military participation was not a matter of if, but only of when. The United States was technically "neutral," and many Americans wanted to keep it that way. However, we already were training British pilots, supplying materials to England, "lend-leasing" equipment to the Allies and diligently training our pilots (as "civilians," of course) in anticipation of the inevitable. People with varied technical skills were offering their services to England, and experienced flyers delivered aircraft across the Atlantic or flew in combat for the Royal Air Force.

In June 1940, the Canadian Privy Council had passed a minute which exempted U.S. citizens from having to swear allegiance to King George VI. This was an action of great magnitude because, after that time, Americans could enlist or accept commissions in the Canadian military forces without the fear of forfeiting their U.S. citizenship. The Clayton Knight Committee - WW I ace Billy Bishop's brainchild - was established. This was a private organization based in New York to disseminate information to men interested in working for, or joining, the RCAF. Of course, the committee did far more than that: it also offered

assistance by drawing up necessary documents, arranging for medical examinations for pilots without current licenses and often providing funds to anyone who needed help getting to Canada. As one can imagine, there were factions in the U.S. that protested. To circumvent these objections a second organization was created, a "front" known as the Dominion Aeronautical Association. However, for all intents and purposes, the recruiting continued and U.S. officials

simply averted their eyes.

The group operated out of the Waldorf Astoria Hotel in a thinly-disguised cloak-and-dagger atmosphere - just about as inconspicuous as a naked lady on Fifth Avenue in the Easter Parade. Were they effective? Almost 9,000 Americans enrolled in the RCAF and, of these, more than 5,000 declined to transfer to U.S. forces when later offered the opportunity.

When I contacted Errol Boyd, a Knight Committee recruiter, at the

5a The boy from the USA. A publicity/recruitment photo taken not long after my arrival in Canada. Note the prominent "USA" patch on the top of the left sleeve. (D. Armstrong collection)

19 Fleet, known in Canada as the Finch; most Canadian versions were equipped with canopies. (Courtesy of National Aviation Museum, Canada)

Waldorf he interviewed me immediately, checked my logbook, called a couple of my references and arranged for me to leave as soon as I could do so.

On September 7, 1940, I arrived in Ottawa and was provided with a delightful room in the beautiful Chateau Laurier Hotel and told to put all of my meal charges on the bill. The next day I was interviewed by the RCAF, given a most thorough physical examination and briefed about such things as life insurance (minimal) and remuneration. On my third day in Canada I was reassured that I would not lose my U.S. citizenship, took the

slightly modified "oath of allegiance" and was commissioned a pilot officer and promptly "promoted" to flying officer (equivalent to a U.S. first lieutenant) in the Royal Canadian Air Force.

In addition to my room and board I was also given a uniform allowance - with a list of approved tailors - and $5 per diem expense money. I chuckled as I remembered that my first flying job paid me $5 per week, so I was showing some improvement. Lectures and military etiquette sessions helped fill the time it would take for the tailors to complete my uniforms, and wandering around Ottawa revealed that it was a truly beautiful city. The uniforms were finally delivered and, on September 22, I received my orders posting me to Toronto's Manning Depot.

For the next two weeks the officers and NCOs at the depot made a noble effort to turn my roommate, F/O Tex Harville, and me into instant military types - with debatable suc-

cess. We drilled, marched in parades and attended indoctrination classes from daylight to dark. I don't know how Tex felt about this, but I do remember feeling I'd had enough, and that I was ready to get back to flying. On the fourth of October we celebrated with six or seven other officers at a great dinner party at the Royal York Hotel in Toronto and on the fifth I was on my way to Trenton - to fly!

Trenton, Ontario, is on the north shore of Lake Ontario and was the home of the Central Flying School where I was assigned to flight refresher training. The first RCAF aircraft I flew was an old friend, the 125-hp Kinner Fleet, exactly the same as those I had flown at Dallas, except some of the Canadian models had canopies because of the cold. The same day I was also introduced to a North American Yale (BT-9) and became comfortable with the flight pattern, paperwork and procedures. Throughout the next two or three

31 Consolidated PBY, Catalina, known in Canada as the Canso; flying boat; two Pratt and Whitney, R-1830-92, 1,200-hp radials. (Courtesy of San Diego Aerospace Museum)

weeks I thought that I'd gone to heaven. I flew hours and hours in the noisy, but now famous, North American Harvard (AT-6), doing aerobatics, instrument, night and formation flying as often as the schedule permitted. I was as high as a kite!

The base adjutant's office helped me find a tiny apartment at the Hotel Clarendon, in nearby Brighton, making it possible for LaVerne and Donnie to join me. When they arrived she brought the good news that, in the spring, if I was still somewhere in Ontario, my dad was planning to visit. I was sure that I could get permission to show him around the base wherever I was stationed and knew he'd thoroughly enjoy seeing the planes I was flying.

Twin-engine aircraft were entirely new to me, but my familiarization was simplified by the use of an old, fabric-covered Avro Anson. Today it would be called "user-friendly," but in 1940 I felt it was a "kitten." Ansons

were very forgiving airplanes, and I would have a hilarious experience in one several months later.

My next three twin-engine aircraft were Lockheeds: Models 10, 12 and 212. Although all of them were fine aircraft, I liked the Model 12 best because it was smaller, lighter and had better performance than the more familiar Model 10. I spent a lot of time practicing simulated engine failures, single-engine approaches and feigned emergencies of almost every conceivable nature. It was definitely a wonderful learning experience for me.

The winter snow at the airport was handled in a most interesting manner. It was not plowed away - it was packed down by huge rollers forming a hard surface, almost as though it had been paved. The rollers were covered with short, spike-like projections which created little holes

22 Avro Anson, "Faithful Annie"; navigational trainer; multi-seated, low-wing, monoplane, retractable gear; two Armstrong Siddeley Cheetah, 325-hp radials. (Courtesy of National Aviation Museum, Canada)

in the surface that helped prevent cracking and improved the traction. This method was considerably faster than plowing, eliminated the hazard of snow piles and ridges and was especially valuable when the "lake effect" dumped heavier-than-normal snow on the area. I found they used the same system in Ottawa when I was transferred back there just before Christmas 1940.

21 North American AT-6, "Texan," known in Canada as the Harvard; advanced trainer; tandem, two-seat, canopied, low-wing, monoplane, retractable gear; Pratt and Whitney Wasp, R-1340, 550-hp radial. (D. Armstrong collection)

29 Northrop A-17A, known in Canada as the Nomad; tandem, two-seat, canopied, low-wing, monoplane, retractable gear; Pratt and Whitney (twin-row) Wasp, R-1535, 750-hp radial. Designed as an attack/dive bomber but used in Canada primarily for target towing. (D. Armstrong collection)

32 "Towing the `Pinocchio' [Bolingbroke IV on floats] home after being damaged during tests." (D. Armstrong collection)

Ottawa was a living postcard that winter. The snow stayed a pristine white nearly all of the time, and the Parliament buildings and downtown area glistened in the sun. Uplands Airport, where I was flying, throbbed with activity all day, and most of the night, as hundreds of bright-yellow Harvards took off and landed. LaVerne enjoyed the city while I instructed students in advanced flying and aerobatics. This was to be the only class of fighter-pilots I would teach while in Canada, and they were a fine group of young men.

One terrifying incident was burned into my memory when two students had a mid-air collision. The wing of one Harvard broke away a large portion of the rudder on the other. Each pilot stayed calm, regained control and, with the combination of luck, skill - and angels riding on their shoulders - landed safely. I often wondered if they fared as well in combat.

To identify them as volunteers from the States, all American serving in the RCAF wore a "USA" patch on the sleeves of their tunics, just below the shoulder. This highly-vis-ible designation often meant that many of us were used in publicity photos and newspaper stories. High-ranking officers from Air Force Headquarters frequently ate meals at the Uplands Officers' Mess and (as I was told later) noticed that "I knew how to eat," used the appropriate fork or a fish-knife, and displayed proper manners. My dad had, of course, given me suitable training in these things as I grew up. What Dad and I hadn't foreseen was that this polish, combined with the "USA" on my shoulder, would lead to my being invited to many social functions throughout my service with the RCAF.

His Excellency The Governor General and Her Royal Highness The Princess Alice, Countess of Athlone invites F/O and Mrs. D. Armstrong to a reception at Dansanton on Saturday, 18th of January, 1941, at five o'clock.

This reception, although rather dull, brought me to the attention of several of the staff officers who want-

ed to take an inspection trip to three training fields in the Maritime Provinces. There was a Boeing 247 at the Rockcliffe airport and, although it was kept on active status, no qualified pilot was currently available for such a flight.

At breakfast one morning I was asked if I thought I could check myself out in it and be ready, in a day or so, to make a trip "down east." I studied the pilot's manual, found the aircraft in excellent condition and, with the help of the crew chief, familiarized myself with all the controls and instruments. The sergeant must have decided that I was OK, because he sat in the co-pilot's seat on my first flight. It was an easy plane to fly, but an interesting aircraft since it had no flaps to assist in approaches and landings. However, that must not have proved unacceptable because several airlines used 247s quite profitably. The trip took us through Nova Scotia and New Brunswick and was a real vacation for me. I received exactly the same VIP treatment as my passengers, and realized later that it never hurts to have friends in high places.

Not long before leaving Uplands I also had an opportunity to fly the great Noorduyn Norseman. I remember thinking it was a little odd that I checked out in the plane on skis, having never before flown it on wheels. (Later I would fly it with wheels and floats, as well.) It was definitely a pilot's airplane, and I understood why it has always been considered a bush-pilot's dream.

The Ottawa River separates Ottawa (Ontario) and Hull (Quebec) and most of the pilots went across the river to the Standish Hall Hotel for their graduation parties. When my class of pilots graduated I, of course, joined them at the party and had my first introduction to the Australians. Like my guys, the Aussies had just finished fighter-pilot training and were expecting to be posted to combat squadrons very soon. They had consumed large quantities of beer and were up on the balcony, looking down onto the dance floor, when one of them was playfully pushed over the railing. On the way down, he did a one-and-a-quarter flip and landed flat on his back on a table below - destroying it and scattering bottles, glasses, chairs and people everywhere. The room instantly became deathly quiet. The Aussie, who had not even dropped his liter of beer, stood up, shook his head, looked up at his friend and said, "You barstid," and walked back upstairs.

My class graduated and, expecting to be assigned to other duty in the very near future, I took some leave and, with LaVerne, went skiing at Camp Fortune in Quebec. Once again, I was ready for something new.

On March 1, 1941, I was ordered to Trenton for the second, and final, time. My assignment was again at Central Flying School, this time training new instructors in the Tiger Moth, Fleet, Harvard and Anson. The teaching would be different for me because the RCAF had instituted a "patter system" of flight instruction. In order to utilize newly-graduated pilots as instructors it was vital that everyone use a standardized method of teaching. To facilitate this, the instructors memorized and used specific words and phrases to demonstrate, explain and teach every action the student pilot would encounter in flight. We recognized that "teaching by rote" had obvious drawbacks; but combat attrition was extremely high, and there were

20 North American BT-9, known in Canada as the Yale; basic trainer; tandem, two-seat, canopied, low-wing, monoplane, nonretractable gear; Wright Whirlwind, 450-hp radial. (D. Armstrong collection)

33 Grumman FF-1, known in Canada as the Goblin; tandem, two-seat, canopied, biplane, retractable gear; Wright, R-1820, 750-hp radial. Built by Canadian Car and Foundry. (Courtesy of Grumman Corporation)

not enough experienced instructors to meet the demand. I didn't enjoy this method but tried to give each new instructor all the help I could. On the other hand, I felt that my talents were being wasted and mentioned this fact to the squadron commander.

Shortly afterward (did my "friends in high places" help?), I was assigned the task of preparing an abbreviated pilot's manual for the Lockheed 10. The manual in the airplane was not the one normally supplied by the manufacturer, but rather a verbose and obscure discussion of loading and weight-and-balance limi-

tations. This meant I needed to flight check a lot of procedures and data - and one of the flights almost had a nasty conclusion.

It was my habit to memorize the location of controls and instruments in most of the aircraft I flew so that, in an emergency, I would not have to waste any time looking for a control or an instrument reading. This habit might easily have saved my life: I was in the Lockheed and had about 300-feet altitude following takeoff when the left engine exploded into flames. Without conscious thought I feathered the propeller, hit the fire extinguisher button and remained in total control. I

saw no more flames, but plenty of black smoke, so I made a slow right turn, put the gear back down and landed on the airport. I shut everything off and rolled to a fast stop within seven or eight yards of the crash equipment. I do not remember ever looking for any control or instrument, except the airspeed indicator, during the entire incident. I completed the manual revision while the shop installed another engine.

The majority of the requests to participate in small social functions at the officers' mess seemed to fall on three of us from the States. Frankly, these were a damn nuisance, many times interrupting flight schedules and always intruding into our private lives. We understood, on the more important occasions, and attended willingly; but we resented being put on display at insignificant events. One day we had been "asked" to attend an affair at a large, very posh Toronto hotel, with literally dozens of other officers. The purpose of the party has long been forgotten, but I'll bet there are people who still laugh out loud when they

25 Lockheed 212; a modified Lockheed 12. Ordered by the Netherlands with both turret and forward-firing guns. (Courtesy of National Aviation Museum, Canada)

remember what happened.

The three of us had driven to Toronto early that evening and bought two-dozen live chickens and arranged to get them later that night. At about 9:30 we picked them up, put them in three burlap sacks and went back to the hotel. The introductions, meaningless speeches and toasts were over; and the free, open bar was being well used. Our absence had clearly not been noticed. We waited a few moments until the way was clear and then released the chickens into the ballroom - through three different doors, at the same time.

It was absolute bedlam! Chickens were squawking and running all over the place! Feathers were flying! Ladies were screaming! Waiters were trying, with no success, to catch the birds! And most of the men were, by now, howling with laughter. One over-dressed dowager was standing on a chair being supported by a rather stuffy gentleman who was doing his best not to laugh, while we managed to maintain an appropriate image. It was absolutely hilarious!

It took at least a half-hour to restore a semblance of order but, of course, the party was over. The best moment of the entire event was when a well-decorated group captain got into the elevator and said, "That was the best damn party I've been to since WW I." We never were accused of being the culprits; however, there were a few fairly accurate guesses.

Once a week a mechanic ran up the engine on a Northrop A-17A that was on the field, but I had never seen it in the air. My next assignment was to fly it, make an evaluation and prepare a set of check lists. I had the Northrop moved into the shop and asked the mechanic to cycle the landing gear to make sure it would function properly in flight. We also cycled the flaps and checked all the other systems. (The flaps were unusual because they looked like slices of Swiss cheese - full of circular holes - and I was to learn more about these flaps at Douglas in 1943.) After the mechanic and I were both satisfied that everything functioned as designed, I spent about an hour in the cockpit memorizing where things were. Then I had it wheeled out, started it up and did some taxi tests. Ground handling went well, so I took off and flew around for a while to get the feel of it.

The following week was devoted to becoming totally familiar with the aircraft and pinpointing, as accurately as possible, stalling, climbing, approach speeds, etc. That information, plus the data from the engine manual and my personal observations, gave me enough material so that I could prepare the check lists, a very abbreviated pilot's manual and an eval-

23 Lockheed 10, Electra; ten-seat or cargo, low-wing, monoplane, retractable gear; two Pratt and Whitney Wasp Junior, R-985, 450-hp radials. Used by early airlines. (D. Armstrong collection)

uation report. This assignment gave me a sense of accomplishment, but it also showed me how little I actually knew about planning and conducting flight tests to obtain useful and accurate data.

Soon it was spring, we were still in Ontario and my dad was on his way up for his promised visit. It was at this time that a most bizarre series of events took place. Every now and then, because there were fewer aircraft in the traffic pattern, I used the Picton airport, and a couple of times spent the night there. During one layover I caught a terrible cold, so I flew back to Trenton. On landing I requested and

received some medication and, without stopping to notify anyone, went home and went to bed, fully expecting to be back at work the following morning.

At the same time, there was another pilot at Picton - also from the States, also with the surname of Armstrong - who unfortunately had crashed late that same afternoon. His Harvard had gone through the ice on the lake, so neither his aircraft nor his body had been recovered.

The next morning Dad was en route from Long Island and stopped to phone me at the air base because we had no home phone. He was told, "F/O Armstrong's missing." Since he could not phone our home or obtain any further information, he kept driving, hoping that somehow there had been a mistake.

I had awakened that morning with a terribly high fever, so LaVerne asked a pilot who lived in the same building if he would advise someone in my squadron that I was ill and would not be at work, but he left on a flight without relaying the message.

LaVerne and I knew nothing about the crash, or the mixed-up identities, until flowers started being delivered to her and some of the women came over to console her and offer their help. Visitors or flowers arrived every fifteen minutes or so.

One of the wives immediately phoned my squadron and advised them that I was, in fact, alive. A second stayed with Donnie and me so LaVerne could meet my dad when he arrived at the visitors' gate. Around

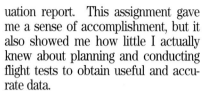

28 DeHavilland Moth - Gipsy; basic trainer; tandem, two-seat, some with canopies, biplane; Gipsy I, 100-hp in-line. Tiger; same as Gipsy; Gipsy Major, 130-hp in-line. (D. Armstrong collection)

noon LaVerne had the situation under control and brought a very relieved and happy father to see his son. After I recovered I requested a couple of days' leave and obtained permission to take Dad out to my squadron and show him around. I did my best to sneak him into a Harvard with me, but we couldn't get away with it. Just before he left he did see me practice formation-aerobatics with Sgt. Pilot Henderson in preparation for an air show, and thoroughly enjoyed it. It was a very timely visit because I was transferred to the Eastern Air Command in Nova Scotia soon after Dad returned to the States.

Dartmouth is across the river from Halifax, Nova Scotia, and in July 1941, was the home of Number Five (Bomber-Reconnaissance) Squadron to which I had been posted. Signs of tension were everywhere. The sheltered harbor was a major departure point for Allied shipping; therefore, extremely high security precautions were in effect. Most military personnel were acutely aware that they were facing a dangerous trip across the Atlantic, and an assignment to combat when they reached England. Posted near every public telephone was a sign warning the user not to discuss shipping information, unit designations or even the weather. Blackout regulations were displayed in all public buildings. Sabotage, or submarine-attack, warning posters added to the total awareness that "there was a war on."

German U-boats had attacked and sunk ships within sight of the harbor entrance, and would have penetrated the harbor itself had it not been protected by a submarine net. The major deterrent to offshore sub attacks was the presence of the coastal-patrol aircraft, most of which were flying boats (either the Consolidated PBY Catalina/Canso or the Supermarine Stranraer).

The Stranraer was a biplane powered with two sleeve-valve, Bristol Pegasus engines of 1,060 hp each, and had a seven-man crew. It carried four 500-pound depth charges, weighed 30,000 pounds and had fabric-covered wings. Because the wings were shorter and the hull higher in the water, many of us felt that it would be more seaworthy than the Catalina if forced down on the ocean. Only fifty-seven of these flying boats were built and, it's my guess, they were used in Canada because they would have been sitting ducks if flown within the range of German fighters.

I don't remember that the Stranraer had any particularly bad habits so it must have handled normally. On the water it taxied well, and that's a plus for any seaplane. But I do remember the pneumatically-operated automatic pilot – very well. Most autopilots I had used made no noticeable sound, but the one in the Stranraer hissed and gasped every time it made an attitude correction. Some pilots claimed that it helped them stay awake on long convoy-escort flights.

32 Bolingbroke IV (Bristol Blenheim manufactured by Fairchild of Canada); two Bristol Mercury VIII, 920-hp radials. Experimental, the only Bolingbroke ever fitted with floats. (D. Armstrong collection)

While flying the Stranraer a strange phenomenon happened to me almost every time I left the copilot in charge and went aft to sit in the main hull compartment for a cup of coffee or a sandwich. Had I remained there for more than five or ten minutes, the barely-perceptible motion of the aircraft would have made me air-sick! Quickly realizing this, I had my meals and naps "up front" and it never caught up with me. In more than fifty years of flying there has never been any other aircraft, whether I was the pilot or a passenger, in which I felt even queasy!

Bombing practice was fun and, because I had never had the opportunity to do it before, I needed every minute of it. The target was a float or raft anchored off shore. After my first or second run I could drop a small, practice bomb close enough to the target to, at the very least, have given a sub crew a good scare. On one run I actually hit the target and was promptly told that when anyone scored a hit he had to "stand for a round of beers" that night. I didn't mind at all. We had a ball.

My request for a checkout in the Catalina was approved, and during one of the flights a pilot made the remark that convoy-escort duty was boring. I was dismayed at his attitude because, to me, it was a frightening responsibility! If I, or my crew, missed spotting a periscope or a sub, it might have resulted in the loss of a ship, all those aboard and vital cargo. And if a troop carrier had been torpedoed, thousands of men would have died. I was never "bored."

The weather around Halifax during the summer of 1941 was either cold or miserable; I wore a rubber-lined raincoat every day but three in my three-month tour. There was so little sun that the locals took on an almost gray complexion, and instead of referring to themselves as "Haligonians," the term got changed to "Hell-and-gone-ians." Personally, I found most of the residents to be helpful and hospitable, even though they certainly had a difficult few years when their city was inundated with thousands of military and supporting personnel who must have frequently gotten under foot.

Everyone has used, or heard the expression, "it's a small world," and I have a classic example. Please, keep in mind that there were thousands of military personnel in the Halifax area at any given time, and very few Americans. I only used the ferryboat, which crossed the harbor from Halifax to Dartmouth, for two or three crossings in the short time I was stationed there. On my second trip I literally bumped into a young man, Don Beale, who had been in high school with me in White Plains, New York. He was an RCAF sergeant, still a U.S. citizen and in Halifax awaiting transportation to England. We were both amazed at the overwhelming odds against our meeting under such circumstances. I took him to dinner, and he was already gone the next day when I tried to reach him by phone. I know he received his commission and married an English girl, but I never learned if he survived the war.

In Halifax, the more intensely-felt urgency of the war hadn't totally eliminated social functions such as a reception for the Australian ambassador. I, as one of a very few "USA" officers in the Eastern Air Command, was invited to most of them. One day I attended a luncheon honoring the king's brother, the Duke of Kent, at which he presented the squadron with an official emblem.

I was to be seated "in sight of the head table," and had worn a freshly-pressed uniform, but neglected to change out of my hand-made, black, half-Wellington boots.

27 Noorduyn Norseman; eight-seat or freight, high-wing, monoplane, wheels/floats/skis; Pratt and Whitney Wasp, R-1340-AN-1, 550-hp radial. Most famous "bush plane" in Canada and Alaska. (D. Armstrong collection)

26 Boeing 247; civil transport; ten-seat, low-wing, monoplane, retractable gear but no flaps; two Pratt and Whitney Wasp, 550-hp radials. (D. Armstrong collection)

When the formalities were over, it was customary to stay for twenty or thirty minutes and "be available" - in the event that the guest of honor wanted to have a specific officer presented to him. The adjutant introduced me to the Duke, who cordially asked where I was from and a few questions about my present duties. Then, to my surprise, he asked to see my boots. (The station C.O. was shocked that I had not worn proper shoes and, even more so, that the Duke had called attention to the fact.) I put my foot on a chair and raised my trouser leg. The Duke of Kent looked at my boot and laughed, put his foot on the chair, raised his trouser leg and displayed an almost identical boot! He shook my hand, laughed again and made a comment about both of us having excellent taste in footwear!

[Historical note: The Duke of Kent, George Edward Alexander Edmond, fourth son of King George V, born in 1902, was a member of the Royal Air Force after 1940. He was killed, while on active service, in an airplane crash in Scotland in 1942.]

An attempt to develop faster coastal-patrol seaplanes for the RAF/RCAF while utilizing existing and available aircraft resulted in an experimental test of floats on the famous Bristol Blenheim light bomber. The Blenheim was manufactured by Fairchild of Canada, and called a "Bolingbroke." The Edo Float Company of Canada designed and constructed the floats. The Bolingbroke normally carried a crew of three, was powered by two Bristol Mercury engines of 920 hp each and weighed 15,800 pounds. This was the only Blenheim/Bolingbroke ever built with floats and, in August 1941, I was asked to conduct the water-handling, takeoff and landing tests at Dartmouth.

The aircraft was a truly amazing seaplane. It handled well on the water, got up "on the step" quickly on takeoff, flew easily in the air and, because the center of gravity was lowered by the weight of the floats, was extremely stable. It also landed well, even in a fully-stalled attitude. My initial evaluation report was very favorable and further tests were scheduled.

This was to be a very interesting few weeks for me since I knew very little about how to obtain the necessary

30 Supermarine Stranraer, "Stranny"; flying boat, long-range coastal patrol; crew of seven, biplane; two Bristol Pegasus X, 1,060-hp radials. (D. Armstrong collection)

32 Noorduyn Norseman (Courtesy of National Aviation Museum, Canada)

information. I contacted one of the aeronautical engineering officers by calling Air Force Headquarters in Ottawa. He was able to help me because the tests were limited in scope and much of the data I was seeking was merely comparative to data already available for the same aircraft on wheels. The engineer suggested specific test flights, which I conducted to the best of my ability.

The final tests were to be take-offs and landings in progressively rougher seas until, in the wording of the request, "something bent." I borrowed a football helmet - yes, a football helmet - padded the seatbelt and went to work. Everyone - the engineers, the Edo people, even the crash-boat personnel - was astounded at the punishment the aircraft and floats

withstood. I, too, was astonished, and fairly well bruised from my neck to my ankles. By the time a float strut "bent," and dents and rivet-losses appeared on the floats, I was very happy to call it quits. Once again, these tests made it obvious to me just how little I knew about the theory of test-flying, but I wouldn't have missed the opportunity for anything. I learned a lot and the tests were fun!

Number 118 Squadron operated from the Dartmouth airport and had a dozen or more Grumman FF-1 biplane fighters. Fifty-odd of these unique airplanes had been manufactured under license by the Canadian Car and Foundry Company. The Canadians designated it the "G-23 Goblin." It was unusual because it had been the first U.S. Navy fighter to have a retractable landing gear and an enclosed cockpit. It had a pot-bellied fuselage to provide space for the retracted gear and was a rugged and formidable plane when first built in 1931. It took a fair amount of talking, but I finally conned someone into letting me fly one - and it was well worth

the effort. The short wingspan made it exceptionally fast on rolls and it was equally responsive in other aerobatic maneuvers. I must have put on quite a show, so I was asked to fly it again to do some more aerobatics for a group of visiting VIPs the following week. I still feel it was a privilege to fly that rare U.S. Navy biplane fighter.

On October 12, 1941, I was transferred to the Test and Development Establishment at Rockcliffe Airport at Ottawa, Ontario, where my dreams would come true, at last.

Hold fast to dreams, for if dreams die
Life is a broken-winged bird, that cannot fly.
Hold fast to dreams, for when dreams go
Life is a barren field, frozen with snow.

Langston Hughes

32 Noorduyn Norseman (Courtesy of National Aviation Museum, Canada)

CHAPTER 6

PER ARDUA AD ASTRA
Test and Development Establishment
October 1941 - October 1942

[Historical notes: *Per Ardua Ad Astra* (Through Adversity to the Stars) - the official motto of the Royal Canadian Air Force.

Whenever it is used within this book, the term "establishment" may be construed to be synonymous with "squadron." A squadron, consisting of several flights, was usually attached to a wing which, in turn, was part of a group. The Test and Development facility (during WW II) was more directly linked to the RCAF Headquarters and, though comparable to a squadron, was designated an establishment.]

Most of us have had our lives enriched by a very special person - someone who has had a significant and profound influence upon us. As a youngster I had been inspired and nurtured by many of aviation's giants; as a newly-licensed pilot I had flying opportunities seldom afforded a novice, and I remain grateful for each and every one of them. Then, when I was twenty-one years old, circum-

6x The Flying Bicycle. While at McCook Field, Dr. William F. Gerhardt built this bizarre apparatus (in 1923). It had seven wings, was mounted on the frame of a bicycle and the propeller was driven by foot pedaling. In the collection of memorabilia presented by Mrs. Darlene (Crist) Gerhardt to the History Department of Wright-Patterson Air Force Base (formerly McCook Field) there is footage of its first flight. It rose three inches from the ground, for a distance of twenty feet. (Courtesy of YEAR, Inc.)

stances placed me under the tutelage of a truly great man who took me under his wing like a mother hen. His impact upon my career as a test pilot almost defies description.

He painstakingly and diligently instructed me, not just in the methods to be used, but in the rationale behind the methods. If it was possible, when I flew to practice the techniques he had explained to me, he went up with me - to critique the flight and suggest ways I could improve my skills and broaden my understanding of what I was doing. I already was an experienced and competent pilot; but in the months we had together he molded, polished and turned me into a knowledgeable and confident test pilot. In order to better

understand the significance of what I was able to accomplish in the following few years you, the reader, must first know something about this man who was my teacher, my mentor and my friend - the man I fondly called "Doc."

William Frederick Gerhardt was born in 1896, received military pilot training in 1917-1918 and remained an active Air Corps Reserve Officer until 1939. He attended Whittenburg College, then earned his Doctorate in Aeronautical Engineering at the University of Michigan. (In the early 1920s only two schools offered degrees in aeronautical engineering - MIT and the University of Michigan.)

In 1922, at McCook Field (Dayton, Ohio) Gerhardt joined Dr.

Georges DeBothezat, working in great secrecy, on the design of one of the first successful helicopters - initially flown on October 19, 1922. On April 17, 1923, it left the ground in a sustained, stable and controllable flight while lifting four men. The May 1923 issue of the *Aeronautical Engineering Review* documents these events, complete with photographs.

While he was Chief of Flight Research at McCook Field, Dr. Gerhardt designed and flew the seven-winged "Cycleplane," making the first "flight by manpower" in July 1923. This notable invention was not an official project of the Engineering Division; rather it was

assembled in the helicopter hangar by Gerhardt and volunteers, working in their spare time. It was a valuable contribution to the field of aviation in that it helped determine the limitations of manpower. Engineers subsequently recognized that flights of any endurance would probably require continuous mechanical power.

Dr. Gerhardt was employed as a professor of Aeronautical Engineering at the University of Michigan in 1924 and, during his tenure there, also became director of the Curtiss-Wright ground school at the Grosse Isle Airport. It is an interesting note that when he and Darlene Crist were married in Boston on December 3, 1924, the attendants for

the ceremony were Lieutenant and Mrs. James H. Doolittle.

In 1927, while working with an associate, Lawrence V. Kerber, Gerhardt co-authored a definitive book, *The Manual of Flight-Test Procedures*. This volume details the readying of an aircraft for flight test, including the installation and calibration of test instruments, as well as establishment of the research and performance test plans. It outlines the collection, computation and reduction of data, and how to determine and eliminate error (in both obtaining and presenting the data) and was probably the first book of its kind to cover both research and production test flying.

[Author's note: Other texts state that this book was originally issued by the University of Michigan. However, the University library (in 1993) could not locate any record of it. The Library of Congress lists two copies: Card No. 28-27120 and Call No. TL 671.G4. The San Diego Aerospace Museum, in its archives, also has a copy.]

Dr. Gerhardt was invited to chair the new Department of Aeronautical Engineering at Wayne State University (Michigan) in 1930, and continued on the faculty, taking a leave of absence in June 1941, for "military service" - at which time he

47 Airspeed Oxford, "Ox-box"; advanced trainer; low-wing, monoplane, wheels/skis; two Armstrong Siddeley Cheetah, 355-hp radials or Pratt and Whitney Wasp, 450-hp radials. (Courtesy of National Aviation Museum, Canada)

accepted a commission in the RCAF. He was attached to the Test and Development Establishment at Rockcliffe, Ottawa, Ontario, Canada, and held the rank of flight lieutenant, equivalent to a captain in the USAAF.

It was here that our paths would cross.

No words can adequately describe my feelings when, on October 12, 1941, I arrived at the Test and Development hangar and offices at Rockcliffe. (Coincidentally, Lloyd Child, who later would be instrumental in my transfer to the Curtiss-Wright Corporation, was demonstrating a P-40 at Rockcliffe that same day.) When asked, many children say that when they grow up they want to be firemen, cowboys, soldiers or whatever they momentarily fancy; but since the age of seven or eight I had repeatedly told my parents I wanted to be a test pilot.

Now I was going to fulfill my dreams. I understood and accepted the fact that I was not, by any stretch of the imagination, a qualified test pilot but, at the same time, I knew I had the will and skill to become one. Even now I can't explain why I felt as confident - not cocky or arrogant - as I did that day. I just knew it was going to work out. It wouldn't happen quickly, or easily - but I was primed and "yearning for learning!" That very afternoon I first met Doc Gerhardt and, before I knew anything about his qualifications

35 Blackburn B-6 Shark; carrier-borne torpedo bomber; biplane, nonretractable gear; Armstrong Siddeley Tiger, 700-hp radial. Built by Boeing Aircraft of Canada. (D. Armstrong collection)

36 Fairey Swordfish, "Stringbag"; early torpedo bomber; biplane, nonretractable gear; Bristol Pegasus, 690-hp radial. Wings folded back alongside fuselage for carrier storage. (Courtesy of San Diego Aerospace Museum)

or background, I liked him. He was quiet, unassuming and obviously cared about his work and the people around him. He radiated confidence and graciously accepted the respect given him by his fellow officers. Within a few days I knew a great deal more about him, from our talks together and from the engineers, mechanics and other pilots. When we discussed my flying experiences - my playing at flight testing in the OX-5 Travel Air and the Cub, the work I had done on the Northrop A-17 and the Lockheeds and the tests I had done in the Bolingbroke on floats - I was completely frank and up-front with him. I related what I had done - and how little I knew about what I was doing - and he must have sensed how sincerely I wanted to learn.

I first got my feet wet when Doc Gerhardt set up a couple of simple rate-of-climb test flights, told me how to do them - and why - and then climbed into the right-hand seat of an Anson and helped me do them. After we landed he showed me how to complete my report, then had me "help" him prepare the graphs and check the data. He flew with me several times in the first two or three days, and on each flight I tried, and learned about, something new. On Friday he gave me some test reports and graphs to study over the weekend and, on Monday, offered to really help me learn how to bring down good results. To say I was thrilled, fascinated and totally enthralled would have been the understatement of the year. I was hooked! I had arrived! It was happening! I was on my way to becoming a test pilot!

Throughout the next two months I flew a great many performance and handling tests on a marvelous variety of aircraft under widely-diverse conditions. Almost any plane assigned to Rockcliffe, or even those passing through on a ferry flight, could be "requested" by the Test and Development's senior engineering officer, F/L Gerhardt, for "evaluation" purposes. In most, but not every instance, I submitted a brief, but viable written report. It was an almost unbelievable opportunity to familiarize myself with aircraft that I never would have been able to fly under any other circumstances. For example, I was assigned to fly the old Blackburn Shark and the Fairey Swordfish (biplanes), a Northrop Delta (transport), the Handley-Page Hampden and the Douglas DB-18 Digby (bombers) and the Hawker Hurricane and Supermarine Spitfire (fighters), in addition to other routine flights, all in a span of about seven weeks. Only another pilot can possibly imagine the sheer joy of this.

To fly these planes for a few hours would have been pleasure enough but, on each flight, without exception, Doc gave me a test to perform, thereby adding to my testing knowledge and piloting skills. My first longitudinal-stability tests were practiced on the Hampden "Flying Panhandle." My first single-engine rate-of-climb tests in which I laid out, conducted the flight and worked up all the data were in the Douglas DB-18 Digby, with Doc sitting calmly in the right-hand seat. I did speed vs power flights in the Spitfire, stalling speed vs G-load checks in the Hurricane - learning, always learning. Doc was methodically, yet tactfully, broadening my experience and enhancing my skills while permeating me with an overwhelming desire to "do it safely, analytically and intelligently."

By December Doc and I felt I was ready to do some tests entirely on my own. So, on the 15th, I flew a Lockheed 14 (awaiting special equipment at the Ferry Squadron in the next hangar) to DeHavilland's field, near Toronto, to conduct some canopy tests on a Tiger Moth trainer. The tests were to determine if the canopy could be slid back easily in most emergency flight conditions, permitting the occupants to abandon the aircraft rapidly, if necessary. If the hood could be operated quickly and easily, a more costly emergency release could be eliminated from future production.

I, and an observer in the front cockpit, would operate the hoods in level flight, dives, inverted flight, spiral

dives and spins; then report the length of time and degree of difficulty required to do so. As anticipated, the only time the hood was more difficult to operate was in high-speed dives or when the aircraft was spinning. We did the tests with no serious problems - except that the poor observer's stomach couldn't tolerate the inverted flight or the spins. (Even though I felt sorry for him, there really wasn't much that I could do to help him. He did learn, very quickly, not to eat anything until the day's flights were completed.) After several days, and many hours of flying, the factory engineers were prepared to recommend that the emergency-release mechanism was not needed.

Then suddenly, I smelled a fish in the pickle-barrel - these tests had been with an aircraft straight off the production line, and had new, clean, unworn canopy roller-tracks. A Moth, used for instructional purposes, would show the wear and tear of an untold number of rough, student-pilot landings while accumulating dirt and grime from a few hundred hours of taking off and landing on a dusty field. Doc had impressed upon me that, for

50 Fleet Fort; trainer; tandem, two-seat, canopied, low-wing, monoplane, nonretractable gear; Jacobs L-6MB, 285-hp radial. Rear seat was elevated for excellent visibility. Only ninety were built. (D. Armstrong collection)

a test to be viable, it should be performed with the equipment, and under the circumstances, that was as close as possible to what would be used or encountered in actual situations.

I suggested borrowing an older, similar plane - one actually in use by an elementary training squadron - and repeating the tests. (I definitely was not very popular with my observer, or the clean-up crew!) However, the results were entirely different! The worn, dusty tracks almost doubled the time necessary to open the hoods, causing me to recommend that the emergency-release mechanism be

40 Hawker Hurricane; fighter; single-seat, low-wing, monoplane; Rolls-Royce Merlin, 1,185-hp V-in-line. (Courtesy of National Aviation Museum, Canada)

retained on future aircraft. The T & D Senior Engineering Officer (Doc) concurred and production continued with the emergency release included.

The diversity of investigations T & D was requested to perform is best illustrated by my next series of tests. Railroad tracks converge on most cities, making it easy for a bomber, by following them, to go directly to an industrial complex - especially at night,

39 Douglas DB-18, Bolo, known in Canada as the Digby; bomber; low-wing, monoplane; two Wright R-1820-53, 1,000-hp radials. Adaptation of the Douglas DC-3/C-47, Dakota. (D. Armstrong collection)

with bright moonlight. The Canadian National Research Council had been requested to develop some type of material which the final car on every train could easily and economically spray, or drip, onto the tracks that would dull their shiny-steel reflectiveness. On several clear nights, when the moon was more than one-quarter full, I took some of the NRC people aloft, in a Norseman, to see how effective their latest camouflage was in hiding the tracks. In my opinion, I thought their efforts only marginally effective; but I was too busy to follow up the project

and never learned if the research continued.

The old, reliable Fairey Battle was frequently used by the air-gunnery training squadrons for target towing and, after gunnery practice, the sleeve (a target which looked like a big, elongated windsock) was dropped. It took considerable time to land, taxi, hook up a new target and take off again, so T & D was requested to experiment with ways in which a new target could be snatched up without having to land the aircraft. Working with a couple of men from one of the gunnery groups, we made some modifications of the equipment. I then made a short series of flights, ascertained that the equipment worked as planned and prepared a brief manual of the flight procedures involved.

It was an enjoyable project, primarily because the challenge was to devise a snatch hook that was simple and trouble-free. Anyone, especially a "sliderule freak," can develop a complicated gadget that would do the job. The trick was to solve the problem with something truly fundamental. In this case we did, and had fun doing it. I'll never forget the gestures and the "we're-laughing-at-you" antics of the

ground crew whenever I missed with my pickup hook. Our shop guys were a fine crew and, in the year I worked with them, they never let me down.

Since there was an excellent rapport between the officers and all the NCOs and enlisted men, the morale of the group was exceptionally high. Nobody griped when we needed to fly before dawn or late at night; and when we had a light workload, the guys could get off early or have a day or two of unscheduled leave. Rank, discipline and protocol were diligently observed; but what I liked was that they also felt perfectly free to joke with me, or kid me if I goofed.

One unique aspect of flying in Canada was the use of ski-equipped planes. Almost all of the older planes were certificated for use on skis; but there was a major effort to develop emergency skis which could be easily fitted to newer planes, enabling them to be evacuated from snow-covered fields. So skis were adapted to "fit over" the wheels and, while some were unsatisfactory, others proved to be functional. The installation on the twin Cessna Crane (C-78 Bobcat) was one of the "usable, but not-so-good" designs. Here's a partial quote from my report dated March 13, 1942:

Flight tests were then carried out and the skis proved satisfactory for emergency use. They remained in trim in all attitudes of flight, i.e., climb, level flight, stall and glide; however, in all flight conditions the aircraft was so excessively nose-heavy that full nose-up trim could not compensate.

In direct contrast, the emergency skis on the twin-engine Airspeed Oxford worked well, as shown in my report of April 6, 1942:

Air-handling was entirely satisfactory; however, it was necessary to taxi with the tail in the air to prevent the tail wheel,

42 Lockheed 14, Super Electra, known in Canada as the Hudson; bomber/transport; two Wright GR-1829-G102A, 1,000-hp radials. Originally built for the British as a military conversion. (D. Armstrong collection)

which had no ski, from sinking into the snow and possibly damaging the empennage. *The aircraft handles well in this condition without building up too much ground speed because the increased drag of the skis nearly compensates for the increased throttle setting necessary to raise the tail... The skis are satisfactory for their designed use.*

I also flight tested skis on two other aircraft that might facilitate landing covert-forces personnel and equipment in Nazi-occupied Norway. The first was on the twin-engine Bolingbroke (Blenheim) light bomber. The skis were well designed and, although huge and reducing the speed of the aircraft dramatically, were entirely satisfactory. I was the only pilot ever to have flown a Bolingbroke on wheels, floats and skis.

The second test was on the versatile and powerful Westland Lysander. Because of its superb short takeoff and landing characteristics, the Lysander had made innumerable flights into occupied territory (especially France) dropping agents and resistance personnel. It was felt that it could be further utilized to good advantage, in Norway, if fitted with strong, easily-installed "interchangeable" skis. I flew it to northern Ontario because, in April, there was still more than four feet of snow on the ground. Even though a ski-equipped Lysander would have provided a tactical advantage in Norway, my report clearly demonstrates how poorly designed these skis were:

In taxiing, ground control was extremely poor and sometimes dangerous... The aircraft ground-loops rapidly and severely, resulting from the small amount of keel-surface on the front skis, coupled with the fact that the tail ski is free-swiveling... The small size, high-loading of all the skis allows the front skis to sink into normal snow from 8-14 inches, and the tail ski up to 20 inches, causing the tail to be supported on the snow by the stabilizer and elevators... The high boost [power] needed to taxi in deep snow causes high cylinder-head and oil temperatures. The aircraft is almost uncontrollable and dangerous during takeoff especially if one ski is on the surface and the other has sunk up to 15-20 inches in the snow... On landing, the last third of the run is extremely dangerous, the plane uncontrollable and the pilot merely a passenger... After completing over 100 takeoffs and landings, I believe it would be decidedly dangerous to use the aircraft operationally for any purpose whatsoever... The skis are unsatisfactory.

Needless to say, the Lysander on these skis was never used, in Norway or anywhere else. Out of the four different tests, one was good, two were acceptable and one was unsatisfactory. You win some and you lose some.

On our return to Rockcliffe we sported quite a tan - acquired in the "tanning pit" we'd dug, about six feet down in a snow drift, where on many days we had lunch, in our shorts. The trip had been fun, but I was ready to go down to Fort Erie, Ontario, for some stability and control tests on the Fleet Fort trainer. For transportation down and back I used one of my old friends, the Fleet biplane, this one powered by the Armstrong Siddeley Civet engine. It was great fun to fly IFR - "I Follow Railroads" (not Instrument Flight Rules!) - with no radios, just loafing along and enjoying the spring scenery.

The Fort was a totally new design with a low wing, a Jacobs 285-hp engine and the rear seat raised above the front seat to provide optimum visibility from either cockpit. The aircraft had good stability and control characteristics around all three axis-of-flight and handled very well. I enjoyed the project, but was disappointed when I learned, a few years later, that only ninety of these fine planes were built. It could have been an effective, economical primary trainer; and an excellent instrument trainer, as well. I guess it was just built at the wrong time.

Before going back to T & D, I took a couple of days' leave and made a quick trip to Buffalo to do some shopping. When I crossed the Ontario/New York border I was surprised, and deeply touched, when people recognized my RCAF uniform with the USA patch and pilot's wings. A U.S. Customs officer shook my hand and said "Thanks." The taxi driver wouldn't accept pay for taking me to the hotel, and when I went downstairs in the hotel to eat, the manager sent over a complimentary bottle of champagne.

The U.S. had entered the war less than five months earlier and, unlike in the Korean or Vietnam conflicts, almost every family had someone who was already in uniform, or expected to be soon. If not in military service, at least one family member was working in a war industry. People were proud to be patriotic, proud of their men and women in uniform, proud of our flag and proud - although sad - of the gold stars already displayed in their windows. (For those too young to remember, the gold star signified that a family member had been killed in the war.) How different it was then. How sad it is - now - that many Americans have never felt that same, deep sense of pride in their country and their fellow Americans.

A USAAF C-47 (Douglas DC-3) was at Rockcliffe when I returned, and Doc had arranged to have me fly it. To pilots who have never flown one, I can only say that you have missed flying one of the true work-horses of aviation. It does nothing exciting, but there is (to me, at least) a strange feeling of capability about the plane. After ten minutes of flight I felt comfortable - it was almost like putting on an old, familiar pair of slippers.

Soon afterward I had a few, not-so-busy days and helped out a couple of nights by flying a "Faithful Annie" (Anson) for some celestial-navigation students. If only I had known what a kidding I'd take as a result! Two students had been taking celestial "shots" through the navigator's dome and the instructor was checking their technique and numbers. I - with far more ego than intelligence - thought I could do it, too, because Dad had shown me how to use a sextant when I was only thirteen or fourteen. So, I confidently asked if I could try.

After a brief instruction I did what I thought was correct, read my numbers to the instructor and returned to the controls. (Remember that we were flying along the Ottawa River, northwest of the city.) I had barely settled back into my seat when I heard howls of laughter coming from the cabin. The men came forward, still laughing. When asked how I had done, they informed me that, by my shots, it appeared we were just a few miles north of the Panama Canal! My

celestial-navigation skills were comparable to my welding skills. As you can well imagine everyone on the base, or so it seemed, knew about it by the next morning. I was called "Star Man," "King of the Navigators" and "Panama Kid." In my incoming-mail box I found a map - of RCAF Station, Rockcliffe - marked in red ink to show me the way from the T & D hangar to the officers' mess!

Early in May I was given an assignment which kept me busy for the better part of the next two months. It was among the most important assignments of my career - primarily because I learned so very much from it. The RCAF had recently acquired Curtiss-Wright P-40E Kittyhawk fighters and felt it necessary to conduct complete performance tests to verify the manufacturer's figures and to modify, if necessary, the RCAF pilot manual.

Before I was assigned to conduct these tests Doc had been assured by the Officer Commanding (T & D) that I would do all of the fly-

48 Bristol Blenheim (Bolingbroke), "Boley"; wheels/skis; two Bristol Mercury, 1,000-hp radials. This series originated with the design of the 1935 commercial Bristol, Type 142. Initial tests revealed it to already be 50-mph faster than Britain's newest fighter. The versatile aircraft saw service as a light bomber, as the testbed for pioneering British airborne radar and remained fully operational until the end of 1943. Over 6,000 were produced. (D. Armstrong collection)

41 Supermarine Spitfire; fighter; single-seat, low-wing, monoplane; wide range of single Rolls-Royce Merlin, 1,030- to 1,185-hp V-in-lines. Probably the most famous Allied fighter of WW II. Earlier models easily recognized by their elliptical wing. Evolved from the early Supermarine racer on floats. (D. Armstrong collection)

ing and would also be involved with any work done to, or alterations made in, the plane throughout the program. This included weighing, determining the center of gravity, ballasting, fabricating and installing all the test instrumentation and, after each flight, following through on all data reduction and preparation of flight-test reports. At the completion of the program I would assist in preparing the final report.

This became a hands-on test-pilot school - a course planned and taught by one of the most qualified and knowledgeable aeronautical and flight-test engineers in North America. Because I was the only student, it was a face-to-face, professor-to-student, one-on-one learning experience. To put more icing on the cake, I was going to do all of my work in one of the latest fighter planes! I had only one regret -

Doc might be leaving before I completed all of the flights as he had applied for transfer to the USAAF. However, he had covered every minute detail with me, along with the flight engineers who would be working directly on the project. I was also saddened that my dad could not be there to observe the flights and my engineering work associated with them.

[Author's note: For the benefit of the non-pilot, I will describe some of the significant features of conducting a series of performance tests - without becoming too technical. For the contemporary pilot, the descriptions of the equipment and methods (considered to be totally acceptable in 1942) may enhance your appreciation of Chapter 17, "Flight Testing – Then and Now."]

Step one was to install a "photo-observer": a box designed by the National Research Council with a separate panel containing an airspeed indicator, altimeter, clock, outside air

temperature and a manifold-pressure gauge, that would take photos of these instruments every four seconds. I operated this camera by depressing the gun-firing button on the control column and, using it only when necessary, was able to conserve film.

The second step was to weigh the aircraft in level flight attitude - first empty, next with full fuel, guns, ammunition and 190 pounds of ballast in the cockpit. (Pilot weight was averaged at 170 pounds, plus 20 pounds for parachute and equipment.) This was done on three scales, one under each of the

38 Handley Page Hampden, "Flying Panhandle," "Tadpole"; light bomber; monoplane; two Bristol Pegasus XVII, 980-hp radials. (Courtesy of National Aviation Museum, Canada)

main wheels and one under the tail wheel, in order to calculate the center of gravity under both conditions.

The aircraft was now ready. The final preparation for flight tests was to

6a Camera recorder (photo-observer) mounted in RCAF Kittyhawk No. 752 that I used for performance and handling trials, Rockcliffe, Ottawa, Ontario (June 30, 1942). (D. Armstrong collection)

determine the differences that existed between, for example, what the airspeed instrument indicated and what the actual airspeed was, at any given time during flight. This calibration could be determined in one of two ways. First, by timing flights over a well-defined ground course of predetermined length, at various indicated airspeeds, and creating a graph which plotted the actual vs indicated speeds. Second, by flying (in close formation) beside a "pace" aircraft, whose airspeed instrument had already been accurately calibrated, and creating a similar graph. Because I had already calibrated the airspeed indicator on a Hurricane using the first technique, we used the "pace-plane" method for both of the airspeed instruments (on my panel and in the photo-observer).

The first performance tests were speed vs power flights. This entailed flying in precise level flight, at an exact altitude, with maximum permissible engine power. In order to obtain a good overall graph I did seven of

these flights, at 4,000-foot intervals, from 1,000 to 25,000 feet.

To determine the best climbing speed at various altitudes, I did a series of timed-climbs, through 1,000 feet, at airspeed increments of 10 mph - starting at 40 mph below and ending at 40 mph above the estimated best climbing speeds. These flights were conducted at 5,000-foot intervals from 5,000 to 25,000 feet. The best climbing speed at each altitude was plotted on a graph and the curved line connecting them would be used to find the best climbing speed at any chosen altitude.

Using the speeds as determined by the previous tests, I then did four, timed "full-power climbs to service ceiling" (the altitude at which a plane can continue to climb only 100 feet per minute). Additional information that we obtained on these timed-climbs included engine oil and coolant temperatures and changes in outside air and cockpit temperature.

Next, I verified the exact stalling speed of the Kittyhawk with the aircraft "clean" and "dirty" (flaps and wheels down, coolant flaps and cockpit open).

And last, we measured takeoff distances and did some timed climbs from the start of takeoff to 1,000 feet altitude.

Academically, here are some of the results (Curtiss P-40, Kittyhawk, RCAF configuration): gross weight, 8,050 pounds; maximum level-flight speed, 328 mph at 16,000 feet; rate-of-climb, 2,510 fpm at take-off power; service ceiling, 30,100 feet; stalling speed - clean, 76 mph and dirty, 66 mph; takeoff distance, 2,035 feet.

Dr. W. F. "Doc" Gerhardt - now, without question, one of my "giants" - did transfer to the USAAF before the tests were completed. However, he stayed in touch with me, by phone, throughout the program. The information about these tests is from my copy of the fourteen-page, official RCAF report, submitted by Squadron Leader D. M. Holman on June 30, 1942. A complete copy, signed by many of us, had been sent to Doc, along with some autographed photographs, a week or so earlier.

The fact that I was able to participate in every phase of this program was, in itself, a remarkable and unprecedented occurrence. Without the fervent persuasion of Doc Gerhardt, the cooperation of Squadron Leader Holman and the authority granted by Wing Commander T. R. Loudon, I probably would have been limited simply to flying the aircraft. For these fine officers, and the associated engineers and staff who patiently permitted me to assist in data reduction and presentation, I express again - over fifty years later - my most sincere thanks. The knowledge and confidence I gained from this project was of inestimable value to me throughout the remainder of my test flying career.

A test pilot is almost continuously making suggestions - hoping to improve an aircraft's performance, make it safer, easier to fly or more effective for its designed use. Test flying stimulates creative ideas: some worth pursuing; others, although innovative, don't quite make it. Illustrative are two ideas that I developed which were investigated by the RCAF, the USAAF, Curtiss-Wright and Douglas.

The first was an automatic rudder-trimming device that used a simple bank-and-turn indicator, activating a small electric motor which would move the rudder trim-tab. This device actually was considered for use by Curtiss-Wright in the XP-60 program (Chapter 8). The other was an instrument named by Doc Gerhardt a "Dynameter." It gave the pilot a stalling-speed indication at any G-load; as well as a personal "black-out" warning, adjustable to the individual pilot. This instrument was tested and seriously considered for use in aerobatic and fighter trainers: Although both proved to be viable, they were not quite good enough. I did, however, get a great deal of personal satisfaction from creating them.

The DeHavilland Mosquito photo-reconnaissance/bomber was an aircraft that I enjoyed flying equally as much as I had the Bolingbroke, in spite of their vast differences. The Mosquito was constructed primarily of wood and had in-line engines; the "Boley" was metal and equipped with radials - and you can't get much different than that! I liked the way the Boley handled: it had a nice, solid feel to it, while responding instantly and smoothly to control pressure. The "Wooden Wonder" was equally solid and responsive, but was much faster. It was also obviously powerful and light and clean in appearance, but these characteristics don't always guarantee a machine that pilots enjoy flying. To illustrate, the Gee Bee racing plane, built in the 1930s, was powerful and light and clean looking but, as one of its famous pilots had commented, it was "a real bitch to fly." The Mosquito, on the other hand, felt like it was not only going to get you to your destination - comfortably and in a hurry - but, more importantly, like it was going to get you home again. Even today I wish that I could have done more flying in "Mossies."

The tests I did in the Mosquito were all related to the high-altitude performance of the plane. My test aircraft had no guns or ammo, no provisions for bombs and an absolute minimum of radio equipment. It did have a ballasted box in place of a high-resolution camera. Our flights were to obtain data on 1) high-speed range vs fuel consumption and 2) maximum range vs fuel consumption, without regard to

37 Northrop Delta; transport; nine-seat, low-wing, monoplane, nonretractable gear; Wright Cyclone, SR-1820-73, 690-hp radial. Built by Canadian Vickers. (D. Armstrong collection)

how slowly it had to be flown in order to achieve it; 3) absolute operational altitude and 4) the best possible combination of the three conditions.

The maximum-range flights were extremely intriguing, especially since very few people believed our preliminary information. We had done meticulous flight testing; and I repeated many of the flights to verify, without question, the accuracy of our figures. But here we were, with hard, indisputable facts in our hands; and still the typical comment heard from the deskjockeys was, "That's ridiculous, it can't be right!" They finally had to accept the fact that

we could squeeze a fantastic range out of the fuel tanks by flying at just the right combination of high power, low rpm and relatively slow speeds. In any event, I liked the plane and had fun doing the tests.

[Author's note: Charles A. Lindbergh verified the high power, low rpm theory during the Pacific war and was able to sell the idea to the long-range fighter squadrons. When I talked to him at the Naval Air Test Center several years later, we laughed because, in the early stages of his investigations he, too, had seen the same looks of disbelief.]

One of the most significant series of flights I made in the RCAF involved highly-secret, night-fighter radar. By 1941 the British had been able to reduce the size of a very effective, rotating radar antenna to the point where they felt it could be used in night-fighters. However, four problems still needed to be overcome. First, it must be remembered that miniaturization of electronic equipment (tubes to transistors) was unknown at that time, so

51 Fleet Fawn, also known as the Civet; Armstrong Siddeley Civet, 165-hp radial. (D. Armstrong collection)

all such equipment was large (huge, by today's standards) and heavy. Second, the equipment demanded an inordinate amount of electrical power to operate and, since alternators were not available, much larger-than-normal generators were necessary. Third, the antenna was slightly over two feet in diameter and had to be housed, in non-metallic material, in the most forward portion of the aircraft. And fourth, in England there was the constant threat that the test facilities and engineers might be bombed.

The first three problems would all be solved by the use of a fast, twin-engined aircraft: this type of plane would be large enough to hold the equipment, each of the two engines could drive a separate generator and the nose of the fuselage could be adapted to house the antenna. The safest location for test and research was in Canada or the United States. Because the Radiation Laboratory at the Massachusetts Institute of Technology (in Boston) unquestionably had the finest research facility, the project was based there.

Early versions of Airborne Interceptor (AI) devices had been fitted on the Mosquito, Beaufighter, Blenhheim and others, so the choice of the Canadian Bolingbroke for use as a testbed was a logical one. More advanced "twins" would be used operationally if the unit proved satisfactory, reasonably trouble-free and could be manufactured in sufficient numbers. Probably because I could work up weight-and-balance information and keep engineering work-orders logged correctly, I was chosen as the pilot. As soon as I was cleared by security and thoroughly briefed on the project I requested a "permanent" crew - men

already familiar with the maintenance and service of the aircraft. I chose Corporal Griffen and Leading Aircraftsman Wilson, both of whom remained with me for the entire program. They, too, were proud to have been chosen, and learning that temporary duty in the States provided them with living expenses, plus a cash per diem, did nothing to dampen their enthusiasm.

We flew the Boley (temporarily designated as No. 9010) to East Boston Airport where a high-security hangar and shop were already cleared, cleaned and waiting. Dr. T. W. Bonner was the director of the project and spent a considerable amount of time explaining his intentions, outlining my responsibilities and introducing me to his associates. Even now I remember how impressed I was by the MIT facility and its staff.

The Statler Hotel was about halfway between the airport and MIT so I was given a comfortable room there, while Griffen and Wilson were housed in a hotel much closer to the hangar. Within a few days Dr. Bonner and a couple of his engineers invited me and my crew to dinner at one of Boston's beautiful and popular restaurants. The three of us were in uniform, and almost immediately after we entered the room, people started clapping. The orchestra stopped in mid-tune, then began playing *There'll Always Be An England*, and several diners came over to shake our hands. It was a very touching experience, similar to the one in Buffalo, and one which was repeated several times with minor variations (using the music of *The White Cliffs of Dover*, for exam-

53 Curtiss P-40 Warhawk, known in RAF and Flying Tigers as the Tomahawk; fighter; single-seat, low-wing, monoplane; Allison V-1710-19, 1,160-hp V-in-line. Famous for the "shark tooth" paint job on the nose. P-40Ds and P-40Es were improved models known as Kittyhawks with the RAF, RCAF and the Soviet Union. (D. Armstrong collection)

ple). Dr. Bonner asked me if I was embarrassed by it. I replied that I was not, that I took it as a tribute - not to me personally - but to all the American, Canadian and United Kingdom servicemen and women who had been fighting the war for two, long, hard years before Pearl Harbor. I was exceptionally pleased when he replied that he understood exactly what I meant.

The installation of the equipment and the oversize, high-amperage generators required hard work, long hours and a lot of patience. Just as the MIT electronic people thought they had a scope or a piece of equipment installed properly, along came a WCO (work change order) and something would have to be moved. Moving the units was easy, but changing all of the wiring was a terrible, time-consuming chore. I frequently stayed on the job to give Corporal Griffen some "authority," should the MIT men start to do something which might adversely affect the plane. But, in reality, my main responsibility was to weigh each piece of equipment installed, or removed, and measure its exact fore-to-aft location in the aircraft, in order to update the weight-and-balance data sheet. To prevent any oversights, I

54 DeHavilland Mosquito, "Wooden Wonder"; photo reconnaissance/bomber; two Rolls-Royce Merlin 76, 1,710-hp V-in-lines. (Courtesy of National Aviation Museum, Canada)

required that my initials be visible on everything added to the plane, and that anything installed, moved or removed be logged so that my updating would remain accurate.

The hangar was kept secure by armed Marines and I'm certain that no person, not even Dr. Bonner or myself, entered the building without being thoroughly checked. Some days I'd go back and forth between the hangar and MIT three or four times and, every time, they acted as though they had never seen me before. Finally, the aircraft and equipment were ready to be checked. Everyone breathed a deep sigh of relief, but there were plenty of crossed-fingers, too.

Surprisingly, there seemed to be more apprehension about the generators and power-supply units than about the AI components, even though the rotating antenna had given cause for concern in England. But all initial fears proved groundless during engine run-ups and for the first few flights. The

most frustrating delays occurred because we had to land to make adjustments to the receiving units. To make matters worse, we'd have to remove the faulty units and take them to the MIT labs since their test equipment could not be moved to the hangar. After several flights, during which an engineer successfully located airplanes flying near us, we were ready for far more precise evaluation. Now it was time for an expert, some-one with actual night-fighter interception experience. After a short delay, our man arrived from England, and we were eager for some actual night-interception trials.

The first few nights we flew mock interceptions, using military or commercial planes departing from, or arriving in, the Boston area. These "interceptions" were easy: we knew where to look, the "targets" took no evasive action and we terminated our approach to them long before the other pilots became alarmed. Then, just as we felt we were ready for more realistic targets, one of the big generators failed. It was severely damaged - enough to halt the tests for three or four weeks. The telephone search for a replacement could be compared to the organized bedlam at the New York Stock Exchange.

To everyone's surprise - and joy - a similar, usable generator was soon located in a warehouse at the

Middletown Army Air Depot in Pennsylvania. However, try to picture the total confusion created by a civilian request... for USAAF military equipment... on behalf of the RAF... to be installed in a Canadian military aircraft... to facilitate highly-secret tests conducted by the Massachusetts Institute of Technology... for a British procurement agency! It was far too complicated! Not a single person was willing to stick his neck out and authorize shipment of the generator. Every person contacted deftly passed the buck. The only redeeming feature of this comic opera was that Dr. Bonner learned precisely where the generator was - right down to the location in, and the designation of, the specific warehouse in which it was stored.

MIT "obtained" a blank requisition form, and I was asked to fly to Middletown to persuade someone to release the generator. We had discussed (off-the-record, of course) trying to bluff them out of it, and the decision was that I'd play it by ear. A hare-brained scheme was already running through my mind - one just audacious enough that it might work.

Resulting from my official request, a Marine was ordered to accompany me and "guard" the aircraft, although we had already removed the secret units from the plane. In spite of the fact that I had fuel enough for the complete trip from Boston to Middletown, and return, I filed a flight plan to Floyd Bennett (Navy) Field in Brooklyn, New York, where I would land "for fuel." After topping off my tanks, I filed a second flight plan for the very short flight from Floyd Bennett to Middletown and took off without delay. I intended to arrive there long after normal working hours, before anyone other than the Middletown tower operator might become involved. While en route, I radioed a request to be met with ground transportation immediately upon landing.

My short-notice arrival, at night, in a totally unfamiliar RCAF aircraft, instilled an air of urgency into the situation. Then, when I appeared with an armed Marine at my side, the young - and very apprehensive - "ninety-day-wonder" duty officer was completely overwhelmed. He was visibly relieved that his responsibilities were limited to chauffeuring us to and from the warehouse. Suffice it to say that I - rather imperialistically, I'm afraid - convinced yet another poor guy on night duty to honor my "requisition order" and hand over the generator.

Without looking back - someone might be gaining on me - I quickly filed a flight plan for Floyd Bennett Field while my guys loaded the damn thing in the plane and tied it down. Need I add that I took off without stopping for a cup of coffee? But then, I made a "mistake." I canceled my flight plan for Floyd Bennett and refiled for East Boston, by radio, "overlooking" the fact that I was supposed to wait for special clearance before entering coastal areas at night.

Ten or fifteen minutes later most of the lights below us went out. Unknown to us, at that moment we had unintentionally caused a blackout!

However, by the time we arrived near "home" and had our tower on the radio, someone apparently decided that I had no intention of bombing Radio City Music Hall and the lights were on again. We landed, tired, but happy as hell. The blackout bit was hushed up without difficulty, and I'm absolutely positive that the paperwork at Middletown conveniently "got lost"–especially if they thought they might ever have to try and explain why the signature on the requisition order read, "F. D. R. Churchill, F/O, # 9010"– the President, England's Prime Minister, my rank and the serial number of my Boley. I never was, officially, asked for the specific details about exactly how I obtained the generator, but the sliderule-types nearly fell out of their chairs, holding their sides laughing, when I told the complete story at lunch. The young Marine, who had played his part to perfection - with an absolutely straight face – was thanked with dinner for two at a popular nightclub and became the envy of the rest of his detachment. The new generator was installed and tested and, after one more test flight, we could

hardly wait for the next dark night.

Dr. Bonner arranged for a suitable "target" plane, supplied by the USAAF, that would arrive in a restricted, offshore area at a specified time, with all its normally visible lights turned off. My radar operator almost immediately spotted the target on his scope, and the rest of the interception was child's play for him. Both of us were tickled pink!

We broke away and asked the target pilot to take moderate evasive action and again, within minutes, we'd worked ourselves into an easy-kill position just astern of him. Because our confidence had grown with every successful flight, our next target was a bomber whose crew had been ordered to spot and try to avoid us, if they could. However, seated at the scope of the Boley was a combat-experienced night-fighter operator. His instructions to me for the heading, speed or altitude changes were precise and accurate. It was absolutely no contest.

From my standpoint, it was an amazing experience: I knew another plane was out there somewhere. But

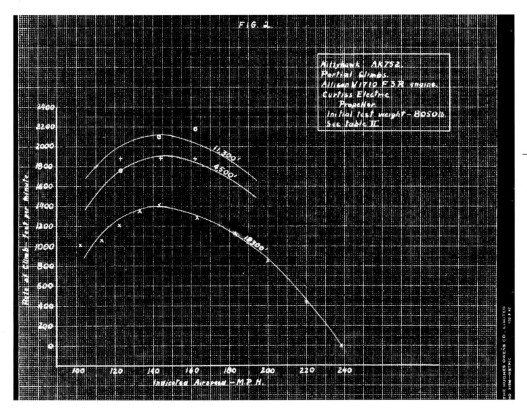

6b Curve graph - Kittyhawk, No. 752 - partial climbs (June 30, 1942). (D. Armstrong collection)

in which direction? Higher? Lower? Then, in my headphones I heard, "Speed: steady. Heading: 268 degrees. Climb: 1,000 feet." Different corrections every few minutes... then every minute... then very small corrections, with lots of "Steady!" commands... and "Reduce speed: twenty." Now I could feel the buffeting from the target's slipstream! "Approaching minimum range"... and finally, the operator switched from intercom to radio and said, "Lights on, target." The target was in my face... right in my gunsight!

In 1994, no one can begin to imagine the effect this had on me, or anyone sitting in the right-hand seat. Currently, such technology is commonplace but, in the spring of 1942 I was awed and, at the same time, completely agog by what was happening.

The equipment we were testing was state-of-the-art for that era. There was only one unit like this - and it was a rare privilege to be the pilot, to work so closely with the men and women of the Radiation Laboratory of MIT. The rest of my time in Boston was anticlimatic. We did tests to ascertain the range of the equipment; its accuracy in clouds and precipitation; how much "ground-effect" was involved (damn little!); if the equipment was affected by high G-loads (it wasn't!). Then we took several U.S. and Canadian VIPs for demonstration flights. The unit was a success and, although no specifics were ever discussed, it was generally understood that the equipment went into priority-procurement status within days after our tests were completed. We went home tired, happy and proud. I never crossed paths with Dr. Bonner again, but have remembered for fifty years how tactfully and efficiently he administered

this vital, and most-difficult, project. It was another great learning experience.

My promotion to the rank of flight lieutenant (equivalent to that of a USAAF captain) was posted on my return to Ottawa. Naturally, I was very pleased because this meant that I was now the senior engineering test pilot. But I sensed a change in the people around me and, for a couple of weeks, couldn't quite put my finger on what was different. I eventually realized that in September 1942, there was a feeling of relief in Canada and England. They no longer felt alone - finally, help was on the way. The industrial colossus of the United States was gearing up rapidly, churning out every conceivable tool of war: guns, ammunition, tanks, ships, planes, planes, and more planes. The despair from the Battle of Britain and Pearl Harbor was changing into hope

and confidence - the Americans were in it now!

At the same time, there was an underlying current of relaxation; a tiny tendency to fall back and regroup, to get rested, to get back into it again, when the men and materials from the States became fully available. Aviation research and development had shifted to American companies, and it was obvious they would supply the vast majority of the planes to the United Kingdom and Russia. These U.S. companies sorely needed test pilots, especially those with specialized training and experience. I literally ached when I thought about it - but I had made a commitment and I would honor it.

Routine tests kept me occupied. The only interesting flights I can remember were made in a little Stinson 105 observation plane, to investigate

ways that pilots could improve their short takeoff and landing techniques. While I was doing these, and some gun firing tests on the Kittyhawk, Lloyd Child made another trip to Rockcliffe. Lloyd was the chief test pilot for the Curtiss-Wright Corporation and, because of his devotion to his profession, a great guy to talk with. (It was not unusual for manufacturers to send test pilots to military units, for a multitude of reasons. Bob Stanley from Bell Aircraft, who later was the first U.S. pilot to fly a jet, had also visited T & D.)

Knowing that I was from the States, Lloyd questioned why I had not transferred to the USAAF when the opportunity to do so, at an equivalent or higher rank, had been presented. My

49 Westland Lysander, "Lizzie"; observation/ liaison; tandem seating, high-wing, monoplane, wheels/skis; Bristol Perseus XII, 905-hp radial. Short take-off/landing capabilities. Was also used for covert operations. (D. Armstrong collection)

45 Fairey Battle; target towing; three-seat, low-wing, monoplane; Rolls-Royce Merlin, 1,030-hp V-in-line. Best remembered as the first RAF aircraft to shoot down a German aircraft early in WW II. (D. Armstrong collection)

answer was that there was no guarantee of an assignment to a flight-test facility, and therefore I remained at T & D. He understood.

A short time after he returned to Buffalo, I was called to Group Captain Hurley's office to discuss a formal proposal, submitted by Lloyd on behalf of Curtiss, suggesting that I be permitted to resign my Canadian commission and accept a post as a test pilot with his company. The group captain agreed that I could probably make a more valuable contribution to the war

effort at Curtiss and offered me a short leave to go to Buffalo and thoroughly investigate the proposal. I was also given permission to accept a position there and was assured that my resignation would be accepted, if that was my desire. I still marvel at the empathetic attitude and the total cooperation I received from the RCAF.

On October 12, 1942, following over two years of service and exactly one year from the time I had reported to the Test and Development Establishment, my resignation from the Royal Canadian Air Force was accepted. I had a single hope then, and still do now, that I had been able to contribute as much, or more, than I learned and received.

This chapter cannot be con-

cluded without a final thought about my mentor, William Frederick "Doc" Gerhardt. Although Doc could fly, he knew his piloting technique left much to be desired. Years later I often wondered if he might have been trying to create in me that which he wanted to achieve himself. In any case, I was the beneficiary, and I hope he was pleased.

55 Stinson 105; trainer; cabin, high-wing, monoplane; Continental, 75-hp opposed. Classified as "nonspinnable." (D. Armstrong collection)

CHAPTER 7

CURTISS, IN CIVVIES
October 1942 - July 1943

In the fall of 1942 my transition from military to civilian life was the opposite of most young Americans. I was making a change because I wanted to - many other young men were making theirs because the war forced their hands. I was coming home to the States - they had no idea where they might be sent. I would have my family with me - they would be leaving theirs. I faced a new job with confidence - many others didn't even know what their jobs would be. However, I think we all had one thing in common - a desire to do our best.

Someone in the housing department at Curtiss found a comfortable home for us in Kenmore, a short drive from the Curtiss-Wright plant at the Buffalo airport. The problems I encountered in finding my way around the huge factory, getting flight equipment, obtaining security passes and clearances to permit me entry into the developmental areas and experimental flight test hangars were almost beyond belief. It took seven days before I was ready to fly!

Lloyd Child and I had agreed, before I left the RCAF, that, in order to familiarize myself with the Curtiss system, I would assist in the production flight test department the first two months I was with the company. (They didn't have enough production pilots at that time.) When not on the flight schedule, or on bad-weather days, I was expected to be at the experimental flight test department and learn their procedures, study the test programs and get to know the engineers and pilots.

While learning about the various departments and programs, it became apparent that there was a considerable difference between a military test pilot and a civilian test pilot. The **military** pilot worked for the **buyer**, whereas, the **civilian** test pilot worked for the **seller**. *The planes I had tested, as a military test pilot in the RCAF, had all been extensively tested by civilian pilots, before I flew them!* I had helped develop other tactical uses for, or tested the

7a A publicity caption says "new face among Curtiss test pilots." My scrapbook caption reads "Note `Mr. Glamorpuss' crash helmet and all. Ain't he beautimuss?" (D. Armstrong collection)

7b "The Rogues Gallery." From left to right-
Jean "Skip" Ziegler, yours truly, Herb
"Fireball" Fisher and Johnny Seal.

effects of modifications of, or additions to, a proven aircraft. Test pilots, before me, had done the experimental flying, had demonstrated to the military that the aircraft would live up to certain specifications and then, after production, had done a check flight on all systems before delivery. Now, I was going to do all these things at Curtiss - I had become a **civilian** test pilot!

At this point I want to digress and identify the specific responsibilities, in the 1940s, of an experimental test pilot, a demonstration test pilot and a production test pilot.

The **experimental** test pilot attempts to prove, and improve upon, the theories of the designers and engineers, from the initial flight of a prototype aircraft, until it is accepted or rejected. This is a long, sometimes tedious process, requiring hundreds of hours of extremely precise flying and thousands of hours of engineering work.

Performance, maneuverability and the general characteristics of an airplane can be approximated by calculation, comparison and ground testing. Then it falls upon the experimental test pilot to fly the aircraft, testing every phase of each of these deductions. Very few prototype aircraft perform or handle as well as anticipated. Many can be modified successfully, thus resulting in an acceptable product. Some never quite make the grade. Luckily, only a few end as bad memories.

A good illustration of the number of hours flown, and the time consumed, solely on flight testing a new fighter plane can be found in the history of the Curtiss XP-60D. The aircraft was delivered to the experimental flight test section on September 21, 1941. Nineteen months later, on May 6, 1943, after test flying for more than 251 hours, it crashed. Believe it or not, this was considered to be a very short program!

Experimental flight tests continue, even after a prototype has been tested, demonstrated and accepted, in an attempt to improve the product. Compare early WW II fighters to their later models and notice the fuselage changes in the newer planes, modified to accommodate the full-vision bubble canopy. Think about the addition of superchargers, improved dive brakes, more powerful engines or different armament. Also, remember that inevitably problems show up during use, especially in combat, and must be remedied. Every one of these things requires flight testing by an experimental test pilot.

The advances in the aeronautical and structural sciences have dramatically improved upon the methods which were used to develop a new aircraft in the early days of aviation. My dad was flying in 1910, and many of his friends flew in the early 1920s. From them, and from what I have subsequently read, I learned that during those years a new aircraft was designed, built and test flown by what I call the "Four-G Method: by Guess and by God, Get in and Go."

There has been tremendous progress since man's first powered flight, less than a hundred years ago, but the fact remains that experimental test flying was, and is, an extremely dangerous profession. Many aircraft have cost the lives of more than one test pilot, and every test pilot accepts this risk as part of the job. Physical conditioning, training, education, experience, reflexes and skill all help to create a professional test pilot; but, occasionally, even the gods cannot

protect the "giants."

Edmund T. "Eddie" Allen was truly a giant! He was regarded by his peers as the most capable multi-engine test pilot in the world, and the Institute of Aeronautical Sciences awarded him the Octave Chanute Award in 1939 in recognition of his many accomplishments in aviation. Yet, despite his consummate professionalism, he perished as a result of mechanical failures beyond his control during the experimental program of the Boeing B-29 Superfortress on February 18, 1943. Unfortunately, he is but one of a long, long list.

The **demonstration** test pilot (called a "contract test pilot" in some texts) does exactly what the name implies - demonstrates that the aircraft will actually comply with all of the contractual specifications, especially those of a structural and aerodynamic nature. To put it simply: prove that the aircraft will stay in one piece, and be controllable, under all of the circumstances required by the contract.

This pilot must fly the aircraft to the calculated, absolute limits of speed and structural load and verify that it can recover from unusual situations and attitudes, like extremely high-speed flight or inverted spins. These are the ultimate tests of the aircraft and require uniquely precise piloting skills, excellent judgment, exceptional reflexes and a hell of a lot of good luck. Extremely dangerous, it is without question the highest risk of all flight test work.

I was fifteen in March 1935 and vividly remember the shock I felt when my dad told me that Jimmy Collins had been killed when the Grumman XF3F-1 he was testing disintegrated on the final dive demonstration flight. Several years later I was even more shocked and saddened. The man who had befriended me when I first joined the experimental flight test department at Curtiss, Byron A. "Baggy" Glover, lost his life in a dive demonstration of the SB2C Helldiver, when he bailed out of the dive bomber after a structural failure.

His parachute became fouled in the wreckage on his way down.

Far more test pilots lost their lives in the experimental development of aircraft than in demonstration flights. However, the ratio of fatalities-per-hour-flown is considerably higher during demonstrations.

After the development and acceptance of a newly-designed aircraft, the **production** test pilot does a check flight on every plane as it rolls off the production line. In reality, it is

a flying, final inspection before delivery to the customer. The pilot checks the operation of the power-plant(s); all of the controls; the instruments; radios; electrical, hydraulic and mechanical systems; and that the aircraft handles properly.

These flights have their risks as well: a damaged O-ring in a hydraulic line can prevent extension of the wheels and cause a belly

61 Curtiss C-46, Commando; troop carrier/cargo; two Pratt and Whitney R-2800-51, 2,000-hp radials. Several hundred survived the war and served in a commercial capacity for many years. (Courtesy of San Diego Aerospace Museum)

landing; an improperly-wired toggle switch can keep an electrical circuit from functioning, or a loose fuel-line fitting can result in a fire. While doing a production flight, my friend Burt Purnell was seriously burned prior to bailing out of a flaming P-40 that crashed through the roof of the Curtiss plant at Buffalo, New York, and killed several workers. A simple fuel-line leak or fitting failure was thought to be the cause.

No matter how well an airplane is designed, constructed and inspected, there will always be some things which are not quite perfect. The production test pilot tries to make certain these problems are found and corrected before turning the aircraft over to the customer.

And the military - in many, but not all, contracts - stations one of their pilots at the factory. It is his job to make a second check flight on each aircraft before delivery. This is usually referred to as the "acceptance flight" and, to a lesser degree, repeats what the production pilot has already done.

Remember that these were the definitions generally applicable during the fantastic expansion of military aviation during WW II. The basic division of tasks remains true today, but it should be understood that many responsibilities probably overlap when smaller flight- test staffs are used.

Production flight testing in the high-performance aircraft I was flying at Curtiss was more joy than work. I was flying our P-40s, the Curtiss-built Republic P-47 Thunderbolts and the Bell P-39 Airacobras from the Curtiss Modification Center. Most of the flights were routine. "Crabs" (the term used to refer to whatever needed to be adjusted, repaired or replaced) were usually minor - malfunctioning instruments, misaligned controls, inoperative radios, poor brakes, etc. - but occasionally something nasty happened, reminding everyone this was a serious business. After Burt Purnell's burning P-40 crashed through the roof of the plant, everyone on the production line became even more acutely aware of how one, tiny mistake could end in a terrible disaster.

In the following case an assembly-line mistake, fortunately, resulted only in a surge of my adrenalin flow. It was November 19, 1942, I was in a P-40K and for the first thirty minutes everything went as expected. I had cycled the wing flaps, constant-speed propeller, cowling flaps and the landing gear a couple of times when the tail wheel and left wheel went down and locked; the right one partially lowered, but did not lock. When I put the landing-gear control into the "up" position, neither of the main wheels would retract, and a tower fly-by confirmed that the right wheel was, indeed, dangling about halfway down. One of the engineers, Mr. Frank Lakowitz, made several suggestions by radio, but everything remained the same. The emergency hand-operated, landing-gear hydraulic pump had no effect whatsoever and the prospect of a one-up-one-down landing, or a bailout, didn't appeal to me at all.

As a last resort, I rolled it over and flew inverted, still trying to retract the gear and, strange as it may seem, noticed that the hand pump felt as though there might be a little pressure building up. Remaining upside down, I quickly placed the control into the "down" position, pumped like crazy and was pleased - and surprised - when the right wheel joined the other two wheels in the down-and-locked posi-tion. When I rolled into normal level flight, the hand pump was once again useless. I made a safe, no-flap landing and, on inspection, we found an improperly-assembled hydraulic valve that had, for no logical reason, permitted the system to work while the plane was flying inverted.

Inverted flight was more commonly used to "clean" the cockpit of nuts and bolts, metal shavings, rivets or miscellaneous debris that fell into the fuselage during construction. Most of the pilots would open the hatch, roll the plane over and let the junk fall, or get blown, out. I liked to roll my planes over with the hatch closed first - just to see what would show up. If it were all trash, I'd roll it back to normal flight, open the hatch and roll it over the second time and let it dump out.

During forty-five or fifty flights I accumulated a wide variety of stuff, including screwdrivers, soft-drink bottles and caps, a hacksaw blade, a package of condoms, a couple of good fountain pens, several packs of cigarettes, a pocket knife, a pair of side-

58 Curtiss XP-40Q; same basic plane as Chapter 6, Number 53 (Curtiss P-40 Warhawk), with the addition of a bubble canopy. When the wings were later clipped, the speed increased to 422 mph at 20,500 feet, making it the fastest of the P-40s. (Courtesy of San Diego Aerospace Museum)

cutters and a wallet. The wallet was easy to trace, of course, and I personally returned it to the man who had lost it. He was amazed at how I had found it and said that when he came to work the next day he'd bring a surprise for me and my family. The following morning I received a call requesting that I meet with one of the security officers. He sent a car for me; and when I arrived at his office, the man whose wallet I had found was waiting with a package for me. As a way of saying "Thanks" he had brought me a large pan full of Polish stuffed cabbage!

The first two months passed quickly, and I moved my gear into the experimental flight test hangar. I already knew Baggy Glover, Herb Fisher and several of the flight engineers quite well and, soon after I started flying experimental tests, Johnny Seal and Jean "Skip" Ziegler joined the team. It was a real pleasure and privilege to have such fine men as my associates and friends.

Herbert O. "Herb" Fisher was a quiet, pleasant and very efficient test pilot, and I remain proud to say I flew with him and that he was my friend. At Curtiss he flew thousands of production and experimental test flights and, in my opinion, was primarily responsible for getting the big C-46 Commando transport plane into general use by the military. His accomplishments are legendary and are recounted with great insight and sensitivity by Martin Strasser Caidin in Chapter 11 of *Test Pilots: Riding the Dragon* (Bantam Air & Space Series).

He was an exacting taskmaster, but always fun to work with. Among my favorite memories of our times together are the days when we flew "Flying Tiger" P-40s in some movie sequences, "doubling" for the stars and trying our best to keep the director from making too many technical mistakes. We repeated one scene - a formation takeoff from a grass strip - so many times that the last take was flown at dusk instead of at dawn. When I pointed out that the sun was now in the wrong place, they simply rewrote the script in order to use the shot.

Herb checked me out in the C-46 and I was very impressed and pleased with the amount of time he spent with me, making absolutely certain that I understood the Commando's many idiosyncrasies and emergency systems. Our philosophies were similar - do it right, or don't do it at all - and, perhaps, that's why we both survived our aviation careers!

On another occasion Herb asked me to hold down the right-hand seat on a series of takeoff tests in the C-46 which, at that time, was notorious for leaking hydraulic fluid. (Remember the "all electric houses"? The C-46 was an "all hydraulic airplane" - and equally bad!) Everything was powered by hydraulics - landing gear, flaps, flight controls, cowl flaps, brakes, oil-cooler flaps - and they all leaked. In the airplane, on most flights, there were at least three, five-gallon cans of hydraulic fluid. This would be used to replace what had leaked out and was essential just to keep all the components operating or to get the gear and flaps down for landing. On the takeoff tests, because the gear was going to be retracted and extended so many times, we had an extra forty-five gallons of fluid, and one of my jobs was to add some when necessary. Later Herb kidded me about it, saying that he used me as his copilot because he figured a guy called "Armstrong" could manhandle those cans better than anyone else! However, I learned a lot from Herb and thoroughly enjoyed being around him.

[Author's note: Happily, Herb Fisher was one of those fortunate test pilots who survived his profession and lived well into his eighties.]

Skip Ziegler was another very special pilot, and a dear friend. When he joined Curtiss (from the military) he was a relatively inexperienced test pilot but his enthusiasm, piloting skills, unassuming attitude and charming personality quickly won him the respect of the engineering staff. He was my chase pilot on many of the XP-60 tests and, far more than that, always was avail-able to talk with me about the problems I had on these extremely difficult flights. Our friendship went beyond the confines of our professional association and when he married his long-time sweetheart, a "preemie" nurse fondly called "Punk," I was honored and happy when asked to be a part of their wedding.

Skip left Curtiss to work for Bell Aircraft and went on to fly their famous tadpole-shaped X-5 research airplane. On July 16, 1951, he made the world's first in-flight wing sweeping. A few days afterwards, he successfully swept the wings a full sixty degrees, thereby proving that the variable-sweep concept was feasible.

Two years later, in May 1953, Skip Ziegler lost his life on a test flight of the Bell X-2 when a twenty-five cent gasket failed and the aircraft exploded while still attached to the B-50 launch plane. The explosion also killed Frank Wolko, one of the crewmen. The Bell test pilots, William Leyshon and D. W. Howe, managed to get the B-50 down safely, but the aircraft was so horribly damaged by fragments from the explosion that it never flew again.

[Historical note: The X-5 was retired in 1955 following its final flight by Neil Armstrong and is now in the Air Force Museum in Dayton, Ohio. The rocket-powered Bell X-2 was the first aircraft to exceed Mach 3, three times faster than the speed of sound, when it attained 2,094 mph! Test pilot Mel Apt was at the controls and was killed during his return to the airport.]

Performance testing requires a very high level of concentration, and a soft touch on the controls, in order to obtain data which is consistently accurate. Because of the meticulous training I had received from Doc Gerhardt in Canada, I had a distinct advantage over many other pilots. Before many flights I prepared graphs showing the conditions of the test and put them on my kneepad. Then, while flying, I plotted each point on the graph. At the conclusion of the test runs, if the resultant curve (the line connecting the data points) looked good, I knew I had obtained accurate information. On the other hand, if a point or two looked questionable, before landing I would repeat that portion of the flight. This procedure frequently assured that the tests would not have to be repeated in a day or two. The data curves I obtained in this manner were only an indication of the accuracy of my piloting - they needed to be corrected for altitude, temperature and instrument error - but I saved many hours of "damn-it, do-it-again" flying since I could check up on myself, without having to wait for a flight engineer to do it for me.

By 1943 perspiration was an integral part of preparation for high-altitude flights at Curtiss. ("High altitude" was then defined as anything above 35,000 feet for longer than fifteen minutes.) Some people believed, in those days, that pilots flying at high altitudes would be subject to the "bends" - nitrogen bubbles forming in the blood stream. Exercising while breathing pure oxygen before takeoff was supposed to prevent this from happening. So, for most high flights the pilot first rowed a rowing machine for thirty minutes while breathing the pure oxygen, then continued to breathe it until the flight was completed. Now, fifty years later, I have to admit that I don't know whether or not the galley-slave program helped to prevent the bends, but it sure helped keep us trim and slim!

In February we experimented with a series of P-40 timed climbs at various weights, speeds, power and propeller settings. We found how we could dramatically improve long-climb

performance - reaching 35,000 feet, or higher, as quickly as possible - and were delighted to get favorable comments back from the combat squadrons. I did the majority of these tests, and the rowing machine took off about ten pounds!

Although I was already working on the XP-60 program, I continued to do tests on various models of the P-40. One day I was east of Buffalo in a P-40F at 22,000 feet doing a two-position turbocharger speed check. Without warning, the engine literally blew itself apart, filling the cockpit with smoke. In no time at all I had shut off the fuel supply, wondered if the fire would go out, given a Mayday (emergency) call on the radio, thought about bailing out and looked quickly for a place to land. I knew I was over Geneva, New York, and that there was a short, hill-and-dale airstrip west of town where I thought I could belly-land - if the fire went out and if I could see well enough through the smoke to locate it.

I pulled the nose up, banked steeply and kicked almost full opposite rudder, putting the plane into a steep, slipping spiral. I had decided to bail out if the fire got worse or hadn't gone out by the time I descended to 5,000 feet. When the altimeter read 5,000 feet all I could see was smoke, but no flames, so things were looking better. I was able to spot the farm

where the strip was, took a guess as to wind direction and mentally set up an approach to land. Then one of those strange, fleeting thoughts, that comes out of nowhere, popped into my head - I wonder if Dorothy is home?

At this point I was committed to land so I tightened up my belt, got some flaps down and the hatch open. Just as I slowed up and got level, I saw a small flame up near the propeller. By now I had no choice: I had to get it on the ground. The strip was tiny, terraced and, luckily for me, muddy and wet - there was even standing water in a couple of places. As I bellied it in, the nose cowling scooped up water, mud and wet grass and put out the remaining fire. The "giants," again, held me in the palms of their hands!

Five years earlier, when I was a student at Cazenovia College, my steady girlfriend had been Dorothy Kean. A couple of times her family had invited me to spend my vacation with them. The airstrip I had used for my emergency landing was on their farm, so consequently I knew exactly where the field was in relationship to the house and the highway. No, she was not there when I landed; but, yes, about twenty minutes later Dorothy and her mother returned home. After recovering from the shock of the unexpected method of my arrival, Mrs. Kean took me into the kitchen and fed me some pie and milk. I also used their phone to inform the plant of my whereabouts and what had happened to the plane.

The urgent need for planes by the U.S. and Allied forces had placed demands on aircraft manufacturers that were unrelenting. Anything which slowed down the flow from a production line was almost intolerable. But,

at the same time, there was a very real need to be able to incorporate changes in an aircraft when improvements became available. The Curtiss Aircraft Modification Center was a specially-created facility that did nothing but contract for modification work on existing aircraft. For instance, if the original manufacturer did not have the space, or a system, to do its own modifications without disrupting normal, high-speed production, it was more practical to have the work performed elsewhere. Or, if the necessary work was to be done on a "short run" - say, one hundred planes - it was more expeditious to send that work to a separate plant that was already keyed to such projects.

The Bell P-39 Airacobra was one of the planes that underwent modification at Curtiss. The aircraft were consigned to Russia, where they would be used primarily in very cold weather for ground attack against tanks and troops. Many were to be flown by U.S. pilots - from New York, across Canada to Alaska for refueling; then by Russian pilots - from Alaska, across Siberia to Russia. As the designated planes came off the Bell production line, they were given a brief flight check by a Bell production pilot and immediately flown over to Curtiss (a short hop from Niagara Falls to Buffalo). There the modifications to the oil and engine cooling systems, engine preheating and oil draining equipment, to name a few, were made in preparation for the long ferry flights and cold-weather operation. A final production flight check was handled by Curtiss pilots.

Usually because of weather delays, production flight testing would occasionally fall behind the output of the main plant and the "mod" center. Herb Fisher and I tried to help them catch up whenever we could and often ended up flying the P-39s. I remember having more than one nasty thought about the Bell pilots, because I felt they made rather perfunctory production test flights (knowing the planes were to be modified and test flown again). For whatever reason, we did have an inordinate number of "crabs" on these flights.

One flight was particularly interesting, to say the least! Immediately after takeoff I had flipped the landing-gear switch and, while picking up airspeed, noticed that the control stick felt very "scary." Fore and aft movement (the elevators) was fine, but lateral movement (the ailerons) was almost as though a student was also holding the stick and over-controlling terribly. I had to make a concentrated effort to hold the stick in the neutral position. At 1,500 feet altitude, when I pulled the nose up and let the stick go, the ailerons went to the full right position, producing a rather rapid roll. I recovered easily and found that to tap the stick on either side resulted in a full deflection of the ailerons - they were drastically overbalanced. The mod center had made no changes to any controls, and I will never believe that this condition could have been overlooked during the initial production test flight or the delivery flight. Maybe I could understand (but not accept) one careless pilot; but for two pilots to miss something as obvious as this was ridiculous - and dangerous!

The C-46 production line was rolling out aircraft at a pretty good clip, and most of the hydraulic problems had been fixed, or at least, greatly improved. Although the produc-

tion flights on a "big bird" averaged two or three hours - over twice as long as on the smaller planes - I tried to help whenever I could get away. I had a copilot only if one of the P-40 production pilots was free and wanted to get some right-seat time in the larger aircraft, but mostly it was a "do-it-yourself" flight. On the infrequent occasions when I had to add more hydraulic fluid in order to land, there were all the elements of a three-ring circus. (Remember, I was alone in a twenty-three ton, twin-engine cargo plane!) If the autopilot was working properly, the procedure was simple enough: engage it, go back and add the fluid. But, if the autopilot was not functioning properly, I had to trim the aircraft for level flight, but a little nose-down; run aft; dump in the fluid and run back to my seat. Though this only took a few minutes, it seemed much longer. In my haste I had ruined a good pair of shoes and pants with splashed hydraulic fluid; but, thereafter, I had enough sense to wear old sneakers and flight suits.

Production test pilots were desperately needed by most aircraft companies, and Curtiss was no exception. They were few and far between because nearly all qualified pilots were in the service. George Matteson was a P-40 Warhawk and Hawker Hurricane pilot attached to the RCAF Ferry Squadron at Rockcliffe. My Test and Development unit had been in the next hangar. He, too, had come from the States and, because of the agreement between the U.S. and Canada, was eligible to transfer to U.S. forces. I talked to him about taking a job at Curtiss and he was willing, so I helped obtain permission for him to bypass the U.S. military and transfer directly to civilian duties at Curtiss. He proved to be a crackerjack production pilot and was definitely an asset to the production flight test department.

When not in the air, experimental test pilots spend a substantial amount of time in the engineering department. The layout of a cockpit is developed by the use of a mockup (a dummy fuselage, usually made of wood) so that controls, instruments, seat positioning,

oxygen fittings, radios, etc., can be moved easily. I was often called upon to suggest improvements because I had flown so many different types of aircraft and happened to be of average height, weight, leg length and arm reach. I had another ability that the engineers appreciated and utilized: an above-average spatial visualization which enabled me to quickly sketch, in an understandable fashion, any recommended changes.

I enjoyed working with the Curtiss mockup crew, and we made many logical improvements in the C-46, the later P-40s and all the P-60s. The pilot and engineers brain-storming together was, and remains, an important phase of prototype development and, in my opinion, is too often neglected. For example, the cockpit in the P-39s that the U.S. supplied to the Russians was so small that anyone above average height felt cramped in it, especially if sitting on a seat-pack parachute. In another fighter I would test a few years later, the anti-G-suit hose fitting was so poorly positioned that it easily became disconnected if the pilot reached down to pick up something from between his feet. And, you can imagine the red faces of the engineers when I pointed out, on still another aircraft, that it was impossible for a pilot to reach the emergency canopy release, even if the G-load was minor.

The XP-60 designers used the standard P-40 pilot protection armor plate behind the pilot and installed it in the mockup. One rainy afternoon after I had studied this, I borrowed a drafting table, designed and subsequently submitted the drawings for an improved armor plate which, with no added weight, increased pilot upper-body protection 25 degrees and knee and upper leg protection by 9 - 11 degrees on both sides. In my opinion, had the P-60 gone into production, this simple change would have afforded the pilot greater protection than previously found in any U.S. fighter plane! Though it was never utilized I have always been very proud of that design job.

The "all work and no play makes Jack a dull boy" axiom didn't apply to Skip and me - we always found time to have fun. After talking with E. R. "Rush" Child - Lloyd's brother - in the aerodynamics department, I had walked through the plant on my way back to the hangar. Seeing several Red Cross and U.S.O. cans (strategically placed to entice people to drop coins or bills into them as they went for a coffee break or to lunch) sparked an idea. As soon as I got back to my office I conned Skip, and one of the shop guys, into helping me find twelve, clean, undented one-gallon cans. Our shop friend made me a two-line stencil: the top line had, in large letters, the initials "O.T.P.B.S."; the second line, just the word "PLEASE." At noon I made a quick trip to a store and bought four-dozen, small, stick-on American flags. We spray-painted the cans white; put the "O.T.P.B.S" and "PLEASE" in black, on two sides and stuck a flag on both sides of each set of letters. Adding a coin slot on the top made our work look passably professional.

During a plant shift change, Skip and I placed the cans conspicuously next to a Red Cross or U.S.O. can, and left them there for a little over a week. When we picked up and emptied the cans we had collected over $400! After recovering from our laughing spell we took our "haul" up to the company newspaper office, told our story and put the money into an existing fund which was used to send gifts to former employees who had gone into the service. The in-house newspaper headlined the story and revealed that the "O.T.P.B.S." stood for a fictional "Old Test Pilots' Benevolent Society." For the next few weeks, whenever Skip or I walked through the plant, we got whistled at and kidded by the workers. It's fun, even now, to think back on it.

I had made the first flight, and several follow-up flights, on the XP-40N; had been back and forth to Wright Field (Dayton, Ohio) to help with some major engine and propeller tests on modified P-40s; had redesigned the production test pilot's card for the Republic P-47 and had continued to help with production flying. Now, most of my time was being consumed by the XP-60 project, and I asked to be relieved of the other duties. I was running into problems that nobody understood and I wanted to be able to concentrate solely on them. I also needed to spend more time with the aerodynamicists and the flight engineers, since it was becoming obvious that I was moving into a far-more exacting and dangerous project.

CHAPTER 8

IT'S GREAT TO BE A CATERPILLAR
December 1942 - June 1943

Shortly after the start of the new year I was asked if I would take over the XP-60D project and stay with it through the preliminary and final dive demonstration flights. The Curtiss engineers believed the P-60 could easily replace the P-40 in combat because they would be faster, have better climb and be more maneuverable. The prototype P-60 looked good, handled well, and most of the people connected with the project were enthusiastic about it. After negotiating, I was offered a contract which included additional life insurance and remuneration for the extra-risk demonstration flights, and I accepted.

Many people have difficulty, fifty years after WW II, understanding why there were so many different fighter airplanes, and why each of them had so many distinct designations. In the early 1940s, the prime need was for quantity - lots of planes and pilots; followed by quality - better planes and pilots. The U.S. logically used what I call "the shotgun method" - threw lots of designs into the air and hoped for a few hits. The successful designs became famous, the others forgotten. The chronology of the Curtiss XP-60 program illustrates how one company did its best to touch all the bases it could, trying for that one, elusive "hit."

The prototype P-60 with the new laminar-flow wing was first flown in September 1941, and had a Packard (Rolls-Royce) Merlin V-in-line engine. Soon after that, however, military procurement people decided that the total output of Merlins would be allocated to the P-51 Mustang program.

Therefore, the next three P-60s were modified to use Allison V-in-line engines and were designated XP-60A.

No XP-60B models were ever completed.

The XP-60C was converted from the Allison to a Pratt and Whitney R-2800 radial engine and fitted with Curtiss electric contra-rotating propellers. (The program originally called for the use of a Chrysler XIV-2220 of 2,300 hp, but this engine was not used because it was far too heavy.)

The XP-60D called for a new Merlin 61 with a two-stage supercharger, a conventional propeller, an enlarged tail section and other minor changes.

The XP-60E was the same airframe as the 'D, but powered with the Pratt and Whitney R-2800 fitted with a single-rotation propeller.

The YP-60E also used the Pratt and Whitney R-2800 engine, but had a low-profile fuselage with a bubble canopy. A fine looking airplane!

The most logical choice as to which plane would be used for all of the dive tests was the XP-60D. It already had the enlarged tail surfaces,

Skyways

a few other structural modifications, and was powered by the original Merlin engine with a conventional propeller. Another plus was that much of the special instrumentation was already on board and calibrated.

The performance testing program of the XP-60s went very well and showed that the aircraft met most expectations. It was a definite improvement over the P-40 series and would have justified a production contract as a replacement for the Warhawk, except for one thing: the ability of the plane to meet the contract specifications of speed and structural integrity was seriously in doubt!

Every manufacturer was striving to develop aircraft that could fly faster and higher than those in combat. But many of the fighter planes in use were already attaining unexplored high speeds, in dives, and encountering unexplainable structural failures. They were reaching a critical dive speed beyond which it seemed that an invisible monster lurked and devoured them. No aeronautical engineer in the world knew exactly what was happening, or how to circumvent it. No structural engineer understood how the unusual loads were being imposed, or how great the stress was; and, therefore, could not determine how to construct suitable components.

On the positive side, because of the insatiable appetite of the war, almost unlimited funds were available for research and development. On the negative side, the experimental test pilot was, and I use the next word deliberately, "terrifyingly" exploring both aerodynamic and structural unknowns - simultaneously! I, together with a surprisingly few other experimental and demonstration test pilots, faced a very difficult and challenging task. Many would not survive.

The inside of the XP-60D cockpit was as familiar to me as my wife's body. I could sit in the cockpit, blindfolded, reach out and touch any con-

trol, or point to every instrument and tell my flight engineer the high and low limits of its range. I knew my airplane, and was totally confident I could instinctively operate any control or device without looking for it, and that my peripheral vision would instantly spot any significant changes indicated on my instruments.

The dive airplane was, of course, meticulously prepared; my engineering and maintenance crews were acutely aware of the critical nature of the tests. Because the laminar-flow wing design was still new, the structural engineers had installed strain gauges to measure the bend or twist of the wing. Flight engineering had installed a V-G recorder (airspeed vs G-load) and a photo-observer to keep track of time vs altitude, airspeed, outside air temperature, elevator position, etc. This instrumentation would remain in place throughout the dive tests. Additional strain gauges might be installed on the tail assembly, and a recording would be made of all my voice transmissions during each dive.

My first encounter with the "monster" occurred in two investigative dives to verify the functioning of the special instrumentation installed in the aircraft and to explore the handling characteristics at airspeeds and altitudes which approached those to be attained in the preliminary dive tests.

The first dive started at 23,000 feet and was to descend to 12,000 feet. At slightly less than 475 mph the aircraft began "porpoising" (nosing up and down, repeatedly) and the elevator control became extremely sensitive. I realized instantly that I should use the elevator control very gently, so I simply let the altimeter unwind until the porpoising disappeared at lower altitude. After landing, the photo-observer data confirmed the porpoising and revealed that it continued even when I had not moved the elevators.

My second dive started at 30,000 feet and was supposed to end at 20,000 feet. The porpoising started earlier, was far more severe, and I found myself strictly a passenger in an

uncontrollable hunk of metal, screaming toward the ground in a highly disturbing manner. I maintained a slight back-pressure on the stick, with no discernible result, and the aircraft finally recovered, by itself, at around 18,000 feet. The monster had revealed its ugly head in no uncertain terms. When I landed, I damn sure wanted to learn more about it!

I arranged for a meeting with a couple of the flight engineers and two or three men from the aerodynamics department and quickly found they didn't know much more than I. This did nothing to increase my confidence! I then phoned Milo Burcham at Lockheed, because I knew there had been similar problems with the twin-boom P-38 Lightning; and Joe Parker at Republic, to find out about his work on the P-47 Thunderbolt. They confirmed similar phenomena on both aircraft. The compressibility effect of the air flowing over the wings at higher Mach numbers was doing some very strange things to our airplanes.

[Author's note: Sadly, neither Milo Burcham nor Joe Parker survived the war. Milo was killed testing the Lockheed P-80 Shooting Star when the jet engine failed just after takeoff. Joe also lost his life in a take-off accident, while working with an Air Force squadron on Ie Shima, a small island off the western coast of Okinawa.]

The term "compressibility" was rather loosely used, especially in the early 1940s, but in simplistic terms it occurs when air "bunches up" ahead of one or more areas of an aircraft as it flies faster than 400 mph. The wings were the most critical area; and when the air bunched up in front of them, it disturbed the flow, moving the center of pressure and causing the aircraft to pitch upward or downward. Then the disturbed air arrived at the tail surfaces, and normal control was disrupted. (Below 400 mph any "compression" of the air had little or no effect upon the aircraft.)

The "Mach number" method of speed designation was named for an

8e "Galley-slave Armstrong" denitrogenizing (reducing the nitrogen content of the blood by replacing it with oxygen) in preparation for high-altitude flight - through exercise. Note Spencer girdle covering the abdomen. With me is Chet Dudzig, Curtiss flight analysis engineer. (D. Armstrong collection)

Austrian scientist, Ernst Mach, who was one of the pioneers in studying supersonic speeds. It is essentially the relationship of the speed of the aircraft to the speed of sound. The speed of sound under standard conditions is 764 mph at sea level and decreases with altitude until, for example, it is 679 mph at 30,000 feet. An aircraft traveling at three-quarters the speed of sound, at any altitude, flies at Mach .75; or at half the speed of sound, at Mach .50.

To obtain a production contract, the P-60 had to demonstrate that it could withstand a specified G-load at selected speeds and altitudes. All of us involved in the project felt the G-load would not overstress the airframe; however, in attaining the required speeds, we might encounter some of the many problems associated with high Mach numbers. We decided to approach the desired speeds in increments not to exceed 10 mph. This would require more dives but, perhaps, we could keep the monster at bay while we learned how to combat it.

Dive number two had unpleasantly surprised everyone, so I wanted to repeat it to see if I could find a way to regain some measure of control when the porpoising took over or, at the very least, get additional data to compare and evaluate. And "repeat it" is exactly what occurred. Porpoising took over at almost exactly the same

Mach number as it had in the second dive, but this time I applied a little nose-up trim, held the stick very steady and the plane became controllable much sooner - at about 22,000 feet. When the data was examined it showed that the porpoising had been more severe - ranging from 0 - 4.75 Gs - although, using trim, the recovery was improved. We decided to start the next dive even higher to give me more room for recovery, but to make no attempt to recover until the speed was about 10 mph faster than we had attained so far.

On dive number four the monster took a real swipe at me. After the expected (but not enjoyed) porpoising started, another nasty little problem cropped up. I'll quote, verbatim, from the test flight report:

...in addition there was a sudden and violent tendency for the aircraft to roll to the left. Upon attempting to correct this condition, the ailerons seemed to over-balance, developing a continuous rolling movement from right to left, etc., until dampened out by the pilot's knees...the pitching oscillations had already exceeded the pullout Gs and the combination of aileron and elevator difficulties was so severe the pilot abandoned any attempt to do anything except recover control of the aircraft...the pilot had to use both hands and both knees to dampen out the churning motion of

the stick, and the aircraft pitched enough to throw the pilot's head violently against the canopy.

The data confirmed all of this, but inspection revealed no structural damage. It was decided to remove some balance weights from the ailerons, change the elevators and repeat the flight. Just above my knees on the inside of each thigh was a dark, black bruise about eight inches long and four inches wide. The monster must have smiled! My fifth dive was somewhat better. The aileron over-balancing had been eliminated and the elevator change reduced the over-sensitivity of the control, delaying the porpoising until we got the speed up to around Mach .72. But I had a real eye-opener - literally! Every time the aircraft pitched upward (the photo-observer showed that it started at Mach .71), I saw "purple sheets" about ten feet long, angling up at about forty-five degrees from the leading edge of each wing. I had never experienced this phenomenon before - contrails, yes - but purple sheets? And, what was causing them?

Another call to Milo Burcham revealed that he, too, had seen something similar, but was rather reluctant to say very much until he could confirm or be more specific about it. We both deduced it was a visible shock wave and let it go at that.

In normal flight, lift is generated when the air flowing over the longer, upper surface of the wing accelerates, reducing the pressure above the wing. In the 1940s aircraft used a relatively thick wing which was not swept back. When these planes flew at speeds exceeding Mach .70 the airflow above the wing approached, or even exceeded, Mach l. The subsonic air tried to mingle with the sonic, or near-sonic, air and created a turbulence, or "flow separation." This resulted in violent and disrupted air currents striking the tail section and causing trim changes, sloppy or exceedingly stiff controls and unusual pitching movements, either upward or downward or oscillations of both. Exacerbating this was the disturbed airflow caused by "compressibility." Attrition of machines and men was very high; and pilots, although not quite correct technically, said these crashes were caused by "shock waves."

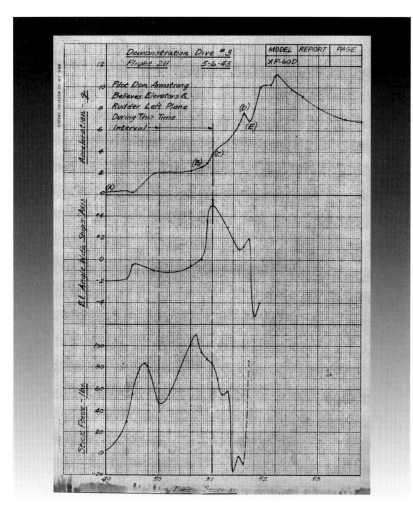

8b Graph presentation of the loss of the tail - XP-60D, May 6, 1943, while doing demonstration dive No. 3, Flight 211. Note: Serious stability/control problems began at 49.5 seconds and tail was ripped away before 51.0 seconds. Also indicates over 11 Gs after the tail failure. (D. Armstrong collection)

The XP-60 was undeniably in trouble. We hoped we could find a fix but we had no definitive information to work from. We were almost, but not quite, operating under my "Four-G system" - and none of us were very happy about that! We were trying our

best, but it was a flying version of Russian roulette! My suggestion that I visit some of the other people who were in the same boat was approved; so I made a few phone calls, packed my flight bag and headed for Long Island, Connecticut and Ohio.

Flight test engineers, aerodynamicists, structural engineers and the experimental test pilots at Grumman, Republic, Vought and Wright Field were, without exception, totally cooperative and equally concerned. To this day I firmly believe that absolutely nothing was withheld from me. Any requests I made to see flight-test reports, proposed aircraft modifications or even memos with speculative conclusions and proposals were granted. I, in turn, had brought along all the available P-60 test data for them to evaluate and did my best to answer their questions. There was no indication of any com-

petition between these companies. We had a mutual problem - pilots, planes and the war effort were all in jeopardy. Everyone was looking for a solution, and all were willing to share what they had learned in a heartwarming and unselfish manner. I was grateful, and very proud of our profession.

One of the things that seemed strange to me on these visits was that, although each company was aware of the common dilemma of higher Mach-number flights, none were particularly well informed as to the extent of the problem. Everyone knew about the structural failures (primarily to the tail surfaces) of their own aircraft and that other companies were having similar difficulties. But, probably because of the obvious need for secrecy, there were only cloaked references to similar failures occurring to fighter aircraft in combat. (It certainly would have been a tactical advantage for the enemy to know there was a good possibility that the tail might break off if he could lure our aircraft into a prolonged, high-speed dive.) Such incidents were kept tightly under wraps. So were the structural failures at the factories, for the same reason. In 1941, when Lockheed test pilot Ralph Virden was killed after his P-38 lost its tail in a high Mach-number dive test, relatively few people knew the details.

We will never know exactly how many planes were lost to the monster, because combat tail-failures could have been due either to enemy fire or in dives, when structural limitations were exceeded. We do know, however, that tail failures occurred frequently enough (in Curtiss P-40s, Bell P-39s, Lockheed P-38s, Hawker Typhoons and Republic P-47s) to fuel rumors which, in turn, created losses. A fighter pilot must have complete confidence in his aircraft. Some became tentative about entering sustained dives, and that involuntary pause cost lives.

When I returned to Buffalo I participated in several long conferences and my four major suggestions met with immediate approval. First, try to install more strain gauges to, hopefully, forecast the approach of excessive

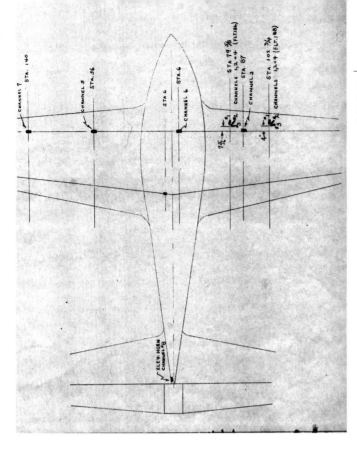

8c "Sketch #1." Schematic of the XP-60D showing placement of the strain-gauge sensors for the oscillograph. (D. Armstrong collection)

loads. Second, watch the tail section for possible vibration or flutter. Third, acknowledge the very great probability of structural failure and attempt to prevent destruction of "on-board" recorded data in the event of loss of the aircraft. And fourth, "make haste - slowly."

From my standpoint, I was prepared to encounter severe control difficulties - extreme sensitivity, ineffectual or "set-in-concrete" controls - any of which could occur, and all of which would be unpleasant. I was fully cognizant, and accepted the reality, of possible structural failure. However, now I had a little more ammunition and knew that I had friends fighting the same battle. I was ready to resume the test dives and give the monster a good run for its money!

My next dive scared the hell out of all of us. Violent porpoising, ineffectual controls and more than 15,000 feet loss of altitude occurred while I was, once again, an unwilling passenger in the aircraft. But all of those things were minor compared to the very sobering data from the strain gauges! We had encountered unanticipated high loads on both the horizontal and vertical tail sections, some of which were close to calculated structural limits! We needed more help.

The aerodynamic and structural engineers suggested another elevator change: to use one which was thinner and, presumably, less likely to permit oscillation. Beyond that, everyone seemed to have a "let's keep our fingers crossed" attitude. In fairness, I must admit that I was empathetic - they couldn't fix something they didn't understand - but it was my neck on the block, and I kept hoping for a solution.

In my search for answers I sought out opinions on what might fail first, how and when it might fail and what gyrations of the aircraft I might expect following such a failure. Without exception, all the engineers agreed: if a structural failure occurred, it would be at the tail just as I moved the elevators to start the pull-out. An engineer, Henry Nagamatsu, had made

8d XP-60C - 3/4 right front view. Note the contra-rotating propellers. (D. Armstrong collection)

quite a study of the characteristics of the laminar-flow wing. He predicted, in the event of a tail failure, the nose would pitch violently upward producing an accelerated-stall condition, resulting in an extremely high-speed snap roll. In addition, he said the snap-roll gyrations would produce very high Gs, and would also pause and reverse direction several times before what was left of the aircraft entered a terminal flat spin. WOW!

Assuming that I could survive the breakup of the aircraft, I still had two very serious problems. First, during such violent gyrations, I must remain conscious. And second, with the anticipated high Gs, how was I going to get out of the aircraft?

"G-suits" were not yet available. All the help I had to prevent the blood rushing from my brain to my abdomen was a primitive corset (made by the Spenser Corset Company) with an air bladder in the front which could be inflated by pumping a syringe before the dive. Henry's guestimate was for "over 10 Gs," and my little Spenser corset certainly couldn't cope with that. We agreed I should leave my seat-belt tight, but my shoulder harness loose so I could get my head down on my knees, retaining blood in my brain.

Neither were ejection seats available. At 10 Gs my body would effectively weigh, in my flight gear and parachute, about one *ton*! It would be impossible for me to climb out of the aircraft. Henry had insisted that possibly as many as three or four roll-direction reversals would occur;

8a Picture number 2634-after the tail came off. "Just as it looked before the crews touched it." (D. Armstrong collection)

so we agreed that I should bend over, get my head on my knees and try to get out during one of the roll-direction "changeovers."

Everyone connected with the project had done his best. There was simply nothing else we could do to improve the plane or to reduce further risk. We had reached the place where the only way to get an answer was to resume the tests. I had accumulated all the information and advice I possibly could. Now it was "put up or shut up" time - what being a test pilot was all about. I knew the monster was out there, waiting; but I was as well armed as I could get - and ready to go.

The new elevator helped, and we did two more build-up dives, reaching Mach .735 and .745, without any new problems, though I felt I was logging far too much "passenger time." We agreed that I should try the big one - if I could reach Mach .76 without the plane coming apart, we'd meet the specs. Then we might be able to improve the controllability and end up with a production order for a new combat airplane.

I don't think I could improve, nor should I embellish, upon the official report of the last flight of the Curtiss XP-60D:

At approximately 2:30 p.m. on May 6 (1943), pilot Don Armstrong took off on the last flight of the final demonstration of the XP-60D. The dive was started at 2:54 p.m. at 26,000 feet, 20 miles SE of the Buffalo Airport from a normal push-over entry. All controls were trimmed for zero load and the initial descent was

without incident. The pilot notified the ground by radio that he was approaching Mach .76 and would start the pullout as specified... Following this and before the actual act of pulling the required acceleration (Gs), a high-frequency vibration developed, accompanied by a severe positive (upward) pitching moment. After a very brief period of extreme tail buffeting, the aircraft went completely out of control. The positive pitching moment became extreme and was accompanied by a violent twisting or snap-rolling in one direction and the aircraft abruptly changed to a climbing attitude. During this extremely violent spinning, twisting and high acceleration - approximately plus 12 Gs - the pilot was unable to move or see what had occurred. He then realized the aircraft was coming apart and, to retain consciousness, vision and possession of his mental faculties, allowed himself to become bent over in the cockpit. Suddenly the aircraft hesitated and a negative (downward) pitching moment was encountered. The pilot immediately opened the hatch and observed the wings were still intact, there was no control in the elevators or rudder, and it would be necessary to abandon the aircraft. Before any other action could be taken another positive pitching moment and violent rolling commenced and he bent over in the cockpit once more. Once again the aircraft hesitated with another negative pitching moment and the pilot abandoned the aircraft.

Upon orienting himself during the fall, the pilot found the aircraft

following him closely. He allowed himself to fall free for over 9,000 feet until the wreckage had cleared away and one of the gyrations of the aircraft caused it to go off on a tangent away from him. The pilot then opened his parachute, causing him to be above the aircraft and in the clear. Due to the high wind (ground wind of 35 mph with gusts to 50 mph)...he drifted to land near Alden, New York. Mr. Armstrong was apparently uninjured with the exception of a sprained or broken ankle which he incurred when he either bounced off a barn or when striking the ground.

The accuracy of Henry's prediction about how the aircraft would behave, minus the tail, has remained amazing to me since the crash. Thankfully, I had talked it over with him - and listened to him. It undoubtedly saved my life!

Two other memories have stayed with me for fifty years. The outstanding one is almost supernatural, and I'm certain that some readers will either not believe me or will reach for a "practical explanation." So be it; but I know what I believe, and that's good enough for me.

Immediately after I bailed out I instinctively reached to pull the parachute's ripcord. At that instant, I vividly saw my friend Baggy Glover and heard him loudly say, "No!" I looked up, and right above me was the main portion of my tailless airplane. Had I opened it, my chute would surely have become tangled with the plane. (Baggy had been killed when his chute became fouled in the wreckage of his Helldiver after a structural failure.) Supernatural? Subconscious? What difference does it make? Baggy held me in the palms of his hands.

The other recollection is the total disbelief on the face of Nathan Sweet, the farmer who watched me come down. I saw him standing near his barn and shouted down to him when I was still fifty or sixty feet in

the air. He looked up at me, ran across Swartz Road to Milton Meyer's farm, watched me bounce off the roof of a barn and helped me get out of my chute when I landed. His mouth opened and closed a couple of times as he tried to speak, and he finally said, "Oh, my God; oh, my God, are you all right? Where did you come from?" Then he realized how funny he sounded and we both laughed - he at himself, and I, because it was so very wonderful to be alive!

He didn't have a phone but helped me into his car and drove me to Stowell's Pharmacy in Alden, New York. I couldn't walk, so I crawled into the store, called the company, and my wife, and waited for the crew to pick me up. The pain medication that pharmacist Ralph D. Stowell gave me was effective, to say the least - I was on "cloud nine" for four or five hours. A week or so afterward, I sent him a note of thanks and a couple of autographed photos; and he wrote me a very touching letter which I still have. He was a hunter, like myself, and sent me a tooth from the first moose he had killed. He asked me to wear it on my flight suit as a good-luck charm, and I did.

Scores of pages were written explaining the crash, but they all boil down to this: as the critical Mach number was reached, compressibility caused the center of lift to shift rearward on the wing, creating a positive pitching moment which raised the nose of the aircraft. The disturbed airflow also sent shock waves toward the tail assembly, inducing flutter or vibration and diminishing the effectiveness of the horizontal stabilizer, permitting the build-up of even more positive (nose-up) forces. The horizontal stabilizers and elevators broke away followed, two-tenths of a second later, by the vertical fin and rudder. This multiple-structural failure can be very clearly seen in the photographs in this chapter. Most of the test-data records were recovered, and I had survived to cooperate in coordinating the information. The data was shared with other manufacturers and, hopefully, helped in improving future designs.

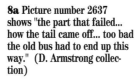

8a In picture number 2636 if you look very closely you'll see "my checkerboard insignia on the side of the cockpit. Also [note] the clean break that the stabilizer broke off, and how the horizontal members took the vertical fin and the rudder with it." (D. Armstrong collection)

8a Picture number 2637 shows "the part that failed... how the tail came off... too bad the old bus had to end up this way." (D. Armstrong collection)

The orders for 1,950 P-60As and 500 P-60Cs were canceled, and the P-60E order was rescinded even before the YP-60E made its first flight. We had fought the monster as hard as we could. The XP-60D had been devoured. Since I had done my homework - and received a lot of help from many wonderful people - I had been able to bail out of the plane. Because of my parachute, I had escaped to fight again, another day.

On May 11, 1943, I received a letter from the Irving Air Chute Company notifying me of my membership in the famous Caterpillar Club and a gold pin, shaped like a caterpillar, with "D. Armstrong, May 6, 1943" engraved on the back. I still have the pin and, on special occasions, wear it with grati-

tude and pride. Membership in the Caterpillar Club is restricted to pilots who have saved their lives by the use of a parachute, and believe me, it's great to be a Caterpillar! With the loss of the XP-60D, the imminent demise of the proposed P-60 series was no longer in doubt. I did a few more performance tests on the contra-rotating propellers in the XP-60C (and enjoyed its no-torque performance and improved rate of climb) and then some comparison tests in the XP-60E and the XP-40Q. The '60E and the '40Q were both very good-looking airplanes and, following the war would, quite literally, "end up" in air racing. In the 1947 Thompson Trophy race the '40Q crashed following an engine failure but Skip Ziegler bailed out, break-

ing a leg. The '60E had a *tail failure* while attempting to qualify, and James DeSanto was also able to bail out. Hence the P-60s drifted into obscurity.

There was no specific project for me so I took some time off and visited Grumman and had the chance to fly their TBF Avenger, F4F Wildcat and F6F Hellcat. At Vought I flew the F4U (I would fly Corsairs, again, later at Goodyear) and at Martin I flew the B-26 Marauder. I also made myself take time to visit New York City and wrote an article for *Skyways* magazine (October 1943) about test flying.

While visiting the other companies I was invited down to Washington, D.C., and offered a position as a flight engineering inspector for the CAA. This rather surprised me, but they insisted they needed a test pilot who could work up his own data. LaVerne had been quite emotionally upset when the P-60 broke up, and the CAA job really appealed to her because it was "probably much safer." I felt that I didn't have much to look forward to at Curtiss anymore and decided to see what Civil Service work was like. It created quite a ruckus because I was a very versatile pilot to have around, but Curtiss finally agreed to let me leave.

Although I had seen the handwriting on the wall, nevertheless, I was shocked and saddened, a few years later, when it became obvious to nearly everyone in the aviation world that Curtiss would never again regain its former status. The P-60 program was almost its last gasp.

My dad had known Glenn Curtiss since their early days of motorcycle racing. He often spoke delightedly of the achievements of the Curtiss company, from its humble beginning through WW II. Thankfully, neither of them would have to witness the lack of insight and preparedness that permitted one of the world's oldest and most prestigious aviation companies to disintegrate and pass into oblivion.

[Historical note: In 1910 Glenn Curtiss won the *New York World* newspaper $10,000 prize by flying from New York to Albany in slightly less than three hours, and the same year founded the Curtiss Aeroplane Company. In 1916 the Curtiss Aeroplane and Motor Corporation was created and, during WW I, built over 5,000 planes and almost as many engines, employing 18,000 workers. Curtiss and the Wright Aeronautical Corporation merged in 1929 and Glenn Curtiss died on July 23, 1930, aged 52.

Curtiss-Wright built over 30,000 aircraft and 220,000 engines in the ten years before the end of WW II, employing over 175,000 people. But sadly, the company seemed to have been totally unprepared for the postwar era, closing down the Aeroplane Division in 1951 and selling out to North American.]

8a The "after" of the XP-60D. (D. Armstrong collection)

8a Picture number 2635 is "another view, from the rear, and it's still a mess; note how the leading edge of the wings folded up." (D. Armstrong collection)

CHAPTER 9

LOW AND SLOW IN THE CAA
July 1943 - March 1944

[Historical note: (CAA) The Air Commerce Act of May 20, 1926, charged the Secretary of Commerce with fostering air commerce, issuing and enforcing air traffic rules, licensing pilots, certificating aircraft, establishing airways and operating and maintaining aids to navigation and entrusted these duties to the Department's Aeronautics Branch, later renamed the Bureau of Air Commerce. In 1936, the Department assumed the important task of air traffic control. In 1938, the Civil Aeronautics Act transferred the central government's civil aviation role from the Commerce Department to a new independent agency, the Civil Aeronautics Authority. In 1940, President Franklin D. Roosevelt split the Authority into two agencies, the Civil Aeronautics Board (CAB) and the Civil Aeronautics Administration (CAA). The CAA was responsible for air traffic control, airman and aircraft certification, safety enforcement and airway development.]

My CAA appointment as a flight engineering inspector on July 8, 1943, began on a disappointing note because I was assigned to the Dearborn Street office in downtown Chicago. The noise and traffic of the city were completely unlike Buffalo, where my office had looked out onto the airport and had been an easy, relaxing drive from my home in a suburban area near Kenmore.

Decent housing was virtually impossible to find in wartime Chicago, so I purchased a comfortable Vagabond travel trailer and located a lovely place to stay in Park Ridge,

Illinois - quite pleasant for LaVerne and Donnie (now four). I knew I'd be traveling throughout a several-state district frequently, but when in Chicago I decided I would commute by train.

The branch of the CAA to which I was attached was the Flight Engineering and Factory Inspection Division. Their responsibilities included not only the testing and certification of new or modified aircraft but - during the war - whenever the division had pilots available, assisting the military by flying acceptance flights at various factories. (The factory inspection aspect was handled primarily by the military.)

Four days after starting work, I was ready to get back to flying. I had absorbed most of the CAA procedures I needed to know and had a good secretary whom I hoped would keep up with the inordinate amount of paperwork that bureaucracies require to justify their existence. So I asked to be assigned to "something useful."

The next morning I was sent to St. Charles, Illinois, and started doing acceptance flights, which should be more accurately described as "production testing." Between July 12 and

October 2, I flew 269 such flights for the U.S. Army and the Royal Navy: at St. Charles in the Fairchild PT-23; at Wayne, Michigan, in the Stinson L-5 and Fairchild AT-19; and at Middletown, Ohio, in the Aeronca L-3, Fairchilds PT-19 and PT-23. I also flew a Fairchild PT-26 Cornell which was powered by the Ranger 200-hp engine. (I would "fly" this Ranger engine again in 1949 - racing in Sprint cars in Florida.) LaVerne and Donnie stayed in Park Ridge most of the time and I shuttled myself around in a CAA Stinson Reliant.

There was very little free time except for days when the weather was too poor to fly. One day I was able to slip away and visit the Curtiss-Wright plant at Columbus, Ohio, where I flew the famous SB2C Helldiver. This was a strange, "glad-sad" flight; I enjoyed flying the plane, but I couldn't forget that it was in the same type dive bomber my friend Baggy Glover had been killed. Another break in my routine came when I had the opportunity to fly the little Culver LCA on a layover in Bowling Green, Kentucky. However,

78 Meyers OTW 160; trainer; tandem, two-seat, open-cockpit, biplane; Kinner R-56, 160-hp radial. (D. Armstrong collection)

80 Funk 65; side-by-side, two-seat, cabin, high-wing, monoplane; Lycoming, 75-hp opposed. (Courtesy of San Diego Aerospace Museum)

the most interesting flying I did during these seven weeks was in Tecumseh, Michigan.

Tecumseh was home for Al Meyers and the Meyers Aircraft Factory. Al had designed and built a fine, two-cockpit biplane - the Meyers OTW ("Out to Win") - with a 160-hp Kinner engine. This required a temporary experimental "NX" designation and complete testing to obtain CAA certification.

I did the airspeed calibration flights on July 23, a set of low-altitude sawtooth-climb tests on the 27th, stability and landing tests at both the most-forward and the most-rearward centers of gravity on the 29th, medium- and high-altitude sawtooth climbs on the 30th, and wound up the project that same day with the spin

tests. Al and his crew were easy and fun to work with, the plane was a joy to fly and it was great doing "real" test flying again!

The OTW was truly a winner and a great credit to Al, and to the people who came from surrounding farms to help build the planes. A few years later Al sold his design of a Meyers 200 (a four-place, low-wing aircraft) to the Aero Commander Company and afterward, as far as I know, devoted himself to manufacturing aluminum boats, jeep tops and trailers.

Paperwork finally got so bogged down that I had to go back to the office on October 3 and write reports, expense accounts and an evaluation of production-testing procedures I had seen. Then, on October 18, I started a two-week series of certification tests on the Waco UPF-7. The concentration necessary to obtain accurate test results would reduce the amount of time I could

spend watching for other aircraft, so I chose to use the field at Joliet, Illinois, to get away from the busy Chicago airports.

While doing the tests on the Waco I had to wear three "hats." I was the mechanic who serviced, did minor maintenance and installed the appropriate ballast or equipment on the aircraft. I was the engineer who determined the nature of, and worked up the data obtained from, each flight. And I was the pilot. A delightful challenge!

In addition to the usual airspeed calibration, sawtooth climb and take-off and landing tests, I had to change weight and balance configurations for each of the stability and control, stall, spin and dive tests. The information obtained from all of these tests required the preparation of many graphs, drawings and reports, and I can't possibly relate how thankful I was for Doc Gerhardt's superb training! After the flights it took three days in the office to put all of the information into presentable form and to submit enough copies to satisfy the voracious appetite of the "system." It had been a most satisfying experience.

Next, I was on my way to Wichita, Kansas. Al Mooney was one

of the era's great small-aircraft designers. This time he had created the Culver YPQ-14A, a "flyable" target drone, to be used by the Army for anti-aircraft gunnery practice. It was a tiny, single-seat, fast and responsive plane that could be ferried from place to place by a pilot and then could be flown by radio control while being used as a target. This time I only had to do the flying while Al and his staff wore the other hats. We did the same tests I had just completed on the Waco, plus some cooling, high-altitude, speed and general performance flights; and Al and I shared some truly excellent steak dinners. (One of his engineers raised the beef.) I recall thinking at the time that this was the first plane I didn't "climb into" - instead, like long underwear, I "put it on!"

On November 18 I borrowed an Aeronca Champ and flew from Wichita to Ardmore, Oklahoma, for one of the shortest assignments I ever had. A local CAA inspector reported that a Piper J-5 Cruiser in his district had encountered "tail buffeting." I flew it, found a faulty airspeed indicator, had it replaced and flew it again. It would not buffet if flown within the clearly-marked limits. He thanked me and I went home. Having me travel all that distance for something so simple was like calling a podiatrist to operate on your foot, instead of looking first and removing the stone in your shoe!

My logbook indicates that my next series of tests was in Grand Rapids, Michigan, on an experimental Driggs 3-95. While writing this chapter in 1993, I could not remember what this aircraft was, or looked like, in spite of the fact that I had flown it for thirteen hours and fifteen minutes. Mr. John Cournoyer of St. Louis, Missouri, saved the day by sending information and photos. The Driggs I tested, NX-592E, was one of twenty built in Lansing, Michigan. It was a two-cockpit biplane powered with an inverted Cirrus 95-hp engine. I did all the usual certification tests and, for some strange reason, over five hours of spin tests! The aircraft was certified, but no further production was ever done.

Before leaving Grand Rapids I did some evaluation flights on a two-con-

trol (no rudder) General Aircraft "Skyfarer." It was the second aircraft to be certified by the CAA as being incapable of spinning. There was also a Funk 65 on the field and, since I had never been in one, I talked the owner into letting me fly it. It flew very comfortably, and I was disappointed to not see more of them after the war.

In July, when I had been testing the Meyers OTW, Al had invited me to return and go hunting with him. My next assignment was in Michigan so I took a few days leave and went over to Tecumseh. There were very few

I flew 120 more acceptance flights at Wayne, Michigan, in AT-19s and L-5s and was pleased to see Margaret Cook again. Women pilots were few and far between in 1943, and those who were around seemed to be utilized primarily to deliver aircraft. There were others, but Margaret was the only female production test pilot I knew, and it was always a pleasure to be around her. I had no way to follow her career and always wondered what she did after the war.

It was paperwork time again, and back to Chicago I went. But

84 Driggs 3-95, Skylark; tandem, two-seat, open-cockpit, biplane; Cirrus Hi-Drive, 95-hp in-line. Only twenty were built. (Courtesy of National Aviation Museum, Canada)

hunters (most of them were in the service) and the corn fields around Al's farm were full of pheasant. He loaned me the clothes and guns I needed and we got some fine birds within walking distance of his house. Then we went up to the Houghton Lake area and spent a couple of beautiful, crisp, fall days deer hunting.

Flying reverted to being low and slow and rather dull between December 20, 1943, and January 19, 1944. As during the previous summer,

86 Howard DGA-15A, "Damn Good Airplane" (known in the U.S. military as the GH-1/NH-1, Nightingale); four-or five-seat, cabin, high-wing, monoplane; Pratt and Whitney Wasp Junior, 450-hp radial. The DGA nickname is currently being used by Doug and Dave Shillen, Texas, fabricators of custom firearms and components, to describe their excellent - Damn Good Actions - bolt-action design. They custom-built a 7mm Rem. Magnum rifle for me, with which I've hunted for nearly ten years. Maybe they knew fellow-Texan, Benny Howard? (Courtesy of San Diego Aerospace Museum)

almost as soon as I got there I was called to St. Charles, Illinois, to make a few flights in the Howard DGA-15A (GH-1). "DGA" was Benny Howard's abbreviation for "Damn Good Airplane." Some pilots thought the Howard was a bit tricky to fly - it got very unfairly tagged with the name "Ensign Killer" - so I reviewed the pilot's manual and made a few suggestions about approach speeds and techniques. I enjoyed the airplane, and it did a great job as a Navy personnel carrier and air ambulance. The Navy had a twin Beech 18 at St. Charles the week I was there, and the pilot gave me a chance to get a couple of hours in the left seat. I felt that it was a good performing aircraft and had a lot of fun making three-point, stalled landings in it. When it was empty, and the center of gravity way forward, it was much easier to wheel-land it!

Then came the straw that broke the camel's back: I was assigned to do CAA certification tests on the Navy N3N-3 trainer. This aircraft was built at the Naval Aircraft Factory and

powered with a Wright 235-hp engine. It was a proven design; a well-built, open-cockpit biplane. N3Ns had flown for thousands of hours, and the only apparent purpose for the proposed program was to change the "NR" registration to "NC" (from "restricted" to "commercial"). In peacetime, I might have understood adhering to the letter of the civil regulations in order to accomplish this but, in my opinion, "testing" it during the war was redundant, bureaucratic nonsense!

Although I objected to the premise, I returned to Joliet, did all the tests (similar to those I had done in the Waco UPF during October 1943), returned to the office, wrote up and submitted all the proper reports. But then, while keeping up to date with petty details, I spent the next month writing letters and talking to friends at Boeing, North American and Douglas.

I had been with the CAA less than seven months and flown almost five-hundred hours, only eighty-eight of which were devoted to engineering tests. My test-flying skills had been

sharpened and I appreciated having the opportunity to hone them. However, my country was at war, and I felt that my talents were not being fully utilized. It was time to move on.

[Historical note: (FAA) The Federal Aviation Act of 1958 transferred the CAA's functions to a new independent body, the Federal Aviation Agency (FAA). In 1966, President Lyndon B. Johnson announced his intent to seek legislative authority for a new cabinet department that would combine all major Federal transportation responsibilities. The result was the Department of Transportation (DOT), which began operations on April 1, 1967. The FAA was renamed the Federal Aviation Administration and became one of several modal organizations within the new Department.]

CHAPTER 10

DOUGLAS AND DOGS
March 1944 - August 1944

Douglas, North American and Boeing were all west-coast companies, and since I had never been west of Texas, I offered my services to all three. Within a short time I received offers from each of them. My feelings were mixed: I would enjoy the new experience of the larger aircraft at Boeing, but I could probably be more valuable testing smaller, higher-performance aircraft at Douglas or North American.

67 Martin B-26, Marauder, "Widow Maker"; medium bomber; two Pratt and Whitney R-2800-5, 1,850-hp radials. (Courtesy of San Diego Aerospace Museum)

Don Douglas, Junior, was in charge of the experimental flight test division of Douglas, at the Santa Monica plant, and his projections for experimental flying in their new dive bombers and twin-engined light bombers sounded enticing. I needed a change, needed to feel useful again, so I resigned from the CAA and left Chicago, with my family and trailer, for southern California.

We wanted to take our time on this trip and planned a week-long visit with LaVerne's family in Dallas. Meanwhile, because I was not yet on the Douglas payroll, I was technically eligible to be drafted and was reclassified. When I arrived at the experimental flight test hangar I picked up the notification with the mail, which had been forwarded to me. A couple

of hours later, Don Douglas, Junior, and I reached General H. H. "Hap" Arnold by telephone and explained the situation to him. He remembered my work at Curtiss and had us hold while one of his aides called some poor clerk at the draft board. I'm sure I sweated and squirmed when listening to the General emphatically "straighten things out." (He could be very emphatic.) A telegram from the draft board arrived before noon the next day, with an "essential deferment," and that was the last I heard from them!

Once again, having my trailer was a godsend. The Douglas Company maintained a staff who had the thankless task of trying to find housing for new employees. Locating space for a trailer was easy. They found a small, beautifully-landscaped park in Pacific Palisades, across the road from the ocean. We were comfortably at home within a few hours and thoroughly enjoyed being on the beach the whole time I was at Douglas. On March 8, 1944 - exactly one month after leaving the CAA - I was checked out in the Douglas A-20G at Clover

Field. I had reported for work on March 1 and spent a week getting security passes, arranging things in my desk and locker and getting acquainted with my new associates and the procedures that I was expected to follow. The other experimental test pilots were really helpful and made me feel welcome and a part of the group in no time. I can't remember who gave me that first check ride. It must have been either Frank Sinclair, Laverne Brown or Gene May; but I do recall liking the A-20 because it felt so solid and responsive. Perhaps it was also the fact that I was flying something with some horsepower once again.

On the 9th and 10th I was able to familiarize myself with the area around Mines, Clover and Long Beach fields by making four delivery flights and on the 11th I was back at work, doing some exhaust-temperature tests on an A-20C. I felt comfortable with the system at Douglas and was happy to be there.

Many other routine tests still needed to be done on the A-20 program and I, being the new kid on the block, was the natural choice for these flights, for two reasons.

98 Douglas A-26/B-26, Invader; bomber; two Pratt and Whitney R-2800-27, 2,000-hp radials. (Courtesy of San Diego Aerospace Museum)

89 Douglas A-20, when converted to night fighter known as the Havoc, known in Canada as the Boston; bomber - Models C and G, two Wright R-2600-11, 1,600-hp radials - Model H, two Wright R-2600-29, 1,700-hp radials. (Courtesy of San Diego Aerospace Museum)

First, it let the project pilots devote their time to more detailed work, and second, the engineers could evaluate my knowledge and skills in order to learn how to utilize me in future flights. So, for the next eighteen days I was "filling in holes in the data" and logged thirty-eight hours in A-20 C, G and H models. Actually, I didn't mind a bit. Since my Doc Gerhardt days I had taken deep pride in always bringing down very precise details, and to do so now was a way of proving myself to the Douglas engineering staff.

Living on the ocean was yet another new adventure for us. Donnie was doing exactly what I had enjoyed at his age - swimming, playing on the beach and being outdoors from daylight to dark. He and his mother loved to beachcomb and pick up shells. In the little free time I had, I joined them walking on the beach,

taking a swim now and then and, any evening I could get home early, cooking and eating outside. After the winter weather in Illinois, Michigan and Ohio, it was wonderful.

A truly delightful change for us was to have friends who were totally unconnected with aviation. Betty and Leslie Charteris lived in a trailer about fifty feet from ours and we shared many happy hours with them. Leslie was the author of *The Saint* mystery stories and brought us into his circle of friends, which included screen-writers, publishers and actors like Anthony Quinn, Spencer Tracy and Pat O'Brien. Leslie's cooking skills reflected his oriental ancestry (one of his parents was Chinese, I think) and our cookouts, when he was "the chef," were absolutely delicious. Betty and Leslie were very good to us, and for us, and I have always had a warm spot in my heart for them both.

Fishing and folk or square dancing have been a big part of my life since my teens. While test flying, both gave me many hours of pleasure and satisfied a deep psychological need to get away from it all. In addition to our newly-found beach friends, an experimental pilot, George DeSonchen, and one of my flight engineers, Bob Lafey, joined me in the California mountains on a few wonderful trout-fishing expeditions. George, from France, always stuck an "s" onto the word trout, so "trouts fishing" it became! Bob and George joined the beach gang a night or two for some Grunion fishing. My name for these hilarious nights was "4-Bs" - Beach, Bonfire, Beer and Bery-wet! (If you've never been Grunion "hunting," you probably don't understand; but it's your loss!)

Folk dancing was mostly with the university faculty, and there were usually far more women than men because of the war. It was fun, relaxing, good exercise and ended early enough so I could get a good night's sleep before flying the next day.

Douglas was building a dive bomber, the SBD Dauntless (designed by Ed Heinemann), which was earning an enviable reputation in the Pacific war. This plane fully used the "Swiss cheese" dive brakes I had first experienced on the Northrop A-17A in the RCAF. In 1935, NACA and Ed had come up with the idea of putting a series of three-inch holes in the original dive brakes of the Northrop XBT-1 to eliminate tail buffet and improve control and stability, and it had worked well. I flew the SBD-3 and SBD-5 on the last day of March 1944, and found them to be a lot like the Curtiss SB2C Helldiver, but with lighter control forces and slightly more visibility.

The Dauntless was fun to fly and, a couple of weeks later, I really shook up the Mines Field tower personnel when I called in and said I was at 12,000 feet just south of the field, requesting a "straight-down" approach. I had to repeat *straight down* a time or two but, since there wasn't any other traffic nearby, I was cleared to do so. I learned later that it startled the hell out of some airline pilots who were listening to the tower frequency.

The next day, April 1, I flew the first U.S. Navy aircraft with a jet engine, the XBTD-2 (No. 04962). This was a weird airplane with a 2,300-hp Wright R-3350 engine and conventional propeller on the nose, and the Westinghouse WE-19XA, 1,500-pound thrust, turbojet engine in the tail. The jet-fuel tank was installed in the bomb

bay, the air intake was on the top of the fuselage behind the pilot's canopy and the engine mounted with a ten-degree downward angle in the rear of the fuselage. Five weeks later I would start testing the BTD-1 - the same aircraft, without the jet engine.

[Author's note: There is a minor statistical discrepancy as to the date of the first flight of the XBTD-2. My pilot's logbook lists the same particulars and the date given above.]

To begin with, the basic BTD was, as I relate later, a "dog," and adding the jet engine did very little to improve it. The extra power of the jet appeared barely to compensate for the added weight and, as the pilot, adding the jet accomplished nothing

except to make an already "blah" airplane more difficult to manage. The jet required totally different fuel and additional control systems - an impractical arrangement, to say the least. After my flights, I was asked for, and offered, my opinions as to the viability of the aircraft. I was not asked to fly it again. I wonder why?

This type of propulsion system - prop on the front, jet in the rear - was not very successful. Douglas, Republic, Ryan and Curtiss were four of the several companies who gave

99 Lockheed P-38, Lightning, "Forked-tail Devil"; fighter/escort/bomber; tricycle gear, twin-boom; two Allison V-1710, 1,475-hp V-in-lines. (Courtesy of Aerofax, Inc.)

the idea a try and Ryan got an insignificant Navy production contract for the FR-1 Fireball.

Republic designed a "mixed-propulsion" fighter for the USAAF called the XP-69. After building only a mockup, the project was abandoned on May 11, 1943. Their second such design, the XP-72, first flew on February 2, 1944, but that project was

76 Curtiss SB2C-1, Helldiver; dive bomber; tandem, two-seat; Wright R-2600-8, 1,700-hp radial. (Courtesy of San Diego Aerospace Museum)

canceled shortly afterward.

Ryan's XFR-1 was first flown on June 25, 1944. However, the program was marred by two fatal crashes, the first on October 13, 1944, and the second on April 5, 1945. Only sixty-six Fireballs were delivered to the Navy.

Curtiss built three prototype XF15C-1s, and no production contract followed. Two were delivered to the Navy in 1945-1946 for evaluation, the first of which crashed on May 8, 1945.

Certainly one of the most colorful pilots at Douglas was Benny Howard. His aviation career could be a fascinating story of its own. He had been a racing pilot, created the Howard DGA, lost one leg in a crash and was now testing four-engine transport/cargo planes for Douglas. His name had been familiar to me for years. He was from Palestine, Texas, and when I told him my first job as a licensed pilot had been in his home

town, we shared several "Hey, did you know...?" coffee-breaks. For me, talking with Benny about some of his early experiences was a flashback to the lives of many of Dad's friends - flyers I had met as a youngster. I buttonholed him at every opportunity and have always regretted that I couldn't keep a record of his wonderful stories. He checked me out in the C-54 and I flew in the right seat with him only once or twice, although I can't remember what sort of tests we did. But here's an interesting story he told me; one that reveals a little about Benny, himself.

After flying the C-54 for many, many hours he thought that he'd found most of the bugs that always show up in any new aircraft. Then he took one across the Atlantic to England and something very strange occurred along the way: the farther he got from land, the more new bugs he found! By the time he arrived, he'd

made a written list of almost one hundred "2-B-fxd" items that he hadn't noticed until the plane was over "all that water, with no place to land." Even the "giants" were human!

Three weeks of doing a wide variety of tests in the A-20 and Dauntless passed very quickly before I was assigned to the XSB2D-1 project and, for the first time in my career, I flew an airplane (April 21, 1944) that I immediately labeled a "dog." The laminar-flow, inverted gull-winged plane was grossly overweight (16,270 pounds) and a ton over Navy specifications. It had a Wright R-3350 engine of 2,300 hp, a tricycle landing gear and was supposed to be an improvement on the highly-successful SBD series. Instead, it had such a disappointing performance that I called it "a brick with wings." Flying the XSB2D was like driving an underpowered, worn-out truck up a mountain, and handling it was like rowing a boat half-full of water. I did *not* enjoy flying it!

When I told the aeronautical engineers that it felt as though I was flying in a partially-stalled condition - all of the time - they simply didn't want to believe me. However, I was convinced that I was right, so I persuaded Don, Junior to have one of the disbelieving engineers "tuft the wing" and fly with me to take pictures of the wing in flight. (Tufting was scotch-taping three-inch lengths of yarn every six inches or so on the upper

93 Douglas DC-4/C-54, Skymaster; civilian/military transport; four Pratt and Whitney Twin Wasp, 1,100- to 1,450-hp radials. (Courtesy of San Diego Aerospace Museum)

90 Douglas SBD/A-24, Dauntless, "S But Deadly," "The Clunk"; dive bomber/scout - SBD-3; Wright R-182 1,000-hp radial - SBD-5; Wright R-18 60, 1,200-hp radial. (Courtesy of Sa Diego Aerospace Museum)

surface of the wing. Any area of the wing where the tufts would not lie flat was, at the very least, partially stalled - not producing lift.) It didn't take five minutes to make a believer out of the doubting Thomas. The results were so dramatically frightening that I thought the poor guy was going to lose his lunch! He was as white as a sheet! Over thirty percent of the wing area in or near the "valley" of the gull-wing was stalled out - in level flight. In a climbing attitude it was horrifyingly worse! And, sadly, that was only one of the problems.

I wish I could say that we eventually ended up with a decent air-plane, but this time we did not. In three months I had flown the XSB2D for a total of twelve miserable hours. Finally, I discussed it at lunch one day, face-to-face with Donald Douglas, Senior, and the designer, Ed Heinemann. I don't know if my comments had any influence on their decision, but after building two examples, the project was scrapped.

The Douglas Company had not gained the respect of the industry by adamantly sticking to something that was questionable so, early in the XSB2D project, recognizing the need for single-seat carrier bombers, they removed the second seat and the defensive armament and built a new aircraft designated the BTD-1 Destroyer. It was hoped that the lessons being learned on the XSB2D would prove beneficial to the new design, but when I was given this project on May 8, 1944, I found myself leashed to a second "dog."

The Destroyer was an improvement upon the XSB2D, but everyone involved with the project knew it wasn't good enough. During the following seven weeks I flew eleven hours and thirty minutes of tests in it, and on every single flight I knew the BTD-1, like its predecessor, was a failure. The Navy contract had been for 358 airplanes, but only twenty-eight were built. Sometime later, Ed Heinemann, when talking about the SB2D and the

BTD, was quoted as saying, "They both were turkeys." In my opinion, turkeys fly better!

[Author's note: Please remember that Ed Heinemann was a superb and highly-respected aircraft designer. I do not mean to imply otherwise! He was the chief engineer of the Douglas El Segundo Division as early as 1938. He designed all of the major Douglas combat aircraft during WW II and subsequently designed the highly-successful AD Skyraider, A3D Skywarrior and A4D Skyhawk. But even the "giants" goof-up once in a while.]

I was a disheartened pilot, but right at the end of my involvement in the BTD-1 program I had an opportunity to fly four different and very good airplanes: the Bell P-63 King Cobra, Grumman's F6F Hellcat, North American's B-25 Mitchell and the Douglas A-26 Invader. The nicest part about these flights was that during them I had the time to wring out the Hellcat and purge some of the frustrations of two months of flying the "dogs." It was like waking up after a bad dream.

Test pilots sometimes offset their tensions with harmless horseplay and, at Douglas, we were no exception. One of our group was a very capable pilot, and justifiably proud of the fact that he had brought down excellent data for quite a long series of flights. Many times external factors - rough air or a malfunction in instrumentation - resulted in questionable information, and several of us had run into minor problems requiring us to make repeat flights. Quite naturally, he needled us and we, in return, with tongue in cheek, accused him of "getting big-headed."

He wore a wig when not flying, but he would remove it and place it in his locker when getting his flying gear on, so his helmet wouldn't mess it up. One day I switched his wig with a much smaller one I had borrowed from a movie studio. When he reached for it, after his flight, every available pilot was in the locker room. He played along and put it on top of his shiny head and loudly conceded that he had, indeed, become big-headed. The following week, on the shelf in place of my helmet, I found a dunce cap; and on Frank Sinclair's desk was a box, gift-wrapped and beribboned, containing a brand new egg-beater with "XB-42" painted on the handle. (Frank was the project test pilot on the XB-42.)

The XB-42 was a very unusual aircraft. It was fast - over 400 mph - with a range equal to that of many heavy bombers. It had two Allison 1,800-hp engines inside the fuselage, behind the bomb bay, which drove a pair of contra-rotating propellers on the *tail*. The only suitable name was "Mixmaster."

Douglas also used contra-rotating propellers in the design of the huge TB2D, which joined the SB2D and the BTD on the "scrappile" in 1945. Republic, Westland, North American, Boeing, Fisher and Hughes also had aircraft on the drawing board which called for similar propellers. Because I had tested contra-rotating props on the Curtiss XP-60C, and Howard Hughes probably knew that I was not entirely satisfied at Douglas, I got an inquiry to see if I might be interested in working for him on a new twin-engine aircraft. Frankly, I didn't think I would be able to get

91 Douglas XBTD-2; torpedo bomber; single-seat, inverted gull-wing; mixed propulsion: Wright R-3350-14, 2,300-hp radial (nose); Westinghouse 1,000 s.t., jet (tail). (Courtesy of San Diego Aerospace Museum)

92 Douglas BTD-1, Destroyer; torpedo bomber; single-seat, inverted gull-wing; Wright R-3350-14, 2,300-hp radial. (Courtesy of San Diego Aerospace Museum)

along with Hughes, and I was able to say "no" without offense by telling him I was still under contract with Douglas. I did hear from him again about a year later.

During the first week of June I went back to Chicago to help out flight testing some minor engine modifications in the C-54-DC. Because Benny Howard had given me a very thorough checkout in the four-engined Skymaster and the tests were almost routine, I felt quite comfortable flying it. (The Douglas plant at Chicago turned out about 650 C-54s during the war.) I repeated the trip and very similar tests in the first week

of July and had time enough to visit the CAA office where I had worked the previous year. The group seemed pleased to see me and hear about my activities at Douglas. Probably the highlight of each of the trips was folk dancing in one of the Chicago Park District halls and going to one of the little ethnic restaurants after the dance for a couple of hours of good food, good wine and good friends.

My last few flights for Douglas were at Muroc - now Edwards Air Force Base test center - conducting some gun-firing tests and an easy structural dive demonstration on the already discontinued XSB2D-1. There was no longer any doubt in my mind - I was just spinning my wheels. It was time, once again, to move on.

After I returned to Santa Monica from Muroc, I visited the folks at Lockheed and flew the great P-38. Then I arranged to have lunch with the Navy representative at Douglas and had an off-the-record chat with him about my situation. Although he was officially not involved, a day or so later I received a phone call from Goodyear Aircraft Company.

When Goodyear's vice-president, Harry Blythe, told me that they

had modified the famous Corsair into the most powerful, single-engine, propeller-driven aircraft in the world and needed a competent test pilot to do all the performance and demonstration testing, I was hooked! Our negotiations were uncomplicated. GAC representatives were delightfully pleasant in all our discussions and eager to give me the help and authority I felt necessary to get the job done. The Douglases said they understood my position and graciously agreed to release me.

Betty and Leslie Charteris had our mutual friends over for a farewell cookout and, when he heard me mention I was leaving, Anthony Quinn said he'd like to buy our trailer and leave it where it was. It sounded like a great idea and, then and there, he gave me a check. Two days later the Armstrongs were traveling east to Akron, Ohio. Things were looking up!

Although we corresponded, regretfully, I never crossed paths with

the Charterises again. Long after I stopped test flying, whenever he was in a play somewhere close by, I made it a point to see Tony Quinn. What a trouper! He made the characters he portrayed come alive in front of your eyes. He is a vibrant human being who loves life and is devoted to his profession. Knowing him was both a privilege and a pleasure.

[Historical note: The Douglas Company was formed in July 1921 and made a name for itself soon afterward by building the plane that made the first round-the-world flight for the U.S. Army. The name was changed to Douglas Aircraft Company in 1928. During WW II the firm operated six complete plants and built almost 31,000 aircraft. Douglas Aircraft Company and McDonnell Aircraft Corporation merged on April 28, 1967, becoming the McDonnell Douglas Corporation.]

94 Douglas XSB2D-1; bomber; two-seat, laminar-flow, inverted gull-wing; Wright R-3350-14, 2,300-hp radial. (Courtesy of San Diego Aerospace Museum)

97 North American B-25, Mitchell; bomber; shoulder-high wing (passing above the bomb bay), tricycle landing gear; two Wright Cyclone R-2600-9, 1,350-hp radials. Used for the famous "Doolittle raid" on Japan. (Courtesy of San Diego Aerospace Museum)

CHAPTER 11

THE HOMESICK ANGEL
August 1944 - October 1944

During the drive from California to Akron, Ohio, with LaVerne and Donnie, I had time to think about some of the ramifications of my new job. My earlier conversations with Mr. Blythe had really whetted my curiosity: the famous Corsair, modified... how could they make an already great airplane even better? Put the pilot in a bubble canopy - add extra guns - give him over sixty percent more horsepower - and what has he got? A fighter pilot's dream-machine!

The Chance-Vought F4U Corsair design, with its innovative "gull wing," had been awarded a prototype contract by the Navy in June 1938, and on May 29, 1940, Lyman Bullard made the first flight of the XF4U-1. It was immediately apparent that the aircraft had great potential and, after many modifications, the initial flight of a production F4U-1 was made by Boone Guyton on June 25, 1942. Between the summer of 1942 and February 1945, before starting production of the F4U-4, Chance-Vought turned out almost 5,000 F4U-1s. In his book *Whistling Death, The Test Pilot's Story of the F4U Corsair* (Orion Books, New York) Boone tells the "rest of the story."

It is interesting to note that, although originally designed as a carrier-based fighter, the Corsair was initially delivered to the Marines for land-based operations. This remarkable aircraft, which became one of the most formidable Navy fighters of WW II, was not used on U.S. aircraft carriers until 1944 - and then only after the British had used their lend-lease Corsairs in that capacity.

Most people in aviation associated the name "Goodyear" with airships (blimps or dirigibles) and it was this extensive aeronautical background that led the Goodyear Corporation to offer its services to the military.

In the winter of 1941-1942, with the war escalating on two fronts, the Navy needed to increase production of the Corsair and ordered a land-based version of the F4U-1 from Goodyear Aircraft Corporation, designating it "FG-1." The first of these took to the air in February 1943. Goodyear built over 4,000 FG-1As and FG-1Ds between 1943 and 1945. (Brewster Aeronautical was also given a similar order, bearing the designation F3A-1. Because Brewster failed to meet delivery dates - they only built 735 planes - their contract was canceled in the summer of 1944.)

Several successful Japanese suicide attacks on our ships and aircraft emphatically foretold - to the U.S. and the world - the magnitude of the threat of the Kamikazes. Convinced that we could intercept many of them with a specialized carrier-based fighter, Goodyear was asked to create - without delay - a variant to their FG-1: one which would climb faster, have greater speed *while utilizing as many components of the FG-1 as possible.* A derivation would have three distinct advantages over an entirely "new" aircraft: it would save design time since the FG-1 was a proven airframe; it would eliminate major retooling, thus facilitating faster production; and it would "look like" a conventional Corsair, perhaps confusing the Japanese.

The most obvious way to accomplish this goal was to use an already-available but more powerful engine - the new Pratt and Whitney R-4360-4 Wasp Major. The Wasp Major developed 3,500 hp at 2,700 rpm with water injection. It was a 28-cylinder, air-cooled radial engine with four banks of seven cylinders each. (In comparison, the engine in the FG-1 developed 2,250 hp with water injection and was about fifteen inches shorter and 1,300 pounds lighter.)

Other design changes would include, at least:

1) A stronger wing capable of handling greater engine and fuel weight.

2) Additional self-sealing fuel tanks to offset the higher fuel consumption.

3) New engine controls.

4) New induction, exhaust, cooling and fuel systems.

5) New engine cowling.

6) A larger four-bladed propeller.

7) A fuselage modification for a bubble canopy.

The program was launched, very logically, by first installing the Wasp Major in a standard F4U-1, thus ascertaining that the proposal was viable. Following this, three FG-1As were to be modified to accept the new engine and subsequently, serious evaluation, development and flight testing would begin. This "new" aircraft was called the Goodyear F2G Super Corsair.

[Author's note: There are very few instances throughout aircraft development when an aircraft designation has been used before, with an entirely different plane. Oddly enough BOTH the designations given to Goodyear fighters, the "FG-1" and the "F2G," had been previously assigned. The Eberhart Aeroplane and Motor Company (a subsidiary of the Eberhard Steel Products Company) had the dubious distinction of building only two aircraft before fading into obscurity. The first was designated as the XFG-1 and made its initial flight in

11a *XF2G-1. From left to right - Warren West, crew chief; yours truly; J. P. West, assistant chief. Note the special test-boom for air speed indicator calibrations (left center of the picture). (D. Armstrong collection)*

11b "Goodyear's XF2G-1 - # 1 'Super Corsair' (photo - 4/28/45). First Fighter with over 3,000 horsepower. Donald Armstrong Project Test Pilot - first flight through demonstration." Pictured from left to right - J. R. Matzinger, instruments; S. W. Pederson, Pratt and Whitney; E. B. "Bart" Myrick, flight engineer; yours truly; Warren West, crew chief; J. P. West, assistant chief; Bob DeLong, "ex-chief, USN." Of special note: the tail surface is covered with tufts, and I'm holding the same kneepad that I was using when I bailed out of the XP-60D. (D. Armstrong collection)

1926. The second, a seaplane version, was designated as the XF2G-1 and appeared in 1928. The entire project was abandoned after an accident that year.]

Until this time (1943) Goodyear Aircraft had been involved in producing the FG-l, but not in developing and testing a heavier-than-air design. They had very competent production test pilots, but now needed a pilot for the experimental, performance and demonstration tests that would be a major part of the XF2G contract.

Their reasoning for hiring me was twofold. First, I had a thorough understanding of flight-test procedures; and secondly, I had a wide variety of flight-test experience. Obviously, Goodyear did not have the time for one of its production pilots to learn how to do this very demanding work - there was far too much pressure to get the F2G combat-ready as soon as possible. Secondarily, but of great importance, I was a highly-qualified and experienced demonstration test pilot. Goodyear hadn't even completed the preliminary demonstration tests on the FG-1 and, after these were done, the final demonstration tests would still have to be conducted for the Navy.

[Author's note: FG-1s were put into service before the demonstration flights were completed. This was logical, and not uncommon, when an already proven aircraft was being manufactured by another company under contract.]

The same prerequisites existed for the F2G - following the experimental work on the prototype aircraft. A total of four complete "extra-risk" demonstrations each consisting of two parts - structural/aerodynamic dives and spins/maneuvers. That meant eight exacting and high-risk programs, *plus* all the experimental and performance testing work on the F2G! It was truly an exciting challenge and one which I embraced with unbridled enthusiasm.

One situation disturbed me - I was being "brought in" from outside of the company. My job, senior engineering test pilot, was newly-created, and none of the existing company pilots, to my knowledge, had been considered for the position. Would this, and the fact that I was only twenty-five years old, be resented? Admittedly, it was all academic, because I had already been hired, but I resolved to be especially considerate and very aware that I might have to smooth some ruffled feathers when I arrived.

As it turned out, I had absolutely no cause for concern. Although the company pilots were skilled and capable professionals, most had only limited experimental, and no demonstration, test-flying experience. Before my arrival, Mr. Blythe (GAC vice-president) wisely sat down with nearly all of them, discussed my qualifications, and explained why the company had no choice but to bring in someone who could facilitate the completion of the programs. When I first met the pilots, I was flattered, and most certainly humbled, by their sincere respect and warm reception and became even more determined to do my very best to earn their support.

The company also bent over backwards to make me feel welcome and wanted. An apartment was waiting for us and someone was assigned to assist me in obtaining security passes, parking stickers, insurance, and to get me on the payroll. Then they scheduled a lunch meeting in the executive dining room, arranged to have me seated at a table with the executives with whom I would be working on the XF2G project, and introduced me to all of the department heads. During the afternoon I was personally escorted through the plant to meet the engineers in the aerodynamic and structural engineering depart-

ments and was shown drawings of a new bubble canopy and the engine installation.

While touring the plant I was surprised and impressed when I discovered that a number of workers, especially in the noisier areas, were totally or partially deaf. I had seen some "signing" when we were walking around, and soon was introduced to a couple of the supervisors in the fuselage-riveting area - one of whom was deaf, although he had an almost uncanny ability to read my lips and could speak quite clearly. When I questioned my escort, he informed me that Akron had one of the largest hearing-impaired populations in the country, and possibly the world. He went on to explain that the U.S. tire industry was centered in the area (Goodyear, Goodrich, Firestone, etc.) and that the plants where tire pressing was done - with huge, extremely-noisy steam presses - made an extraordinary effort to hire and train workers with audio deficits. It is easy to understand why people with restricted hearing wanted

to move to Akron where they would feel comfortable, as well as be confident that they could obtain steady, relatively high-paying jobs. Throughout my stay in Akron, whenever I was asked to give a luncheon or after-dinner talk to civic groups, scouts, schools or clubs, my "signer" and companion, Alice Kuntz, accompanied me.

It was back to the executive dining room the following morning for a meeting with many of the flight engineers, service and maintenance chiefs from the flight-test hangar and most of the pilots. Gene Racine, John Canada, Art Chapman and Ed Elliott (whom I had known at Curtiss) were four I especially remember because each of them was a skilled, competent pilot and a pleasure to work with, even under the most difficult circumstances. I have never been given - before or since - a more gracious and sincere welcome. Frankly, I was overwhelmed! But I loved every single minute of it, too!

My first two familiarization flights at Goodyear were in the FG-l

11c An instrument panel mockup of an F2G.
Note that almost half of the instruments
were for control-test purposes.
(D. Armstrong collection)

91

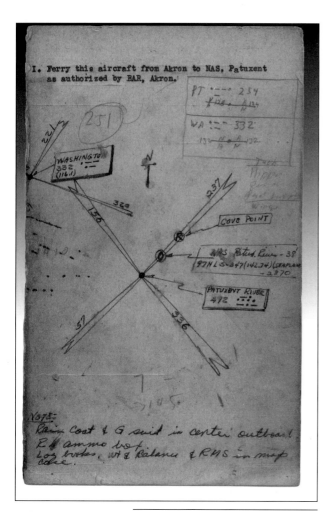

I. Ferry this aircraft from Akron to NAS, Patuxent as authorized by BAR, Akron.

11d Hand-drawn approach chart, NAS, Patuxent (Maryland). I prepared this chart for airplane No. 14692, Flight No. 69, October 25, 1945, and it is yet another example of the rudimentary navigational aides of fifty years ago. (D. Armstrong collection)

and, although I had flown a Corsair only once before - when visiting Boone Guyton at Vought - I was comfortable with the plane after one circuit of the field. In spite of some minor inconveniences caused by construction and expansion, I was also very pleased with the Akron airport which was well situated, with plenty of open space at the ends of the runways. This is always a confidence-builder for pilots, especially those flying with experimental engines, who might have to cope

with an engine malfunction or failure on takeoff.

Before flying, I had taken a few moments to visit the tower and meet the controllers so they would feel like they were talking to someone they knew. I asked them to recognize me by the callsign of "Checker," when I was in an experimental plane, instead of by aircraft type and number. They were happy to cooperate and, in the next two years, assisted me many times when I had a sick engine, hydraulic trouble, an oil leak or needed a low-altitude flyby to check a tail-wheel position, etc.

Since leaving the RCAF, my crash helmet had been painted with a blue-and-gold checkerboard design and most of the experimental aircraft I had tested since then displayed a checkerboard on the fuselage directly under the cockpit or on the nose cowling. Idiosyncrasy or superstition? Who cares? It was something extra my crew chiefs had done for me just because I liked it - and because they cared. I appreciated it!

When the crew chiefs and mechanics saw some photos of aircraft I had previously tested, it was less than two weeks before a tiny checkerboard appeared on No. 092, the bubble-canopy test plane. When the first complete prototype of the XF2G-1 rolled out for its first flight on October 15, 1944, one of my crew

chiefs, Warren West, proudly "unveiled" a checkerboard - a surprise they had kept hidden from me until that moment!

The checkerboard was not an original idea of mine - it dates back at least as far as WW I. One of the earliest checkerboard noses can still be found today on a 1918 Thomas-Morse S-4C Scout at the Cradle of Aviation Museum in Garden City, New York. However, it unquestionably had become my special, personal identification. In 1993, while researching for this book, someone remembered me as "the Checkerboard Kid."

On my second day of flying, the flight engineers had ballasted an FG-1 so that the center of gravity would approximate that of the XF2G and I did a series of longitudinal-stability tests (nose up-and-down movement) and found no unexpected differences. The following day I measured the amount of stick force vs the elevator angle at extreme low speeds, and the amount of stick force vs the aileron angle at maximum level-flight speed. We knew we would have some rudder (directional) control problems with the bigger engine, but the response to either the elevator (pitch) or aileron (roll) was virtually unchanged and entirely acceptable.

The fuselage had been modified to utilize a full bubble canopy

11e Certificate issued by Pratt and Whitney signifying that I was, in fact, the "thirty-sixth pilot of the first one hundred to fly an aircraft powered by a Wasp Major Engine." (D. Armstrong collection)

101 Goodyear XF2G-1, Super Corsair; fighter; single-seat, bubble canopy, inverted gull-wing; Pratt and Whitney R-4360 Wasp Major, 3,500-hp radial. Land-based version with manually folding wings. (D. Armstrong collection)

(not incorporated into standard Corsairs) to give the combat pilot improved visibility in all directions - except down - and I did the first evaluation on my third day at work. It was a remarkable improvement: one which only a pilot who has flown an aircraft, both with and without a bubble, could fully appreciate. Evaluation of the bubble was expedited by "borrowing" an existing canopy from a Republic P-47 for initial design and flight tests. As expected, the concept was highly desirable and practical.

That same day I also did extensive instrument calibration flights on the two test EXF2G-1s (so that performance tests could be started) and also some additional stick-force measurements on a standard FG-1 for comparison. These two XF2Gs carried the *company designation* of EXF2G - the prefix "E" indicating a more-or-less standard FG-1 which had been modified to accept the big Pratt and

Whitney "corn-cob" engine.

The first flight with the big engine was made on my ninth day on the job, August 26, 1944. The plane (No. 471) was a real "kick-in-the-butt" to fly. It had over fifty percent more power than the standard Corsair and three times the power of the P-40s, Hurricanes or Spitfires I had flown. Sometime during the flight I had scribbled a big "H-H-H" on my flight card. When the flight engineers checked to see what it stood for, I replied, "It means `Heading for Heaven in a Hurry'!"

What a wonderful way to cap off my first week and a half with the company. I was totally hooked on the project and could hardly wait to strap myself into the prototype. There was absolutely no doubt in my mind that we had a winner! Not too long afterward, Pratt and Whitney presented me with an attractive certificate indicating that I was the thirty-sixth pilot to fly their new Wasp Major engine. I still have it today, fifty years later.

During the next three days I flew another nine flights: more extensive stability-and-control checks, some rate-of-roll tests; I also checked out a spin-recovery-chute on an FG-1 and measured operating loads on the bubble canopy. I can recall appreciating

how patient Doc had been during my first stability-and-control practice flights in Canada and, once again, it was paying off. In fact, I tried to reach him by telephone to tell him so, but couldn't track him down. Sadly, I never would speak to him again.

Whenever a different engine is installed in a front-engine propeller-driven plane there is another factor, in addition to weight and balance, that is not only insidious, but extremely dangerous - carbon monoxide.

Because the engine controls, the firewall, the exhaust systems and the cowling are not only modified but, many times "hand crafted" (with less precise tolerances), carbon monoxide can more easily work its way into the cockpit. In ALL of my flights in prototype tractor-engined planes, I had ALWAYS breathed pure oxygen the entire time the engine was running - until tests proved the aircraft safe. Even then, I almost lost my life when an oxygen system malfunctioned. But, that's a later story.

[Author's note: Tony Janazzo, flying a modified F2G (No. 457), in

11f *Thomas-Morse S-4B Scout presently on loan to the Cradle of Aviation Museum, Garden City, New York. According to Joshua Stoss, museum historian, the plane has been owned by the same gentleman since coming off the production line. In the photo, ca. 1925, the cowling sports a checkerboard. Although checkerboarding was used in WW I, this is the earliest U.S. photo of the design I have been able to discover and, while the colors aren't the same, it is on the nose cowling - just like mine! (Courtesy of Cradle of Aviation Museum)*

the 1947 Thompson Trophy race at Cleveland, Ohio, lost his life after apparently becoming disoriented. The crash was attributed to carbon monoxide poisoning. He was not wearing an oxygen mask.]

Immediate tests on the EX models revealed life-threatening concentrations of CO in almost every flight condition. This was expected, and temporarily acceptable, because the planes were merely engine testbeds. A warning placard was posted in the cockpit prohibiting any flight without pure oxygen. My tests helped pinpoint some of the sources of the trouble, and corrections were made to the prototype.

With the much more powerful R-4360 engine we also experienced directional-control (rudder) difficulties produced by the increased torque, especially during takeoff or slow-speed flight. For example, the aircraft tended to veer to the left when given full power on takeoff, requiring almost full, right rudder to maintain a straight course. For the moment, until the actual F2G prototype was available, the problem was ameliorated by offsetting the vertical fin slightly - and planning for an enlarged rudder. Although directional-stability tests were satisfactory at any speed above that required for the initial climb, we all knew we had a problem to solve very soon.

Pratt and Whitney must have been very pleased with the success of the R-4360. In fact, several companies had it on the drawing board for future designs. Hughes Aircraft called for the Wasp Major for both the XF-11 and the huge, wooden "Spruce Goose." Because of my experience with the contra-rotating propellers at Curtiss and my impending, extensive work with the F2G, I got another - final - feeler from Howard Hughes. I passed along very favorable comments about the engine, explained my commitment to Goodyear and added that I was happy to remain where I was. In retrospect, my decision was a good one.

By now, word had reached the Navy of the tremendous potential of the F2G, and only a week after my first flight in the testbed, I was asked to bring the aircraft to the Naval Air Test Center at Patuxent River, Maryland, so they could look at it, and perhaps have some of their pilots get a flight in it. So, on September 4, 1944, I made what was to be the first of many trips to "Pax" - even then a fine facility with superb personnel. (I could not know then, or would I ever have imagined, that I would return, as a guest, forty-nine years later, April 1, 1993 - to participate in the Fiftieth Anniversary Celebration!)

[Historical note: Patuxent Naval Air Station was conceived in an effort to consolidate Navy test facilities which had grown, like Topsy, without much direction, for at least thirteen years.

Between 1929 and 1942 an airplane underwent an almost incredulous sequence of events before gaining acceptance by the Navy. First, delivery was made at the Anacostia Naval Air Station (Maryland) where it was flight tested, gun tested and radio tested. Second, it was moved to the Naval Proving Grounds at Dahlgren (Virginia) for dive, spin and bomb tests. Third, to NAS Norfolk (Virginia) for rough-water and/or engine-service tests. Fourth, it was sent to the Naval Aircraft Factory in Philadelphia (Pennsylvania) for catapult and flight-deck landings. And finally, if necessary, the plane went to the Navy Yard in Washington (D.C.) for seaplane catapulting. A minimum of four separate locations in a three-state

104 Fairey Firefly; fighter; Rolls-Royce Griffon, 1,990-hp V-in-line. (Courtesy of San Diego Aerospace Museum)

106 Mitsubishi A6M, Zeke/Zero; Japanese fighter/bomber; Nakajima Sakae 21, 1,330-hp radial. (Courtesy of San Diego Aerospace Museum)

108 Grumman F7F, Tigercat; fighter/bomber; two Pratt and Whitney R-2800, 2,100-hp radials. (Courtesy of Grumman Corporation)

area, with minor duplications of effort (pilot familiarization, for example) at each. Obviously, a time consuming and expensive process.

On November 8, 1939, the head of the Bureau of Aeronautics Plans and Engineering Section recommended that a single site for testing be located and made operational as quickly as possible. Recognizing the threat in Europe at this time, an area at Cedar Point, St. Mary's County (Maryland), was chosen on November 6, 1941 - one month before Pearl Harbor.

The prime contractors were notified to proceed with plans on February 18, 1942; a contract was let on March 1, 1942; and ground was broken on April 4, 1942. Construction started with about 650 workers, grew to more than 6,000 in six months and

peaked at almost 9,000, nine months into the project. This was a magnificent war effort with workmen on a two-shift, seventy-hour workweek schedule. On June 4, 1942, the project was officially designated as the United States Naval Air Station, Patuxent River, Maryland.

Remarkably, three days short of one year from the start of construction - at 11 a.m. on April 1, 1943 - Patuxent River NAS was officially placed in commission!

By mid-August 1943 Pax River (as the station quickly became known) was home for Flight Test, Radio Test, Aircraft Armament and the Aircraft Experimental and Development Squadrons. By the end of 1944, the station had also formed the Service Test, Electronics Test and Tactical Test Divisions. On June 16, 1945, the Naval Air Test Center was established, organizationally separating the test and support functions.]

My flights from Akron to Pax and return were pleasant and uneventful, and the comments made by some Navy test pilots were fun to listen to on the radio - and even more rewarding to hear after they landed. Their radio remarks were guarded because the plane was still "secret," but at the officers' club before dinner they could be candid and comfortable in expressing their opinions. Most were enthusiastic, but all were amazed at how well the plane performed. At the same time, everyone who had flown or evaluated the plane was fully cognizant that Goodyear still had a lot of work to do before it would be ready for combat. The bottom line, however, was that the F2G concept had made a phenomenal first impression, and I was as pleased as punch about that.

Soon after returning to Akron two amazing coincidences combined, and unexpectedly put three old friends in touch–by radio. First, Johnny Seal was flying a Curtiss SB2C at Columbus, Ohio, at exactly the time that Skip Ziegler was testing a Bell P-63 at Niagara Falls, New York, and I was doing some speed vs power runs in an EXF2G at Akron. The second coincidence was that - in addition to each of us being in the air, using the same radio frequency, at exactly the same moment - unusual atmospheric conditions, which might occur only once or twice a year, permitted each of us to hear the others! Skip, recognizing my "Flight Checker" radio iden-

tification, called me, and during our first few exchanges, Johnny recognized us both and joined the conversation. I was 200 miles from Skip and over 100 from Johnny. On the other hand, Skip and Johnny were at least 300 miles apart - yet our low-powered radios were as clear as intercoms. It was one of those once-in-a-lifetime happenings that lights up your world. The *Akron Beacon Journal* even ran a story about it.

At Goodyear all of us were antsy. While eagerly waiting for the first "real" F2G to emerge from the shop, we continued with other tests, and I began investigative flights for the preliminary dive and spin tests on the FG-1.

make things a bit easier when I performed similar, but more dangerous, tests on the XF2G. At least, that's how we rationalized it to each other at flight-test conferences!

Conducting two flight-test programs simultaneously is quite a mental exercise. On many days I would be doing flights in both the FG-1 and the XF2G. The two aircraft looked comparable, but each had disparate characteristics and responded differently in flight. It was like a man with two lovers - sisters, almost identical, but not twins - and you damn well better remember which one you were with! To refresh my memory, and to help me attain the necessary level of concentration before each flight, I requested that the flight engineers prepare a brief written summary of the previous three or four tests which, in addition to my flight-test card, I would review. I also asked the instrumentation crew to locate switches, controls and indicators in exactly the same place in each of our experimental aircraft, thereby making the instrument panels and cockpit layout as alike as possible. While these extra efforts may appear unnecessary, when flying four or five different tests in two or three different aircraft on the same day, they made my transitions far simpler, and much safer (Exhibit 11c).

Frequently, throughout my test flying career I was reminded that the so-called "little things" are often the most troublesome. Many pilots and planes have been lost when a seemingly insignificant part failed. (The Bell X-2 in 1953, and the Challenger in 1986, are classic examples.) Problems can be averted, some of the time, by meticulously checking emergency equipment. Because complacency or assumption have no place in the testing of aircraft, I always insisted on checking a spin-chute before doing spin-recovery tests. A spin-chute is a small parachute attached to the tail of an aircraft. If a plane will not recover

109 Bell P-59, Airacomet; fighter; General Electric J-31-GE-3, 2,000 s.t., jet. First American-designed and built turbojet fighter. (Courtesy of San Diego Aerospace Museum)

Goodyear's contract with the Navy was the same as any manufacturer: the airplane had to complete all the required aerodynamic and structural demonstration tests - push the aircraft to its absolute design limits - before official acceptance. There was an upside, however: we would have the opportunity on the FG-1 tests to work out all the instrumentation bugs and

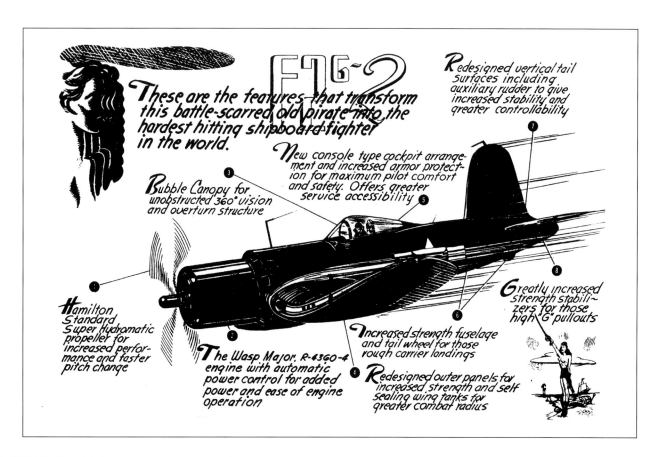

These are the features that transform this battle-scarred old pirate into the hardest hitting shipboard fighter in the world.

F7G-2

Redesigned vertical tail surfaces including auxiliary rudder to give increased stability and greater controllability

New console type cockpit arrangement and increased armor protection for maximum pilot comfort and safety. Offers greater service accessibility

Bubble Canopy for unobstructed 360° vision and overturn structure

Hamilton Standard Super Hydromatic propeller for increased performance and faster pitch change

The Wasp Major R-4360-4 engine with automatic power control for added power and ease of engine operation

Increased strength fuselage and tail wheel for those rough carrier landings

Redesigned outer panels for increased strength and self sealing wing tanks for greater combat radius

Greatly increased strength stabilizers for those high "G" pullouts

11e The "Centerfold!" From the booklet "Introducing the F2G-2" distributed by Goodyear Aircraft Corporation, Akron, Ohio. (D. Armstrong collection)

from a spin, the pilot deploys the chute and the drag pulls the tail up and the nose down, assisting in recovery. The pilot then releases the chute and lands normally.

In anticipation of the spin tests on both the FG and the XF2G, we attached a chute to the tail of an FG and tried it out during slow, level flight four times. The first time the chute simply blew away; the second time it would not open; the third time it blew away and some remaining cable damaged the right-side elevator; and the fourth time it opened properly but would not release from the plane. Each time I landed the plane without any problem, but there were some very red-faced engineers! If we had not made these checks, we certainly would have lost an XF2G six months later.

Brewster (also building Corsairs, as previously noted) sent one of its

engineers to discuss some of their tooling problems with the Goodyear production department. A Brewster pilot flew the gentleman from Pennsylvania to Akron in an SB2A-2 Buccaneer dive-bomber and, while there, kindly let me fly the plane. The mid-wing aircraft, ordered by both Britain and the Netherlands (each called it the "Bermuda"), was probably the least successful combat aircraft put into production during the war. I remember thinking that the plane handled fairly well, but I knew nothing about how its performance compared to that of the Curtiss SB2C or others. Actually, no records exist to show that any SB2As were ever involved in combat.

All the F2G project personnel - from the executives to the refuelers - were hoping to have the aircraft ready to take to the Joint Army-Navy Fighter Conference. However, it would have been a monumental mistake to "push" the final few days trying to do so. I went so far as to make several little posters saying, "Expedite, yes - rush, no" and stuck them on the walls of the hangar.

Then, on October 15, 1944, I made the first flight of the "true" prototype XF2G-1 aircraft (No. 691). All went well, and on the 17th and 19th I

did four thorough shakedown flights, all without incident. This proved that everyone had done their individual jobs well. One of Goodyear's vice-presidents, Dr. Karl Arnstein, asked me what the XF2G was like. My reply was, "It's a Homesick Angel," and the name has stuck to the Super Corsair ever since.

The historic Joint Army-Navy Fighter Conference had started on October 16, at the Naval Air Test Center at Patuxent. I was late, but I joined the group on October 21 - with the new XF2G-1 - just six days after its first flight.

It was an especially exciting event for me for several reasons. To see the sheer joy on the faces of the pilots who flew "my bird!" Also, to fly a wide assortment of the best WW II aircraft - U.S. and foreign. And last, but far from least, to have the once-in-a-lifetime opportunity to fly and/or yak, face-to-face, with some of the world's finest test pilots and engineers.

Our official hosts were Rear Admiral L. B. Richardson, Assistant Chief, Bureau of Aeronautics; Captain A. P. Storrs, Commanding Officer – NAS Patuxent; and Commander Paul H. Ramsey, Director of Test – NAS Patuxent.

The Army Air Forces had representatives from the AAF Proving Ground at Eglin Field and various other test organizations, including Wright Field. The Royal Air Force was represented by Air Commodore N. R. Buckle and the Royal Navy by Commander D. F. R. Campbell. NACA-Langley Field staff included Mr. Hoover, Mr. Gilruth and Mr. Phillips.

Manufacturers included AeroProducts, Allison, Bell, Boeing, Curtiss -Wright, DeHavilland, Eastern Aircraft, General Electric, General Motors, Goodyear, Grumman, Hamilton Standard, Lockheed, McDonnell, North American, Northrop, Packard, Pratt and Whitney, Republic, Ryan, Sperry Gyroscope, United Aircraft, Vought and Wright Aeronautical.

Many manufacturers had more than one test pilot participating in the conference, but I personally remember R. H. Burroughs, Lloyd Child, Fred Collins, S. A. "Connie" Converse, R. W. Foote, Boone Guyton, Bob Hall, W. N. Horan, Charles A. Lindbergh, C. H. Miller, Corwin "Corky" Meyer, Johnny Myers, Joe Parker, Bill Thomas, Ben Towle, E. W. Virgin, M. S. Wittner and Jack Woolams.

I, of course, was Goodyear's pilot, and with me from the company were D. A. Beck, W. F. Burdick, Ed Eichman, Bob Hagar and Ed Shaw.

Having arrived late, I was introduced to the group at lunch and, after making some brief remarks about the F2G, I said how pleased and honored I felt to be a part of the conference. My closing comment was, in effect, "As I look around the room, I wonder how much the war effort would be set back if Hitler dropped a bomb on this facility today." Beneath the surface of what I had said was the undeniable fact that those present comprised the better part of the core of our aviation design and development capabilities. It was, indeed, a noteworthy occasion.

One of the purposes of the conference was to permit pilots to fly and evaluate as many aircraft as possible. I, for example, flew a Royal Navy Supermarine Seafire, Fairey Firefly and DeHavilland Mosquito, even though I'd flown a Spitfire/Seafire and Mosquito before. I then flew a captured Japanese Mitsubishi Zeke, the North American P-51 Mustang, the Grumman F7F Tigercat and the jet-powered Bell P-59. I also flew the Bell P-63 and the Lockheed P-38 once more, for the same reason most people climb mountains - just because they were there.

One rare privilege I enjoyed, and will treasure for the rest of my life, was engaging in a few minutes of "dogfighting" with one of my heroes, Charles Lindbergh. He was in the Lockheed P-38 and I was in one of my favorite planes, the Seafire. After we landed I reminded him of the occasion of our first introduction, and on our way back to the hangar he asked about my father. We also reminisced about the many changes at Floyd Bennett and Roosevelt fields. When the conference disbanded I shook his hand, not realizing I'd never see him again. But he was, and will always remain, a smiling, benevolent "giant!"

From my point of view, the high point of the conference was when I was asked to do a short aerobatic demonstration with the XF2G. What an ego inflator that was! Some of the most experienced and respected test pilots in the world - many of whom were testing planes before I had a pilot's license - were going to watch me fly! Thank God, I had sense enough to do a conservative, although fairly spectacular, show. I let the airplane do the talking and didn't attempt to do anything the plane or I couldn't handle easily. Dad or Mr. Bill must have whispered in my ear - and they both would have been proud of me, too.

I was sorry to see the conference end. There was so much to learn from the meetings and being able to sit down with my peers and discuss mutual problems. The warmth of the fellowship reached deep into our hearts. What a magnificent experience - I am honored to have been a small part of it.

When we returned to Akron, everyone from Goodyear was overjoyed by the enthusiastic encouragement we had received from the participants at Pax. My reaction went beyond that because, for no specific reason, I had a deep sense of confidence in the aircraft. I had flown many different fighters but none had ever given me the feel of unbridled power and the sheer delight of near-unrestricted freedom of movement in the air that I experienced in the XF2G. Just like a kid with a front-row seat at the circus - I could hardly wait for them to get on with the show.

If it is possible to "love" an inanimate object, I was "in love" with the Super Corsair. At the entrance to the Champlin Fighter Museum in Mesa, Arizona, is a plaque which sums it up:

You love a lot of things if you live around them. But there isn't any woman and there isn't any horse, not any before nor any after, that is as lovely as a great airplane. And men who love them are faithful to them even though they leave them for others. Man has one virginity to lose in fighters, and if it is a lovely airplane he loses it to, there is where his heart will forever be.

Ernest Hemingway

CHAPTER 12

THE PILOT'S REACTION WAS NORMAL
October 1944 - June 1946

Following my return to Akron from the Fighter Conference, on October 25, I did a series of longitudinal-and-directional stability-and-control flights on the XF2Gs and some instrument calibration checks on the FG-1. In anticipation of the spin and dive demonstration tests which would be necessary on the FG-1, we did several additional flights to check the spin chute and finally got it to work properly. What no one could anticipate was that we'd go back to square one when we installed a similar chute on the XF2G.

In the interim, however, the Navy had decided to have us test the bubble canopy installation before ordering more canopies from the subcontractor. This involved three dives to the relatively high speed of 450 mph and, while pulling a maximum of 5 Gs at a specified altitude, applying full rudder to achieve maximum yaw. (This had to be repeated with both right yaw and left yaw.) This particular demonstration is one I intensely disliked because if the canopy failed and blew away, my head probably

would have been in it! It is almost impossible to duck low enough to protect yourself and fly the aircraft accurately under these circumstances. What I could do, and did, however, was to change from my normal seat-pack parachute (which was about five inches high) to a smaller back-pack chute; adjusted the seat to its highest position for takeoffs and landings and lowered the seat as far as it would go during the dives. This actually lowered my head about a foot and, had the canopy blown away, it put the odds a little more in my favor. All went well, and just before Christmas I did the flights with no problems whatsoever. The extra-risk bonus made our holiday shopping more fun, too!

Early in 1945 I took the XF2G-1 back to Patuxent for more evaluation flights and, a couple of days after returning to Akron, went to Pax again in the FG-1 so they could inspect the plane prior to the preliminary dive demonstration. Shuttling back and forth so frequently, I left clothes and personal articles at the hotel in Washington so I wouldn't have to carry

things on every trip. In the Corsair, luggage space was limited to the empty ammo boxes in the wings.

The preliminary dives were flights at high altitudes and we needed relatively clear skies. However, the winter weather in Akron is mostly overcast and is usually unpredictable for flight-test purposes, especially in February. Therefore, we decided to take the FG-l to the Goodyear facility at Litchfield Park, hoping for better conditions in Arizona.

The flight west was pleasant and we started the demonstration on March 7. After only four dives I ruptured a blood vessel in my frontal sinus and could not tolerate rapid changes in altitude. Obviously, when I was unable to fly, the flight-test and instrumentation engineers, as well as the mechanics, were all forced to remain idle. If we had been at the plant in Akron, however, they could have been working on the F2G project.

So, we talked it over with the powers-that-be at Goodyear and the Navy, and all agreed to move the tests back to Akron. After waiting a week

12a F2G-2 Demonstration airplane, No. 88459, 3/4 rear view. Note the checkerboard and the pedestal tail. (D. Armstrong collection)

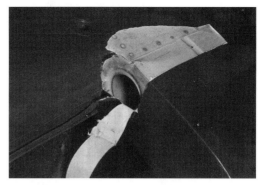

12e Showing rudder failure at outboard hinge (cutout fabric removed) on F2G-2 Preliminary Dive Demonstration airplane, No. 88459, Flight No. 31. (D. Armstrong collection)

to let the sinus problem settle down, the doctor approved my plan to ferry the plane back east, with the condition that I descend slowly prior to each landing, thereby making gradual pressure changes in my sinuses. We both felt I'd be more comfortable controlling my own rate of descent than I would be on a scheduled airline. (Effective cabin pressurization was not in use then.) He gave me some medication to take along, and stipulated that I should discontinue the trip and seek further medical advice if I showed signs of sinus bleeding following any landing.

During a refueling stop I had a cup of coffee and took some of the medication. This proved to be an exceptionally ill-advised, and very dangerous, mistake! In a weak attempt to partially justify the action in my own mind, I halfheartedly tried to point out to myself that the effects of certain prescription medications were not well documented in 1945. In addition, I had acted upon the advice of a well-intentioned medical practitioner. I knew the medication had made me slightly drowsy in Phoenix, but I was so uncomfortable that I took a couple of pills anyway. I've often wondered why I was so irresponsible. Without question, it was a terrible mistake - my mistake - I should have known better. It could have easily led to a disaster.

My flight plan took me from the west into Oklahoma and then, diverting north because of inclement weather, over Kansas City to St. Louis, and continuing via Toledo to Akron. But, somewhere just southwest of Kansas

City, I fell asleep! The Corsair had no autopilot since it was, after all, a fighter plane; but luckily I had it trimmed to fly reasonably straight and level without much attention. So, here I was, fortunately, well above most of the commercial traffic and busting along at a pretty good clip - sound asleep - when I awoke to hear St. Louis radio calling me. The plane had flown, with a sleeping pilot at the controls, for around one hundred miles, winding up approximately twenty miles south of my course and about 2,500 feet higher.

I kept my mouth shut until I knew exactly where I was and what had happened; and then called St. Louis, clicking my mike button on and off as I spoke. They replied, saying that my transmissions were "breaking up," and asked why I had not contacted Kansas City. I transmitted, brokenly again, and asked for a frequency change - never actually stating that my radios were acting up. Frankly, I was scared stiff and decided to make an unscheduled landing at St. Louis. Boy, did I want to get on the ground!

As I dropped my landing gear, the tailwheel-position indicator light showed a malfunction, and created just enough excitement for the airport personnel that my "radio problems" were lost in the shuffle. After making arrangements for securing the aircraft, I went to a hotel and spent the

night. The next day I helped jury-rig the tailwheel so that it remained in the down position and continued the trip to Akron. You can carve it in stone - I did not take any medication during the rest of the trip, or before a flight at any time later, unless I checked with a flight surgeon beforehand. Fifty years later I can still vividly recall how upset I was that night, and how lucky. Once again, my "giants" had held me in the palms of their hands!

It was just shy of a week before I did the remaining three dives, finishing that portion of the FG-1 preliminary demonstration. The "bent-winged bastard" had proved itself - again. We never even popped a rivet!

Next, we had to demonstrate to the Navy that the FG-1 would perform certain slow-flight maneuvers and recover from spins in either direction. Corsair pilots all agreed that the aircraft did not spin in a comfortable fashion; in fact, it was just a tiny bit removed from being violent. But spinning the FG-1 would do a lot to prepare me for similar tests in the F2G. The aerodynamics people had predicted (because of the heavy, extended nose) that spin gyrations of the F2G would be far more intense than what I found in the FG-1. In response to this, I designed an attachment to the seat which would restrict side-to-side movement of the pilot's body in violent maneuvers. If it worked as I hoped, it would keep me more comfortable in the FG-1 and probably be very valuable when I repeated the spins in the Super Corsair a few months later. It was basically a thick sheet of aluminum, about ten inches wide, bent forward around the pilot's

12c Pilot's shoulder brace (my own design) F2G-2 Preliminary Dive Demonstration airplane. The instrument shown is an outside air temperature gauge. (D. Armstrong collection)

12d Showing the checking of the wing fabric on F2G-2 Preliminary Dive Demonstration airplane, No. 88459, Flight No. 20. (D. Armstrong collection)

upper arms and lightly padded (Exhibit 12c). We installed it, and I found it to be quite helpful. Though all the spin recoveries were completely satisfactory, the spins were rough and bruising. More than that, they were a warning of dire things to come - the spins in the big Corsair were going to be tough!

Goodyear was building Corsairs for the Royal Navy, and their Akron representatives had a twin Beech 18 (JRB) which they let me borrow for a second visit to the Martin plant. There I flew a modified B-26 Marauder to reevaluate its slow-speed stability. On the return trip I stopped at NAS Anacostia, had a delicious seafood dinner with friends and went folk dancing. Did I accomplish anything on this trip? In reality, yes. I was able to turn off my brain for a few days before starting a long, demanding sequence of stability-and-control tests which could have a profound effect on the future of the Super Corsair.

For a plane to operate successfully from an aircraft carrier it must have certain control characteristics which, although certainly desirable, are not as essential to a plane taking off and landing from an airfield. Short takeoff distance was one of the F2G's strong points and presented no problem. Short landing roll was not a difficulty either, because the carrier arresting gear would grab the plane and bring it to an abrupt stop. However, during the final portion of a carrier-landing approach the aircraft must be flown at just above stalling speed and, if the approach needs to be aborted for any reason, the pilot must have total directional control. This situation is known as a "waveoff" and that's exactly where the F2G was in trouble.

The raw power of the big "corncob" R-4360 was now about sixty percent greater than the engine of the original Corsair, and translated into an almost equal increase in torque. If full power was applied when the aircraft was flying at extremely low speed, with the landing gear and flaps down, the torque rolled it to the left. Undeniably, there was insufficient directional (rudder) control to overcome it. Adding more rudder area was not the answer because it created other problems; the engineers had already tried, with very little success, changing the offset-angle of the vertical fin. I made flight after flight for them, to no avail, and yet something kept "bugging" me every time I simulated a waveoff. Suddenly I had it - I knew how to fix it!

In 1942 I had submitted a design for an automatic rudder-trimming device to the RCAF which was later offered to the U.S. Army Air Force, in my behalf, by Doc Gerhardt. In my design, it was assumed that sufficient aerodynamic-control area was inherent, and my device simply applied trim when needed.

The heart of the problem with the F2G was not quite the same because, with the dramatic increase of torque and the same vertical area of the original FG-1, there was insufficient aerodynamic-control area to do the job. Yet it was similar enough in concept to give me an idea as to how to resolve it. We needed a method of overcoming the torque only at low speeds and only when the plane was in landing configuration. What was required was a device that would activate additional aerodynamic-control area, apply massive "trim" - automatically - when the landing gear went

down. (When the gear came up, the device must return the extra control surface to a neutral position so as not to have any effect upon normal flight.)

I envisioned setting both the vertical fin and the rudder on a "pedestal" (Exhibit 12a) and, without changing rudder area or the existent vertical fin offset angle, hinging the vertical area beneath the rudder, making it, in effect, a large, movable "trim-tab" which would deflect to the right only when the gear went down. Because the F2G tailwheel had a retracting mechanism, I suggested linking the extra control area to it, thereby making it function only when the landing gear was extended.

After making a couple of representative drawings, I took the idea directly to Dr. Arnstein. He was a highly-respected engineer and designer who almost immediately recognized the potential of my suggestion. He quickly put his people to work determining the height of the pedestal, the amount of deflection of the "tab" and the linkage needed to make it function when the gear was lowered. He predicted that the additional neutral vertical area would also improve the overall directional stability, and it did!

[Author's note: Dr. Karl Arnstein will be remembered primarily for his work in lighter-than-air craft, because he contributed greatly to Goodyear's reputation for having built more airships than any other company in the world. But I held him in my highest esteem for his kind and sensitive personality and his superb administration of the XF2G projects.]

After building and installing the pedestal, only two minor adjustments to the amount of tab deflection were necessary during flight tests. The results were even better than expected. Extreme slow-speed directional

12f The "Checkerboard Kid" and his Super Corsair, September 13, 1945, at the Army-Navy "E" Award ceremony (No. 14692). (D. Armstrong collection)

and lateral control at maximum power were phenomenal - many pilots felt it handled better than the standard Corsair. A full-power, emergency waveoff in the F2G was, as a Navy pilot said a few months later, "No sweat."

When designers and engineers listened carefully to their suggestions, many test pilots have assisted in the development of experimental aircraft. I remain, to this day, pleased and proud of the "pedestal tail," and other contributions I was able to proffer.

Several times I have mentioned visiting other companies, flying their aircraft and chatting with engineers and pilots. This may seem strange because such courtesies are not common today. However, during WW II, it was mutually beneficial to all manufacturers to share with, and glean from, each other. The contractor (the U.S. Government or one of the Allies) raised no objection to these "exchange" visits or flights and, though some pilots did not have much opportunity to travel around, I enjoyed doing so and was never refused a request for a visit or a familiarization flight.

One day I received a call from my old friend, Johnny Seal at Curtiss, who had a few free days and wanted to visit me, see the Goodyear plant and fly the Corsair. It was a nice reunion - we caught up on mutual friends and test developments - and I made arrangements for Johnny to make an evaluation flight in the FG-1. He enjoyed the flight and wrote a report for us - just as I usually did at other companies. We had a nice steak dinner out at Riley's and he went back to Buffalo. I often wished that test-pilot friends had stayed in closer touch, but I guess if we had, we'd have spent a lot of time at funerals.

Because Goodyear's Navy contracts included the latest Corsair, the F4U-4 (the Goodyear designation would be FG-4), one was flown from Vought in Connecticut so I could evaluate it. Like its predecessors, the F4U-4 was a fine fighting machine. And now Goodyear was taking that same basic dream even farther - truly a giant step beyond the "dash-4" - and turning it into the awesome F2G: the most powerful, single-engine, propeller-driven

fighter in the world!

Two weeks after V-E Day (for you youngsters - "Victory in Europe Day" - May 8, 1945) I made another trip to Patuxent to do the official final spin, maneuver and dive demonstration of the FG-1. Although every condition of these tests had already been met in my flights at Goodyear, this was to fulfill the contractual obligations to the government. Whereas there is always an element of risk, whenever a plane is pushed to its design limitations, all the odds were definitely in my favor. The original Vought F4U had been demonstrated successfully, the basic structure of our FG-1 was the same as the Vought, and these were merely repeat flights. And that's exactly how things worked out.

I hit all the specs right on the button and honestly enjoyed the entire two weeks we spent at Pax River. Instead of staying out at Patuxent we (my flight engineers, mechanics and I) stayed in Washington, ate seafood and steaks, went folk dancing and didn't even go to the base unless scheduled to fly that day. Did I accept my "extra-risk"

12g Hydraulic failure (of two aircraft: No. 14695, shown here - No. 14692 lost, with pilot Art Chapman bailing out) forced my belly landing at Akron (Ohio) Airport, December 12, 1945. (D. Armstrong collection)

Left page (Page 41)

PREPARED BY — CHECKED BY PJP — DATE

GOOD YEAR AIRCRAFT CORPORATION AKRON, OHIO

PAGE 41 — REPORT NO. FTR 50;GER 377 — MODEL F2G-2

F2G-2 PRELIMINARY DIVE DEMONSTRATION
FLIGHT LOG   F2G-2, BUNO 88459

Flt. No.	Date	Duration Min.	Changes Prior to Flight	Comments on Flight
13	2/21/46	54	1.Repaired F.A.T. gage 2.Reset left aileron 3.Painted ship	Airspeed calibration by tower method
14	2/26/46	31	1.New right aileron installed 2.Left aileron turned ¼ turn 3.56 new plugs installed 4.Repaired FAT gage 5.Right cylinder head temperature gage repaired 6.Tail hook removed 7.Guns and chutes removed 8.Ballast in wings removed	Aileron selection and instrument check
15	2/28/46	11	1.Installed shoulder brace on seat 2.Painted around battery box with anti-acid paint 3.New brake discs installed 4.Offset stick installed 5.New radio	Adjusting the damping screw of GA and VG recorders
16-19 inc.	2/28/46	17	1.Various adjustments of VG and GA damping screws 2.Standard control stick installed	(Same as 15)
20	3/1/46	31	1.New tail wheel 2.Complete post-dive inspection and dimensional check	Official Dive No. 4 - Satisfactory. Wing and rudder fabric checking.
21	3/11/46	24	1.Fabric dope removed, rejuvenated and painted 2.Installed wooden plugs in gun ports 3.Repaired oil leak in accessory section 4.40# ballast installed in place of oscillograph 5.Complete post-dive inspection and dimensional check	Flight terminated because of fire in accessory section.

Right page (Page 42)

PREPARED BY — CHECKED BY PJP — DATE

PAGE 42 — REPORT NO. FTR 50;GER 377 — MODEL F2G-2

FLIGHT LOG - F2G-2, BUNO 88459

Flt. No.	Date	Duration Min.	Changes Prior to Flight	Comments on Flight
22	3/12/46	36	1.New generator and lines 2.New battery 3.Thorough inspection of oil lines and clamps	Official Dive No. 5 - Satisfactory. (2 dives made) Wing and rudder fabric checking
23	3/16/46	31	1.Checked static balance of elevator 2.Fabric dope removed, rejuvenated and painted 3.Complete post-dive dimensional check 4.Dive angle indicator removed 5.Ballasted for aft C.G. 6.Tightened stabilizer bolts 7.Oscillograph installed	Official Dive No. 6 - Satisfactory (3 dives made)
24	3/19/46	20	1.GA-13 installed 2.Ballasted for forward C.G. 3.Repaired small fabric check on right lower wing 4.Complete post-dive dimensional check	Instrumentation check and practice for the rolling pull-out dive No. 7
25	3/20/46	16	1.Brakes reset 2.Complete post-dive dimensional check	Official Dive No. 1 - Satisfactory. (2 dives made)
26	3/21/46	28	1.Repaired minor fabric check 2.Oscillograph adjusted 3.Complete post-dive dimensional check	Official Dive No. 7 - Oscillograph trace unsatisfactory. (6 dives made)
27	4/2/46	16	1.Post-dive inspection 2.Canopy arch reworked 3.Stabilizer spar stiffened 4.Oscillograph reworked 5.Small fabric checks repaired 6.New hinge bearing in L/H elevator 7.New rudder torque tube attachment bolt 8.Dive indicator replaced	Official Dive No. 7 (Roll to the right) (3 dives made) Oscillograph trace unsatisfactory.

12h F2G-2 Preliminary Dive Demonstration
Flight Log, No. 88459, pages 41 and 42
and Air Maneuvers, pages 63 and 64.
(D. Armstrong collection)

check? You can bet your bottom dollar I did - it helped a whole lot when I thought back to such tests as the last dive of the XP-60!

Between tests, while ballast was being changed, I was asked to address the pilots at Armament Test on "Compressibility and the Effects of High Mach Number." I had planned on devoting an hour or so to my talk, including a question-and-answer follow-up. What a joke that was! The pilots were a really keen, interested and astute group and, with their commander's approval, I spent the whole morning - even ended up going to lunch with them. It was a rewarding experience and I felt privileged to have been invited to share my thoughts with such an outstanding group of men.

Somehow or other, I became involved in developing a portion of a training program, designed to familiarize aspiring demonstration pilots with the piloting technique necessary for various dive and pullout tests. For example, in a typical test the pilot must dive to a specified altitude, arriving there at the moment the desired speed is attained. In anticipation of this, he must have begun, beforehand, to pull out - by applying exactly enough backward stick force to impose the required G-load on the plane. Three conditions must be met at the same instant: desired speed, specified altitude and required G-load. This necessitates practice, total concentration, a "feel" for the plane and a fair amount of skill.

Rolling-pullout tests add still another dimension, literally. At precisely the moment the previous three conditions are achieved, the pilot must also have applied full aileron deflection in less than two-tenths of a second. Four conditions to meet - simultaneously - each with an extremely small margin of error!

When doing either type of test "for real," there is no contractually acceptable "minus" error. Unfortunately, even a small error on the "plus" side can destroy the aircraft. Recall, for a moment, my experience with the XP-60 - a speed increase of less than two percent (even before reaching the design limits or trying the pullout) resulted in total tail failure and destruction of the plane. In the XP-60 case there was no error, but it graphically illustrates how disastrous even a small error could be.

Being a recognized specialist on rolling-pullout demonstrations, I was asked to lay out that portion of the program. I arranged for the loan of a Curtiss SB2C-3 dive bomber, because realistic simulations could safely be practiced at speeds restricted by the dive brakes, and planned a training program. How successful the program was I can't recall. However, in researching material for this book, we found a copy of a letter I had written to Gene Racine, referring to this program and outlining details he should include in an "extra-risk" demonstration contract. I also remember the fun I had checking out my program. I always got a kick out of diving a plane that

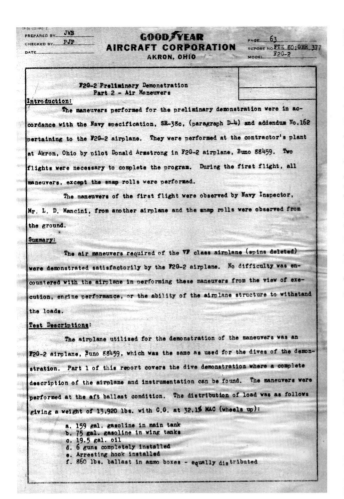

GOODYEAR AIRCRAFT CORPORATION
AKRON, OHIO

PREPARED BY JWB
CHECKED BY PJP

PAGE 63
REPORT NO. FTE EO:OXR 377
MODEL F2G-2

F2G-2 Preliminary Demonstration
Part 2 - Air Maneuvers

Introduction:
The maneuvers performed for the preliminary demonstration were in accordance with the Navy specification, SR-38c, (paragraph D-4) and addendum No.162 pertaining to the F2G-2 airplane. They were performed at the contractor's plant at Akron, Ohio by pilot Donald Armstrong in F2G-2 airplane, Buno 88459. Two flights were necessary to complete the program. During the first flight, all maneuvers, except the snap rolls were performed.

The maneuvers of the first flight were observed by Navy Inspector, Mr. L. D. Mancini, from another airplane and the snap rolls were observed from the ground.

Summary:
The air maneuvers required of the VF class airplane (spins deleted) were demonstrated satisfactorily by the F2G-2 airplane. No difficulty was encountered with the airplane in performing these maneuvers from the view of execution, engine performance, or the ability of the airplane structure to withstand the loads.

Test Descriptions:
The airplane utilized for the demonstration of the maneuvers was an F2G-2 airplane, Buno 88459, which was the same as used for the dives of the demonstration. Part 1 of this report covers the dive demonstration where a complete description of the airplane and instrumentation can be found. The maneuvers were performed at the aft ballast condition. The distribution of load was as follows giving a weight of 13,920 lbs. with C.G. at 32.1% MAC (wheels up):

    a. 159 gal. gasoline in main tank
    b. 75 gal. gasoline in wing tanks
    c. 19.5 gal. oil
    d. 6 guns completely installed
    e. Arresting hook installed
    f. 860 lbs. ballast in ammo boxes - equally distributed

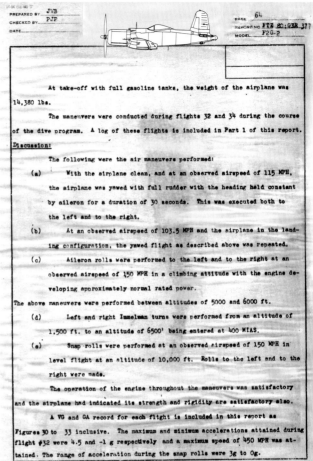

PREPARED BY JWB
CHECKED BY PJP

PAGE 64
REPORT NO. FTE EO:OXR 377
MODEL F2G-2

At take-off with full gasoline tanks, the weight of the airplane was 14,380 lbs.

The maneuvers were conducted during flights 32 and 34 during the course of the dive program. A log of these flights is included in Part 1 of this report.

Discussion:
The following were the air maneuvers performed:

(a) With the airplane clean, and at an observed airspeed of 115 MPH, the airplane was yawed with full rudder with the heading held constant by aileron for a duration of 30 seconds. This was executed both to the left and to the right.

(b) At an observed airspeed of 103.5 MPH and the airplane in the landing configuration, the yawed flight as described above was repeated.

(c) Aileron rolls were performed to the left and to the right at an observed airspeed of 150 MPH in a climbing attitude with the engine developing approximately normal rated power.

The above maneuvers were performed between altitudes of 5000 and 6000 ft.

(d) Left and right Immelman turns were performed from an altitude of 1,500 ft. to an altitude of 6500' being entered at 400 MIAS.

(e) Snap rolls were performed at an observed airspeed of 150 MPH in level flight at an altitude of 10,000 ft. Rolls to the left and to the right were made.

The operation of the engine throughout the maneuvers was satisfactory and the airplane had indicated its strength and rigidity are satisfactory also.

A VG and GA record for each flight is included in this report as Figures 30 to 33 inclusive. The maximum and minimum accelerations attained during flight #32 were 4.5 and -1 g respectively and a maximum speed of 450 MPH was attained. The range of acceleration during the snap rolls were 3g to 0g.

---

was equipped with effective dive brakes!

Just before starting the F2G preliminary demonstrations, I had a nasty experience with carbon monoxide poisoning. Looking back, it's frightening to think, if I had remained in the air for another five or ten minutes that day, I would not be alive to write this book.

As I mentioned in the preceding chapter, I always wore an oxygen mask in experimental aircraft, even for low-altitude flights. In spite of this, during one particular flight, a faulty oxygen demand-valve permitted a large percentage of cockpit air to enter the breathing system. Because I felt peculiar, I cut the flight short.

After landing I wasn't hungry and decided I'd have a small bowl of soup for lunch, and then go home for a nap. I had almost finished eating when I suddenly became dizzy, lost my lunch, passed out momentarily and fell to the floor.

I was taken to the hospital in a very confused state, and the emergency-room physician administered oxygen which somewhat revived me. That night the doctor informed me that blood tests disclosed a "close to fatal" concentration of carbon monoxide in my blood. I went home the next day and, within another day or two, I was fine and did some routine flying - still somewhat frightened by the whole experience. It's one thing to combat something you can see, feel or are aware of; but CO poisoning is none of these, and it damn near killed me. Once more, the gods, or my "giants," lifted me out of trouble!

[Author's note: In November 1946, after I had left Goodyear, the Navy conducted a long series of evaluations on F2Gs at the Tactical Test Division at Pax. Top on their list of suggested "areas for improvement" was that "... carbon monoxide concentration, in the cockpit, was considered too high."]

To improve the structural integrity and accommodate the additional fuel tanks needed on the XF2G (required by the heavier engine and increased fuel consumption) the "old" FG-1 wing underwent several modifications. A production wing was finally available, and we entered almost five weeks of very demanding test flights to ascertain whether the new wing would stand the design structural-and-aerodynamic loads before starting the demonstration program. Also, we would determine that the fuel flow and tank venting functioned in any flight attitude or altitude.

Static loading (placing sandbags on the detached wing to simulate bending load) and dive tests soon indicated that the wing itself apparently was safe, so our efforts turned to the new fuel systems. This mandated that I impose twisting loads on the airframe, high positive and negative G-loads, yawing movements and inverted flight with the new fuel tanks both full and nearly empty. I was doing hours of aerobatic flying in the world's most powerful fighter plane - something most pilots would have given the shirt off their backs to do - but I was getting paid for it!

One afternoon I was at my desk completing a report when D. A. Beck, the project engineer, phoned me. It seemed that some very conscientious soul had called the plant and irately inquired why one of the pilots was "up there, playing around, doing stunts and wasting precious fuel," and "didn't we know there was a war on?" Somehow or other, Mr. Beck had taken the call, and chuckled when talking to me. He was sure that the caller wasn't convinced I had actually been doing necessary test flights. The next day I continued the tests - over a different area.

The XF2G-1 (No. 14692) was ready, and on August 9 and 11, 1945, I did the first two dives in the official preliminary dive demonstration tests. I had a very unusual sense of well-being on these two flights, as if I knew, with absolute certainty, that the F2G was going to perform perfectly - almost as though one of my "giants" was sitting on my shoulder. I had to force myself to observe all my normal, routine precautions. It was an odd, and frightening, sensation. I didn't like it at all - because there's no room for complacency in test flying. I remember my dad telling me, very early in my career, "Airplanes will kill a few pilots, but most accidents are caused by the pilot himself. Take nothing for granted - ever!" Coincidentally, the immensity of the events over the next few days dispelled that feeling forever. I remained totally confident of my ability but, thankfully, that strange complacency never returned.

Then, on August 14, 1945, FDR's "Day of Infamy" was finally avenged. The "Rising Sun" of Japan had been sent to hell by a man-made "sun" of horrifying magnitude - at Hiroshima on the 6th and Nagasaki on the 9th. The war in the Pacific was over!

As though something ludicrous needed to happen to offset the awesomeness of the war's ending, I received a notice from my Draft Board - dated August 14, 1945 (V-J Day) - that I had been "rejected." The original of this notice is still in my scrapbook!

The dive demonstrations continued, and once again my "monster" made its purple presence known. Here's a look at excerpts from the Daily Flight Report of August 22, submitted by flight engineer E. B. "Bart" Myrick:

This was the official dive No. 4 of Addendum SR 119-1. The dive was started at 24,000 ft... the dive angle was variable but did not exceed 40 degrees at any time. Longitudinal instability and mild porpoising was experienced at 12,000 ft at 430 mph. At approximately 475 mph the aircraft behaved with typical Corsair characteristics at high Mach numbers, pitching nose down and also showing aileron ineffectiveness. The aileron stick forces became increasingly left-wing heavy and the elevator control became approximately 90% ineffective... At approximately 500 mph the elevator [position] was 70% aft of neutral. There was an excessive amount of vibration of the entire aircraft just prior to and during the pullout. [After landing] inspection revealed a loosening of the tape on the right-wing fabric and missing tape on the left-wing fabric. These failures were on the upper surface of the wing. No other abnormal conditions were noted. The required specifications were attained. The pilot's reaction was normal.

Only a portion of the wing was fabric-covered and, after removing the affected fabric and replacing it with stronger material, the preliminary dive tests were completed. Yes, the "monster" rode along with me - but never got in more than a few feints and jabs.

Goodyear received an Army-Navy "E" Award at a public ceremony on September 13, with (GAC vice-president) Harry Blythe as master of ceremonies. As secrecy was no longer required, I was asked to perform a fifteen-minute, low-altitude aerobatic demonstration with Goodyear's pride and joy, the Super Corsair. I was delighted to do so and planned a series of spectacular maneuvers which would keep me within easy sight of the crowd and require several low, high-speed passes over the runway. The crew had gussied-up the plane by painting a beautiful blue-and-gold checkerboard which covered the entire nose cowling and polished the plane until it glistened in the sun. The crowd of several thousand got a real thrill out of seeing their "Homesick Angel" perform. But none was more thrilled than I!

Goodyear had built an experimental civilian amphibian (GA-2) known as the "Duck." I was able to talk myself into a flight in it, liked it, and wondered why they didn't make more of an effort to market the little plane.

Aware that the first production F2G-1s were coming off the line, I made a special effort to fly the initial shakedown flights on Nos. 88456, 88457 and 88462. Now I could truthfully say to the world that I'd done it all - from the first flight of the prototype, through the entire experimental development, the final structural and aerodynamic demonstrations (soon to be completed) and the first shakedown of the finished product. I readily admit that the production shakedown flights were wholly, and unabashedly, an ego trip.

At this same time the F2G-2 (No. 14691), suitable for operation from an aircraft carrier, was also ready for demonstration tests, and much of my subsequent dive and spin work was in both the F2G-1 and F2G-2 models.

[Author's note: Although it may seem to the reader that this was an unnecessary duplication of effort, only those tests which required "proof" of different components were mandated by the Navy. Because the flights themselves were almost identical, I'll share only some of the more interesting details.]

The structural differences between the F2G-1 and the F2G-2 were confusing, even to people who built the planes or flew them. Part of the confusion stems from the fact that, in order to expedite testing, one or the other of the models was often used to test components from the other. It really made little difference to those of us who were flying them, and there's a poem about it that I'd like to share:

*Two F2Gs were sitting on the line.
Said one: "What kind of tail is mine?"
Said the other: "The tail that makes you soar
Is the same as the ol' F4U dash-4...
While mine, you see, is strong they say;
It'll hold ten horses and a bale of hay,
And that makes me a dash-2 crate.
But you're a dash-1 - just second rate."
The dash-1 hung his head in shame:*

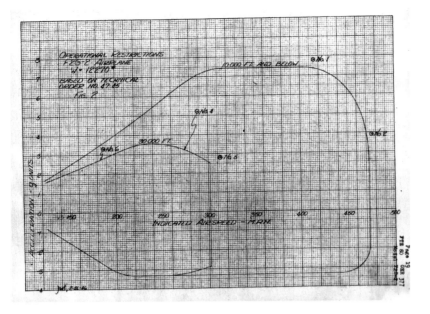

12i Operational/performance "envelope" - F2G-2 - August 26, 1946. Example: Aircraft can be operated at approximately 470 mph at as high as 4 Gs, or at a load of 7 Gs up to 410 mph. (D. Armstrong collection)

"My fin, dear friend, is it the same?"
"Oh, yes, your fin is high and fine.
It has a pedestal just like mine!"
"Are you a land-based job like me?"
The dash-1 said as he looked to sea.
"You fool, I have an arresting gear,"
The dash-2 said with a nasty sneer.
"Do you have a gas tank aft of your seat?"
"Well now, old friend, that's got me beat;
Some say yes, and some say nix.
Now isn't that one hell of a fix?"
The dash-1 laughed and said, "Old bean,
My wings have tanks for gasoline."
"Mine, too," said two, "and my wings fold."
And that one left the dash-1 cold.
"How much do you weigh?" the dash-1 said.
And the dash-2 winked and scratched his head."You mean on paper, or actually?
It makes a difference, don't you see?
The specs say only thirteen grand
But Walderman says the way I stand
I tip the scales at a thousand more,
Including the tiniest access door."
"Where's your C.G.?" asked dash-1.
(He knew that now he'd have some fun.)
The dash-2 blushed and bit his lip,
"The darn thing's clear outside the ship."
The two planes smiled as they shook their props -
"But those Navy guys - they think we're tops!"

Preliminary F2G spin tests were next on the agenda and, believe it or not, the spin chute failed twice more before we got it to function properly. On the first deliberate spin, I recovered as soon as possible and realized that we needed to take some extra precautions before we proceeded. The gyrations and altitude loss were far greater than anyone had predicted, and we had barely gotten started. My dominant impression was, because the gyrations would be so violent, I might not be able to remain spatially oriented sufficiently to recognize how many turns the plane made before attempting a recovery, or even realize my altitude!

Gene Racine volunteered to be my chase pilot and we used two FG-1s to practice the system we would use. The contract specified that the F2G must recover from at least a two-turn spin in either direction. I would enter a spin at 20,000 feet. Gene was to circle about 2,000 feet below me and spiral down around my plane throughout its descent. Immediately when the plane had spun through two turns he would repeat, over and over, the words "Recover... recover..." until he saw the recovery. If the spin continued down another 4,000 feet, he would say "Spin chute... spin chute..." until he saw it deploy. If the chute did not deploy, or if it deployed and the plane still did not recover by the time it had reached 10,000 feet, he was to say "Bail-out... bail-out... bail-out..." until he saw me abandon the aircraft. We tried our system out in a deliberately long spin in an FG-1 and his words came through

loud and clear; I recovered without difficulty.

Then we took a crack at the F2G, ballasted at the normal center-of-gravity position and without fuel in the wing tanks. It was rough! Unfortunately for the average reader, only another pilot can relate to what happened: the nose of the plane went from above the horizon to about ten degrees down past vertical - and back - in slightly more than one turn of the spin! In two turns, the plane lost between 3,200 and 3,500 feet! The recovery did not occur until about 12,000 feet, and although Gene was shouting "spin chute" every few seconds, I couldn't move my arm enough to get my hand on the spin-chute handle! I did not repeat the spin, or do the spin in the other direction.

My "restrainer-seat" probably saved my life. In spite of an extremely tight seat belt and shoulder harness, my crash helmet left paint marks on both sides of the canopy. I was so bruised and sore that I didn't fly for three or four days, but Gene, Bart (the flight engineer) and a secretary came over to my place so that I could dictate the report and not have to go into the office.

The spin in the other direction would be about the same, and the Navy representative agreed that enough was enough. We'd repeat the tests at Pax, with more critical ballasting, for the official final demonstrations. To say that I offered no argument is the understatement of the year!

Inverted spins are exactly what the term describes - spinning, with the plane bellyside-up. Some Navy desk jockey requested that Goodyear attempt an inverted spin in the F2G to see if recovery would be possible. I strenuously objected on the grounds that it was not a contractual obligation and, based upon the problems I encountered in recovering from "normal" spins, it could unnecessarily endanger the aircraft - and me! However, the net result of several phone calls was a reluctant verbal agreement to attempt one entry (it was not certain the gull-winged F2G would spin in the inverted attitude) and recovery, before the plane could really get wound up in a full-fledged spin. If further investigation were indicated, an additional "extra-risk" contract would have to be negotiated.

I had Ed Elliott as chase pilot when I rolled the F2G over onto its back, pushed the stick forward into an inverted stall and punched full right rudder. What the plane did next, I have absolutely no idea - I was far too busy, just hanging on - but it was a gyration so violent that my "restrainer-seat" and shoulder harness could not prevent my head from being smashed against the canopy and cockpit rails. My vision was reduced to a red blur! I needed an almost super-human effort to keep my feet on the rudder pedals and hand on the stick - and, for the first time in my life, I fully understood the meaning of the word "terror!" Without a crash helmet I'm certain I would have fractured my skull. Even with one, I was momentarily stunned. Seconds later I realized that my controls felt exactly as they had when the tail came off the XP-60D - floppy - totally ineffectual! I didn't wait to see what might happen next: I pulled the spin chute, got the nose down, recovered and landed. I was a mess: my bloodshot eyes looked like something from a comic-book horror story, my nose and gums were bleeding and I had a headache as bad as the one following my crash in Texas. Neither Ed nor I could adequately describe the gyration, but I knew that one thing was infinitely beyond any negotiation - I would never attempt that maneuver again in an F2G! There was no incentive - money or anything else - that would change my mind. Dr. Arnstein, D. A. Beck and Ed Shaw all agreed, and the subject was never discussed again in my presence. It was seven days before I could see well enough to fly again, and every morning when I awoke I thanked the spin chute and my "giants" for holding me - no, perhaps this time - carrying me on their backs!

Most people today have little or no conception of how rationing affected civilians during and immediately following WW II. Fuel and tires, for example, were severely rationed and only essential workers without means of public transportation got extra ration coupons. One of my ground

crew named Jim loved to fish and, to save his gasoline to get to the lakes, rode a bicycle back and forth to work (over five miles each way) every day, rain or shine. He was special to me, because it was he who chalked a temporary checkerboard on any plane I flew (unless a permanent one was already painted on the side or nose). When he learned I was going to do a special production shakedown on an F2G, he even rode his bike to the hangar, on his day off, to chalk my checkerboard on the plane before I flew. He and his bicycle were familiar to everyone in the hangar.

One afternoon I posted several notices requesting that all the experimental flight-test hangar personnel be available the next day for a five-minute "special award congregation" at the end of the shift. The crew chiefs put a couple of engine stands together to form a platform; I scrounged a podium from the executive dining room; one of the girls in the office played "churchy" music on an accordion and I stepped up onto the platform wearing a borrowed choir robe. I began, somberly, with the usual, "My friends, we are gathered here today..." and asked that Jim be escorted to the platform. Only three or four other people knew that I had painted a bicycle pedal gold and attached it to a braided cord. I then ceremoniously placed this around his neck while announcing to all that, because of his two-year dedication to checkerboards and bicycles I was, on behalf of all present, awarding him with the "Congregational Pedal of Honor." (I learned a few years later that it was still hanging on a wall in his home.)

Six weeks after the "E" Award ceremony I went back to Pax for the final dive demonstration on the F2G-1. These tests went off right on schedule, were successful in every way, and the Navy's acceptance of the plane was now officially complete - even though the spin demonstration had not been done. There must have been some sort of verbal agreement, or possibly a contractual waiver, permitting us to do only one set of final spin tests on the F2G-2, which would be applicable to both models. This was fine with me

- I was not looking forward to spinning the bent-wing again.

This trip to Pax brought old friends in touch again, because Lloyd Child's Curtiss XF15 was there at the same time. The XF15 project, seemingly doomed from the start, was a mixed-propulsion aircraft similar to the XBTD-2 I flew at Douglas and the Ryan XFR-1 Fireball. Ultimately, three of my old friends from Curtiss were involved in this project: Lloyd, Skip Ziegler and Johnny Seal. Their opinion of the concept was probably no higher than mine.

[Author's note: Lloyd Child and Charles Cox were alternating flights on the first XF15C-1. Lloyd lucked out when Charles was tragically killed during the twenty-third flight on V-E Day.]

I brought the F2G-1 home on November 5, 1945, and the following day started back for Pax in the dash-2 for the final spin demonstration. En route, the engine acted rough and I opted for a precautionary landing at Anacostia Naval Air Station. A Navy mechanic, although not familiar with the Pratt and Whitney R-4360 engine, found some contamination in the fuel and thought that cleaning the fuel lines and filters would do the job. He buttoned it back up, but I decided to keep the odds in my favor and spent the night, not running the risk of more trouble by flying after sundown. (Mr. Bill must have whispered in my ear.)

The next morning, within minutes after takeoff, the engine lost most of its power. The plane would not stay aloft. I made it back to the field but was, oh, so very glad that it hadn't happened in the dark over the middle of Washington, D.C. One of my crew flew down from Akron, made some minor repairs to the carburetor, and I completed my flight to Patuxent with no further problems.

The contract for the spin tests was a tough one. It called for two-turn spins on each side: first, clean; then, fully loaded and ballasted to the most rearward C.G. position. In addition, there were to be one-turn spins on each side with the aircraft fully loaded and ballasted to the most rearward C.G. position; but, now, with the land-

ing gear and flaps down and the canopy open. It was not going to be a pleasant experience.

As usual, the people at Pax were most cooperative and complied with my request for a chase pilot arrangement similar to the one I had used at Akron. Additionally, they provided a second chase pilot, who would remain silent during the flights, to observe the oscillations of the aircraft.

Because the plane would have less time to develop serious oscillations in a one-turn spin, I chose to do those first, and did so without too much discomfort. Recovery was normal and the flight engineer's report once again said, "The pilot's reaction was normal."

The two-turn spins were an entirely different matter. To the right, the spins were not unlike those I had done in Akron, except considerably more violent. The vertical nose oscillations ranged from fifteen degrees above the horizon to one-hundred-ten degrees below it (chase pilot's estimate). The greater oscillation and more violent nature of the spins could have been caused by the heavier loads and/or the different center of gravity and center of mass.

Eleven days later I repeated the spins, this time to the left. Never could I have imagined the effect that these spins had on me physiologically. Without the "restrainer-seat," and an absolutely wonderful Navy chase pilot, I'm certain I'd not have survived. By the end of the second turn I was totally disoriented, and only because I responded, virtually by sheer instinct, to the "Recover...recover... recover" commands did the aircraft straighten out.

After the recovery my flying was very erratic; I could hardly see, was totally confused and unable even to locate the airport. The chase pilot soon recognized my condition and flew alongside of me, talking to me every few seconds. This not only helped keep me aware; but he actually told me how, what and when to do everything. All the way back to the field, during my approach and touchdown, right to the end of my landing roll, he really did it all: "Turn left... hold it steady... reduce power... put your gear down" (sometimes having to repeat an instruction a couple of times). "Get the flaps down... level out some... nose up a little... you're down... keep it straight and let it roll... real easy on the brakes," etc. It was exactly like an old-time instructor with a very frightened, brand new pupil. I don't remember if the landing was rough or smooth - probably rough - but I was down.

When I rolled to a stop, I just sat there while the crash trucks drove up. I couldn't even taxi off the runway until a ground crewman got up onto the wing and directed my every movement - my eyes wouldn't focus on anything. When we got back to the hangar, without the help of two men lifting me, I couldn't get out of the plane. I spent the next couple of hours under the watchful eye of the flight surgeon and the next couple of weeks recuperating - I was that battered, bloody and bruised. I can positively guarantee that the remark "The pilot's reaction was normal" was not included in that report!

The net result: the plane was accepted by the Navy with no further spins required and a recommendation to placard all F2G aircraft - "Intentional spinning prohibited." To be honest, if I had been asked to do the spins again, I would have firmly, but politely declined. You can go to the well once too often!

The first week in December I did some routine tests, then made a flight in a UC-78 Cessna to Michigan and back. However, on the 12th, the roof caved in. A series of events occurred that seemed almost as though they had been choreographed for an aviation melodrama.

I took off at about 3:00 p.m. in F2G-2 No. 14695, for an instrumentation check, and Art Chapman was right behind me in No. 14692. Shortly thereafter, Art flew alongside and asked me to verify that his landing gear was only partially down. He was correct, and I suggested that he do nothing until we contacted the engineering department for advice.

Art followed the instructions to the letter and, after trying the emergency CO_2 gear-extension system, found himself no better off than before. The tail and left wheels were down and locked, but the right wheel still dangled about one-third down. The war was over, so this was no time for heroics. Art, knowing a "one-legged landing" could easily kill him, decided to bail out, and I concurred. Then, almost as though we were rehearsing a script for a really corny play, I suddenly discovered that I had no hydraulic pressure in my plane although, fortunately, my wheels were up, still locked.

After reaching a relatively uninhabited area we circled until the crash crews were below us. Art then took my suggestion and rolled the plane onto its back and dropped free. I followed his parachute down, watched him land safely and made certain the crash crews found him. Then I circled the wreckage until the police and ground crews found it.

Now it was my turn. After completing all standard emergency gear-lowering procedures - except the CO_2 system - I told the engineers that I could attempt to save the plane by making a belly landing, or I could try to blow the gear down as Art had done.

I made certain they understood their two choices: if I ended up with a one-up/one-down situation, I'd bail out. If I brought it in, wheels up, possibly they could more easily find the cause of the failures. After considerable discussion, they finally requested that I try the belly landing, and I agreed to do so.

By this time, the crash crews had brought Art back to the plant, uninjured, and sent a deputy sheriff to watch over the smoking hole in the ground that had been one of my favorite planes - the one with my beautiful checkerboard nose; the one which I had used for a myriad of tests; the one that I'd presented to the public during the "E" Award show.

But, back to the matters at hand: I now directed the crew to the location at the airport where I hoped to slide to a stop and, just before dark, made an uneventful belly landing (Exhibit 12g).

What an afternoon! In two hours, Art had bailed out, his plane had been completely destroyed and I'd belly landed another. A lot of dollars went up in smoke but, thanks to my

12j Falls Eagles Ice Hockey Team, 1946, Akron, Ohio. Yours truly far right, bottom row. (D. Armstrong collection)

"giants" and Lady Luck, no one got hurt.

[Author's note: Ironically, while investigating the hydraulic system, a cable supporting the F2G snapped. The boom of the crane fell onto and broke the back of the fuselage. The Navy decided not to rebuild it and the plane was scrapped.]

Two days after Christmas 1945, I flew a production shakedown on another F2G-2 (No. 88463) and began a six-week stretch of nit-picking flights, mostly to "fill in holes" in engineering data that was needed to comply with Goodyear's contracts. On February 6, 1946, I made certain that I was the pilot who did the production shakedown on the last F2G-2 (No. 88460). Even though there was still quite a bit of experimental and demonstration work to be done before we'd wind up with the Navy, flying the final production F2G-2 was, for me, quite sad.

[Author's note: At the onset of production each airframe was given its BuAer designation, e.g., No. 463. A delay due to an inspection non-con (nonconforming - "necessitating remedial action, reinspection required") would permit the succeeding aircraft to move ahead. It was such a circum-

stance that caused No. 460 to be the last F2G off the line.]

Just before landing I requested clearance from the tower and notified the company that I'd like to do a very brief "show." They announced my plan over the sound system and, while the hundreds of employees poured outside to watch, all work inside the plant came to a screeching halt. Then, just above the runway, I did a 450-mph pass, pulled the nose up in about a seventy-degree climb and did continuous aileron rolls until I was at nearly 7,500 feet - *our* personalized "victory roll," with the last of their "Homesick Angels!"

In preparation for the dives on the F2G-2, I had done several rolling-pullout flights and found that minor modifications needed to be made to the ailerons. While waiting for the new ailerons, I got another lucky break - a trip to Dayton, Ohio.

Wright Field personnel wanted to evaluate the F2G and the Navy agreed, so off I went in No. 88459. On arrival we did some airspeed calibrations (by the pacing method) with a North American P-51 and a short combat demonstration. Then, while some Air Force test pilots flew the F2G, I made three evaluation flights of my own - in a Lockheed P-80 Shooting Star jet, a Messerschmitt Bf 109 and a Focke-Wulf Fw 190. At low altitudes,

none could outclimb the F2G, and of the three, I thought the 190 was more fun to fly.

The Navy Beech JRB was back on the field when I got home. Now that the war was over, the Navy representative asked me to take some of his secretarial and office staff for a flight along the shore of Lake Erie and over Niagara Falls. A couple of these people, I was told, had never taken more than a weekend off for the duration of the war. Was I glad that I could help to say "Thanks."!

It was decided to use No. 88459 (the plane I had taken to Wright Field) for all of the F2G-2 preliminary dive and rolling-pullout demonstrations, and No. 88455 for the powerplant, stalls and slow-flight maneuvers demonstrations. We checked the airspeed calibration (once again) on No. 459, this time by the measured-course method, and then calibrated the airspeed indicator on No. 455 by the pacing method, using No. 459.

Two of the F2Gs had already been lost and, on March 11, 1946, we almost lost the third. Right after the climb to 28,000 feet, the engine faltered and cut back to about twenty-five percent power. To make matters worse, flames were visible under the upper right side of the engine cowling! Suspecting a fuel leak, I shut off the fuel supply, called a Mayday and

122 Messerschmitt Bf 109; German fighter; Daimler-Benz, 1,475-hp in-line. Captured. Displays U.S. insignia. (Courtesy of San Diego Aerospace Museum)

headed downstairs. While reporting what had happened, the flames disappeared and only wisps of light-blue smoke puffed out from where I'd seen the fire. I was within gliding distance of the field and the engine was windmilling, maintaining almost normal hydraulic pressure. Therefore, I could get the gear down so I decided to continue for home. The gross weight that day was about 14,000 pounds and that, combined with a windmilling, four-bladed propeller, gave me the gliding angle of a streamlined brick.

By the time I was on final approach the crash crews were all suited up and in position, but only their moral support was needed because I got the gear and flaps down and made a normal landing. The loss of power and fire had been caused by a two-bit fitting in the fuel supply line to the carburetor, which had evidently split open from vibration. All's well that ends well, but I was beginning to wonder. The spins, the belly landing and, now a fire and dead-stick landing. There's an old aviation axiom, "Bad things always happen in threes." I hoped this portended that I could get back to a slightly more mundane routine.

Between February 21 and May 21, the official preliminary dive demonstration flights continued (Exhibit 12h - four pages). On "Official Dive No. 3" there was failure of the rudder structure at the outboard hinge (Exhibit 12e). On the fourth dive there was minor wing-fabric checking (Exhibit 12d). The highest Mach number I attained was .762 on the second dive. The official reports read:

...The airplane became longitudinally unstable during the course of the dive, prior to the pull-out at 31,000 feet...indicated by the tendency of the airplane to "tuck under"...porpoising began which was estimated by the pilot as 5 to 7 degrees of pitch in amplitude...at the pullup, serious buffeting had occured and of a magnitude exceeding six inches deflection at the stabilizer tips. The pilot's reaction was normal.

My special offset control stick was installed for the rolling-pullout dives and, even with the extra aileron leverage it provided, it took over eighty-five pounds of stick-force to get the job done:

...Full left aileron was applied at 6.8 Gs in .12 seconds. Both the aileron and general structure buffeted severely following the time the aileron was applied, and rudder hinge failure was revealed during inspection. The pilot's reaction was normal.

On April 4 and 9, I tried to help Pratt and Whitney improve the carburetor function and fuel flow on the R-4360.

[Author's note: Carburetor, induction and other "minor" problems plagued the Wasp Major engines for years. For example, when Doug Champlin acquired F2G No. 454 for his museum, the Corsair was in Norfolk, Virginia. After expert mechanic Jerry

Devine meticulously replaced the engine, Dwain Trenton ferried the plane from Norfolk to Enid, Oklahoma. Doug comments, "He (Dwain) became highly proficient at airstarts along the way, as the engine quit every ten or fifteen minutes."]

In 1946, dive demonstration programs were planned to verify that an aircraft could aerodynamically attain, and structurally withstand, certain combinations of airspeed, altitude and G-load as specified in a contract which had been awarded following approval of a design proposal. (Compliance might result in a manufacturing contract if a need for the aircraft existed.) In addition, the parameters thus established would be represented in graphic form, the result passably resembling a drawing of a hot-air balloon on its side (Exhibit 12i). This, having been proven by demonstration flight tests, would become known as a "performance envelope." Envelopes for different altitudes, loading conditions, etc., were quick references for the pilots. Once the airplane was in general service, those pilots who "rode the edge of the envelope" were at risk - those who deliberately, or accidentally, flew the plane "outside the envelope" were lucky to survive.

Each dive in the F2G "proved" only one of the "dots" on the graph. Some were, for example, slow speed at very high G-load, whereas others were just the opposite, very high speed at low G-loads. Some were at maximum Mach number, others were at maximum rate of roll. All were precisely "on the edge!"

Folk dancing opportunities had been few and far between around Akron, so I found many relaxing moments playing hockey. It was good exercise, lots of fun and certainly took my mind off dive tests and spin chutes. The few semi-pro teams in the area were starved for players because most of the young, physically fit guys were in uniform. Probably fewer than one in five players got paid anything, and then it was mostly "gasoline money." Those in critical occupations were only able to skate when work-schedules permitted it - coaches never knew who was going to show up for prac-

123 Focke-Wulf Fw 190; German fighter; BMW 801C, 1,600-hp radial. Looked amazingly like a Curtiss P-36, Hawk 75. (Courtesy of Aerofax, Inc.)

tices or games - and all the teams were short-handed. Without the sponsorship of local businesses, few sporting events could have survived.

It was quite a combination: seventeen-year-old kids, a couple of guys my age and two or three men in their forties who hadn't played in years. I played several games, got cheered a lot when fans recognized the test pilot whose name and picture frequently appeared in the Akron paper - and even scored a few times!

The hockey fans were great, they made up in spirit what they lacked in numbers. Every spectator sensed that the coaches and players were giving all they had to give and overlooked how poorly the teams or individuals played. They stomped and cheered as though each game was for the Stanley Cup. I had *fun*, and for a few fleeting minutes after I scored or made an assist - I was a star!

But my hockey "career" didn't last very long. Team pictures were on a poster board near the entrance to the rink so that fans could order them for autographs. One of the Goodyear engineers bought one and showed it to Dr. Arnstein, thinking he'd be pleased. However, within an hour, my hockey playing was brought to an abrupt conclusion because, as the good doctor said, "We can't take a chance on your getting injured, Donald. Please desist." Oh, well - I'd never have made it to the NHL, anyway.

My contract with Goodyear called for "all the flight demonstration tests required by the company and/or the Navy." Even though the war was over and production was grinding to a halt, I still had several more official tests to make, including the powerplant and air maneuvers demonstrations.

We used my old friend, F2G-2 No. 88459, that had so faithfully performed for me in the previous dive work. The flights were fun because everything went so well and I was getting paid to do a pleasant series of aerobatic maneuvers to demonstrate that the engine would perform as required in "unusual attitudes, simulating those encountered in air combat." The official report concluded:

...All maneuvers were performed as required and no malfunction of the powerplant or the aircraft was encountered. The pilot's reaction was normal.

In looking through my scrapbook, I found the invitation I had posted welcoming all "members of the

Flight Test Engineering Department and the Navy observers and inspectors" to a Demonstration Completion Party at the Akron Mayflower Hotel, May 23, 1946. Looking at six of the photos taken that night, I remember what a wonderful group of people they were! Supportive, understanding, uncomplaining, willing to work crazy hours and do everything in their power to make my job safer and more pleasant. I could never thank them enough; it was an honor to have been associated with them.

An agreement was reached between the Navy and Goodyear whereby, because the war was over, the company did not have to complete the official final demonstration tests on the F2G-2 at Patuxent. The plane was accepted on the basis of the preliminary demonstrations done at Akron and certified, in behalf of the Navy, by Commander R. E. Bly of the local Bureau of Aeronautics office. This meant that my contractual obliga-

118 Goodyear GA-2, Duck; amphibian; three-seat, high-wing, monoplane; Franklin, pusher, 145-hp opposed. (D. Armstrong collection)

tion, insofar as extra-risk demonstrations were concerned, was complete. I had made the last dive on May 21, the final performance flights on May 23 and, because I had not taken any vacations during my time with the company, I took a month of paid leave, starting May 24.

My files show that I got paid for a charter flight in a Lockheed Ventura on June 2. On June 14, 1946, I wrote my last letter to Dr. Karl Arnstein, requesting payment of my extra-risk bonus for the last demonstration tests. Dr. Arnstein kindly arranged for me to remain on their payroll until all of my vacation time was used up. A few days later, on a brief trip to Washington, I made my last military-aircraft flight - while still on the Goodyear payroll - in a P-80 at Anacostia. For the life of me, I can't remember why I took it up, other than, once again, just because it was there.

At the end of my flight back, "Flight Checker" called the Akron tower for the last time. I landed, taxied up to the Experimental Flight Test hangar and walked, very slowly, to my office. It seemed like a huge catacomb without the West brothers, Bart Myrick, Bob Davy, "Pappy" Papaneck, Bob Delong, Charlie Golding, Bob Jacobs, George Kuhn and all the rest who had taken such good care of me for the past two years.

After clearing out my desk and locker, I took my checkerboard crash helmet, shook a jillion hands and, with tears in my eyes and a very heavy heart, drove away from my reserved parking space for the final time.

This was a very bittersweet time for me. I was, on one hand, glad to be away from the stress of test flying and, oh, so very grateful that I had survived. On the other hand, I was sad because I was leaving so many wonderful friends: all the great people at Goodyear, my peers in the other companies and the folk dancers and many Navy friends in Washington and out at Patuxent. A few of these relationships had gone far beyond that of friendly acquaintance - some had become as close as any family could be. While I'd never see most of the people again, thirty years later I did have the good fortune to be reunited with some of my dancing friends.

When I sat down for supper that night, it really hit me - way down, deep inside - and I couldn't finish my meal. There was a devastating emptiness - an overwhelming sadness with a tremendous sense of loss - solely because I realized that, from this moment, I'd probably never fly my magnificent "Homesick Angel" again.

---

121 Lockheed P-80, Shooting Star; fighter; two Allison J33-A-9, 3,850 s.t., jets. (Courtesy of San Diego Aerospace Museum)

CHAPTER 13

A TOTAL CHANGE OF PACE
May 1946 - March 1951

The gods do not deduct from man's allotted span the hours spent fishing.

Babylonian proverb

It seemed forever since I'd done anything except think about aircraft, the next test flight and all the problems associated with my work. I wanted to escape from suits and ties and executive dining rooms. I needed to do something entirely unrelated to flying. My good times fishing and hunting seemed almost like dreams. I wanted to hunt and fish again, work with my hands, spend some time outdoors and be with my family.

I remembered that while doing some flight tests for the CAA in 1943, I had hunted deer and pheasant with Al Meyers from Tecumseh, Michigan. I had also fished a little while testing the Driggs 3-95 and a Skyfarer at Grand Rapids. So, in 1946, when things were winding down at Goodyear, I borrowed a beautiful little OTW biplane from Al and flew over the central part of Michigan. I really liked the lake area around Clare and Cadillac and when Al said he hunted and fished up there every year I decided to do much more than just a fly-over. By the time I said my farewells at Goodyear, I had purchased 1,120 acres of land containing a private lake of over 100 acres, three streams and an old two-story building I intended to convert into a hunting and fishing lodge.

The property had been privately owned, posted and protected for more than twenty years. The lake had lots of bass, perch and pike, and the woods were well populated with deer, rabbit and grouse. That part was great. But there's always a downside: the house was a mess! Standing in the cellar, I could see daylight through two floors and the roof. The lake had no dock. And it was half a mile from the county road into the house with only a rutted trail to drive on. I must admit that LaVerne was less than enthusiastic, but it was ours. We decided to continue to call the place "Doc and Tom's" because the lake had been given that name when the first-cut lumbering

operation was headquartered there.

As soon as I repaired the roof and created a clean, dry living space, I asked Dad and my uncle to come and work with me for a while. This became a real family effort: grading a road and an airstrip, building a bunk house for guests, driving pilings for the dock and turning the old house into a very presentable lodge. The dining room table was long enough to seat twenty-eight people and was made by a neighbor everyone referred to as "the whittler."

My father was not a hunter or fisherman but he truly loved the out-of-doors. He was what most Americans thought of as a "typical" Englishman - a quiet, reserved man who always looked neat and controlled, no matter what the circumstances. He thoroughly enjoyed being with the group, especially on the porch, sitting quietly in the rocking chair and smoking his pipe. And it sure was fun for me to see his eyes sparkle at the "ones-that-got-away" or the "I-don't-know-how-I-missed-him" stories.

One of those beautiful, late-fall, deer-hunting days, about eight of us returned to the lodge for a hot lunch and a few minutes rest and relaxation on the porch. Dad was contentedly savoring his pipe when we heard the honking of a large flight of Canada geese coming over the near end of the lake. He pointed them out to us and said, "Son, why don't you get us one for dinner?" I was the only one who realized he was putting us on, but I played along, took my rifle from the rack and made a big production of stepping down into the yard, loading it, squatting down, aiming and squeezing off a shot.

I don't know who was the most surprised: the goose, the hunters, my dad or me. The second goose on the short side of the "V" fell out of the sky and landed about ten feet from the dock! I rose to my feet, ejected the empty shell and, as nonchalantly as possible, went up on the porch and placed my rifle back on the rack.

As long as I live I'll remember exactly what happened next: Dad, with an absolutely straight face, slow-

ly took his pipe out of his mouth and said, "Dropped it a little far from the house, didn't you, Son?" Then, without as much as a smile, he put his pipe back in his mouth and kept on rocking that chair, back and forth, just as though the dropping of that goose was an everyday event.

You may be certain that we had the goose, along with a venison roast, the next night for dinner. And, you can bet your bottom dollar that I *never* tried a shot like that again!

We were also cutting and selling cedar posts, Christmas trees and house logs. Later we built several log cabins at nearby Lake George and had the 4-H Club or Future Farmers help us plant thousands of seedling pines. As busy as I was, I enjoyed taking the time to share some of my flying experiences with nearby civic organizations and schools. The "rubber chicken" dinners hadn't improved over the years, but the audiences still seemed to appreciate hearing about my test flying.

I had my wish: I was with my family, worked with my hands, spent almost all of my time outdoors and enjoyed some fine hunting and fishing with my son. I also had time to teach him how to handle a hockey stick and improve his ice skating. What a great privilege it was to share with young Don some of the same activities I had been involved in when I was his age. But I found myself getting restless about the same time Dad and Uncle Murrell needed to return to their own lives; so in the early summer of 1948, I sold the place, shaved off my beard and moved to Florida.

My mother's family had owned property in Port Richey, Florida, since 1925. It was a pleasant, sleepy little town on the Pithlachascotee River within sight of the Gulf of Mexico. We liked the area and bought the house adjacent to the family home. While remodeling I frequently spent the night in our place just to keep an eye on things, because some of my tools and materials were stored in an unlocked shed. One night I awakened to find a man sneaking down the driveway with a case of my shotgun shells on his shoulder. I kept a shotgun with me for just such an occasion, loaded with light-load, very small shot. When he wouldn't stop or respond to my warnings, I peppered him a few times until he was well out of range. He dropped the shells after the first shot!

The local doctor was also the mayor, and he telephoned me about an hour later wanting to know if I was going to press charges. I decided that the shock of being hit, combined with the pain of the removal treatment, was a sufficient deterrent. The mayor agreed. A few weeks later the man, a local mullet fisherman, was in the barber shop relating what had happened and I overheard him say, "If you ever walk near Armstrong's house at night, you better be carrying a damn bright lantern and whistling Dixie as loud as you can." The word must have spread throughout the area because I never had any further problems.

When I had been contemplating my move from Michigan, I had asked Dad to tell me his feelings about building a trailer park in Florida. I remembered hearing him tell my mother, as early as 1939, that trailers would be the recreational units of the future. Since I had lived in my trailer while testing for the CAA and Douglas, I had some innovative ideas that I felt would work out well. I bought some nice property and built a ninety-six unit park. We were both right: my investment proved to be an immediate success. Dad was pleased that I was building the trailer park, since it was a vicarious fulfillment of his ten-year dream. However, he only lived long enough to see it begun - and to share my joy at the birth of my daughter, Terry Lynn.

The park had a nice recreation hall, but it needed activities to keep the snowbirds entertained. Since I had square danced and called for dances since my teens, I started having dances there a couple of times each week. In a short time I had another career for myself - teaching and calling square and folk dances. This is really another story, but suffice it to say that this activity would take me to all fifty states, over forty foreign countries and every continent except Antarctica!

While building the trailer park, flying remained in the background, although I maintained my license and kept my physical up-to-date. I had had some fun doing aerobatics in a Stearman and sometimes used a friend's Tri-Pacer for short trips around Florida to go quail hunting. Once in a while I'd fly out over the Gulf to spot schools of mackerel for some of my commercial-fisherman friends, but that was about it.

Before WW I, Dad had been a flyer and a motorcycle racer of considerable renown. I guess it was quite natural for me to try my hand at racing as well. I started in Midgets, played around with Stock cars a little and did absolutely nothing to brag about. Then I got into Sprint cars on half-mile, banked, dirt tracks and had a ball!

Soon I was asked to drive for Pop Hukle's team on the Florida circuit. His cars were powered by Ranger air-cooled aircraft engines, and as long as the driver kept the rpms wound up and drove smoothly, they were practically unbeatable. When I had been testing

aircraft for the CAA, I had flown many hours behind this fine engine in a Fairchild PT-26 Cornell trainer. At the end of the war the Ranger engine was available on the surplus market, and the Hukles wisely built a race car to use them. The Ranger had plenty of power, did not require much modification, never had cooling problems and was extremely reliable. As far as I can remember, I never dropped out of a race with engine trouble; and I won several races, rarely finishing farther back than third place. It was fun!

But calling square dances all over the U.S. and Canada was keeping me on the road, and racing was beginning to lose its challenge. I could no longer do both. My choice was to drop out of racing. What I didn't know then was that I would be test flying again very soon. Or that it would be in a Navy jet fighter!

13a Hukle's Ranger 99 (chauffeured by me) appeared on the Florida "big car" racing circuit in 1949-1950. Newspaper articles suggested that I had "a fondness for daredevil speeds," "the wildest-driving leadfoot on the clay half-mile" and "tried to take off in the Ranger more than once, when all four wheels were off the ground through the turns." (D. Armstrong collection)

CHAPTER 14

A FREE-LANCE JET JOCKEY
March 1951 - March 1952

It was hard to believe that almost five years had passed since I'd been in touch with any of my wartime associates. Frankly, I have no recollection of phoning or corresponding with any of my test-flying friends. I hadn't contacted any aircraft manufacturers other than Al Meyers, and only to check up on hunting or fishing. Nor had I sought employment in the field. My new life was enjoyable and fulfilling, and I had no reason to think about high-performance aircraft except to reminisce with friends around a campfire or over an after-dinner coffee and brandy.

Then "big brother" revealed my whereabouts to Don Garges, and with one phone call he kicked my adrenal glands into high gear. Don had been an engineer at Curtiss while I was working on the XP-60D project. He had later worked for Grumman, and eventually became chief engineer of East Coast Aeronautics, a small company designing and fabricating aircraft components from magnesium. Don wanted me to do the contract dive demonstration on a Grumman F9F-2 Panther jet fighter that would be fitted with magnesium outer-wing panels of a radically different design.

At first I was astounded and pleased that he wanted *me* to do the work and that he had been able to track me down. Then reality set in: I knew virtually nothing about magnesium's use in aircraft manufacturing and I had never seen an F9F up close, much less flown one. In fact, I had time in only two all-jet aircraft– the old Bell P-59 and the Lockheed P-80. The full extent of my experience in either had been short evaluation/familiarization flights.

The whole situation caught me completely by surprise. Thankfully, Don surmised this and didn't pressure me for an immediate decision. Since the wing panels wouldn't be ready for several months, I had some time to think it over. He offered, in the interim, to send me information about the use of magnesium and some background on the Panther, as well as a pilot's manual. Our conversation

ended with his arranging to be in touch in a few weeks.

The package he sent was both informative and helpful and, while I can't claim to have become a metallurgist, I did develop increased appreciation for magnesium. In 1951 magnesium was classed as a non-strategic material and, because it was a light ductile metal weighing about one-third less than aluminum, had already made tremendous inroads into aircraft design and construction. Magnesium could be united to other parts and metals by all accepted techniques and worked by extrusion, spinning, drawing, bending, etc. Equally important, it could be fabricated - by casting, forging or in sheets and plates

- into commonly-used forms.

Its use in the 1940s was not limited to secondary items (Exhibit 14a). For instance, in a typical bomber there was approximately 1,000 pounds of magnesium. Within ten years, the amount was increased to over 15,000 pounds in a long-range bomber. In retrospect, it was logical that the next step would be to fabricate larger components, such as wing panels or tail surfaces, out of this versatile substance.

I knew that the Navy's famous aerobatic team, the Blue Angels, used F9Fs. This, in itself, was a significant credential since they always got the Navy's best. Beyond that, however, my

14a Advertisement appearing in the February 1952 Aeronautical Engineering Review promoting the use of magnesium in aircraft manufacturing. (D. Armstrong collection)

GRUMMAN

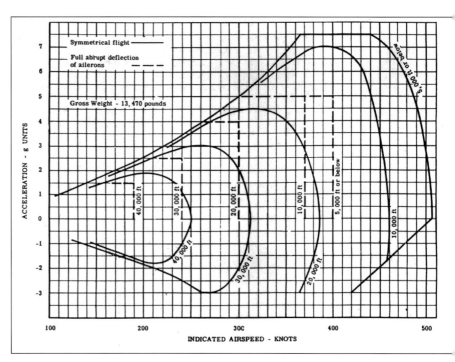

knowledge of the Grumman jet was minimal. I would need to know a lot more before committing myself to conduct the dive tests in one.

Five years after the initial flight of the world's first turbojet, the German Heinkel HE 280, Grumman was awarded a prototype contract (April 22, 1946) for a four-jet, two-seat night fighter–the XF9F-1. It was never built. Subsequently, the design evolved into the single-seat, single-engined XF9F-2 which was first flown by my friend Corky Meyer on November 21, 1947.

[Author's note: Corwin H. "Corky" Meyer came to Grumman in 1942 via MIT and the Civilian Pilot Training Program. He was the project test pilot on the F6F Hellcat, F7F Tigercat, F8F Bearcat, F9F-2/5 Panther, F9F-6/8 Cougar, F10F Jaguar, F11F Tiger and the Mach 2 Super Tiger. Corky retired in 1978 as Grumman's senior engineering test pilot. Without question, a most impressive career! Happily, Corky is enjoying himself in Florida. His help in researching for this chapter is deeply appreciated.]

The first production F9Fs rolled off the line in 1949, having been delayed by problems with stability, the rear fuselage, its powerplant and low-speed handling. In spite of these growing pains, it matured into a fine fighter plane.

The dash-2 was powered by a Pratt and Whitney J42-P-8 jet which produced a maximum of 5,750 pounds of thrust, and developed a top speed of around 600 mph. Because it was gaining an enviable reputation as a rugged and reliable airplane, I phoned Don Garges and asked for more specifics about the wing panels, the aircraft and the dive demonstration requirements.

After the war the government had modified its economic policies and encouraged major contractors to disperse defense work among sub-contractors. At the same time, East Coast Aeronautics, recognizing the possibility of increased utilization of magnesium, proposed fabricating new outer-wing panels for the F9F-2. It is probable they chose the Panther because the experimental panels could easily be attached

to the wing "stub" that was integral to the fuselage. This, coupled with the structural integrity of an already-proven airframe, made the F9F a highly-desirable testbed. The timing was perfect, and ECA was given a nod - and an F9F-2 on which to install their wings.

The most prevalent wing-panel construction at that time was to cover a staunch "bridgework" of internal spars and ribs with a relatively thin skin of aluminum. With this method the majority of structural strength was internal. Conversely, the ECA magnesium panels were to be formed into a very thick outer surface which really could not be labeled a "skin." Therefore, most of its structural integrity was external. In 1951 this was an innovative concept.

The Navy demonstration specifications were unusually practical and based upon plain, old common sense. There was no need to redundantly demonstrate compliance re: maneuverability, performance or spin recovery because the external configuration of the demonstration aircraft was exactly the same as other F9F-2s. The ECA plane's only modification was that its outer-wing panels had a different internal design and used magnesium instead of aluminum. Therefore, the Navy required only a minimal number of demonstration dives, solely to prove the structural integrity of the outer panels. If the wings were as strong as static testing already indicated, the terms of the contract would be satisfied. This made sense to me,

so I was ready to talk it over.

On March 8, 1951, Don Garges flew to Tampa. We discussed, and tentatively agreed upon, the basic terms of an extra-risk contract. Don was easy to get along with, sympathetic to my situation, and our negotiations were pleasant and uncomplicated. My conditions about "commuting" took him by surprise. However, after attending one of my dances at the Gulfport Casino, he understood and readily agreed.

There was still one more question for Don: "Why me?" He explained that he remembered how meticulously I planned and conducted the dives in the XP-60D and, after further inquiry at Pax about my F2G work, felt I could handle the job while maintaining a good rapport with factory and Navy personnel. I have no qualms about admitting that I was flattered.

No binding agreement had been signed, but Don and I had come to a "hand-shake, probably-will" meeting of the minds. Now the ball was in my court. The only reservations were mine.

Over the next few days I had some serious discussions with the inner me. I was as busy as a bee. I hadn't flown a high-performance plane in years. And, LaVerne was extremely upset at the prospect of my diving again.

So, why would I even consider jousting with the monster one more time? Why would I accept the risks? I really didn't need the money. Was I being fair to my family?

And ever present was the nagging question: could I rekindle my ability to focus solely on the test - at the moment of truth, at the pushover into the dive?

It may seem strange to some people (pilots included), but I didn't have the slightest shadow of a doubt that I could fly the plane well, or whether my skill would be there when I needed it. To me, this was a given; I knew I could handle the mechanics of it.

In the end, there was more for than against taking the job and I definitely wanted to do it. I knew that once I made up my mind I could live with the decision. Therefore, my answer would be "Yes!"

After signing a formal letter of agreement, I spent some extra hours in any plane that was handy, diligently studied the Panther pilot's manual and laid out a preliminary plan as to how I would approach the final dive demo. Then, in the early fall, I made arrangements for some time in the F9F simulator at the Naval Air Station in Jacksonville, Florida.

The simulator work was fun and interesting. When compared to an old Link Trainer, it was unbelievably realistic. After just a couple of minutes it was hard to remember that the whole apparatus was bolted to the floor. The sound and vibration - even the stall-warning "shaker" on the control stick - helped. I was allowed all the time I needed, and the Navy personnel were most gracious to me - even if I was "just a civilian." Soon I felt confident I would have no trouble in handling the real thing.

Meanwhile, the wings were completed and the aircraft, No. 123057, had been taken to Floyd Bennett Field for final assembly. When everything was ready, I went to check it out.

That the plane was at Floyd Bennett was a good omen: to me, it was a special place. Dad and I had walked hand-in-hand at that airport when I was only five or six years old. In every corner there would be fond memories of a number of my "giants." It was a fitting place to begin what - regardless of the outcome - could very well be the end of my test-flying career.

During my first flight in the Panther I was amazed by my feeling of deja vu: how completely at home in the cockpit I was, how right the plane felt. It was pure joy to realize that, once again, a fine airplane and I were

128 Grumman F9F-2 Panther; fighter; Pratt and Whitney J42-P-8, 5,750 s.t., jet. My test aircraft (No. 123057) was equipped with experimental magnesium outer-wing panels. (Courtesy of Grumman Corporation)

one and welcomed in a friendly sky. On my second flight, I rolled and swooped, did wing-overs and Immelmanns - playing like a child with a new toy. My "giants" must have smiled and shared my pleasure. Only one thing could have made it better: to have had Dad or Mr. Bill there, too.

The obvious differences between the F2G and the F9F were, of course, in landing gear (taildragger vs tricycle) and propulsion (prop vs jet). Other less visible items were that the Panther had far more gadgets and poorer initial rate of climb but higher top speed. The high/low weight spread in the jet also surprised me. Depending on fuel and external stores, it could vary from a low of around 10,000 pounds to a high of over 19,000 pounds.

The stalling characteristics of the Corsair were normal for its era and gave the pilot plenty of warning. The Panther gave a pilot so little warning that a "stick shaker" was employed to alert the pilot. Unfortunately, even this device was unreliable; my first few landing approaches were made with frequent references to the airspeed indicator. In the jet the approach speeds were also higher.

Not unexpectedly, it took a few days and several check flights to pin down the usual niggling problems with the aircraft. Most were little things such as inoperable navigation lights, hydraulic leaks, faulty radio or indicator lights, ailerons or trim controls that needed adjustment. While the "crabs" were being cleaned up I went home to Florida. I returned when the plane was ready to be ferried to Patuxent for final calibration of the test instruments.

Anticipating a fast, "no sweat" flight to Pax, I departed from Floyd Bennett at sundown. It was a clear night, and at my altitude the lights below me were soft and beautiful. At first all went well, but it suddenly became apparent that I should have waited until morning. Just before overflying the Dover Air Force Base,

Delaware, all my lights and radios went out! It was a major electrical failure and affected some flight instruments as well.

In a Panther all of the electrical reset buttons and switches are on the right side of the cockpit and a fuse panel is almost behind the pilot's right elbow. As in the past, I had memorized the location of nearly everything in the cockpit. So, I fell back on the Braille system and my small flashlight, but none of the recommended reset procedures helped. Oddly, the problems seem to cover sections of both the main and the essential bus-bar systems.

Fortunately, because the flight controls were conventional - the aileron boosters, landing gear, flaps, brakes and canopy all operated hydraulically - flying the plane probably wouldn't pose a problem. But I had no radios, and without my lights other pilots could not see me. I was in very busy airspace just east of Washington, D.C., and a hazard to other aircraft. Also, there wasn't any way to know whether other systems were affected; so I felt it prudent to land as soon as safely possible.

The runway at Dover was well lighted and those lights were a comforting sight. However, I couldn't call the tower and had no idea of what traffic was in their pattern. I kept a real close watch as I let down and circled the field while high enough to be above local traffic. When fairly certain I could make a safe approach, I ran through my checklist, landed and taxied to an open area near the control tower. Imagine my utter amazement when I realized that nobody - not even the control tower operator - had seen me land!

I shut things down, got out and found my way into the tower. One enlisted man was there, contentedly reading and totally unaware that I'd landed until I walked in.

Then the fun started. "Who the hell are you?" "Where'd you come from?" "You ain't supposed to be up here!"

That was just the beginning.

Picture his confusion when I told him that I was a civilian pilot, flying a Navy fighter and I had landed and parked the plane right in front of his nose.

To make matters worse, I was dressed in an old, scruffy flying suit, had no documents other than a Florida driver's license, and there was no flight plan to Dover AFB. He was ready to call the base police!

Finally I got him calmed down and suggested he contact the duty officer. A frazzled, young lieutenant arrived, and the comic opera's last act opened with his calling Pax. Someone there verified and closed my flight plan and confirmed my identity. The curtain came down when he got me a room in the visiting officers' quarters. I made a couple of phone calls and got a good night's sleep.

The following morning, after quite a lot of improvising with the external APU starter cables, I fired it up. Everything that was essential checked out O.K. so I flew on to Pax - sans radios and instruments. Hopefully a bad start would assure a good ending. Whatever, it was great to be back at Pax again!

[Author's note: Someday soon, I'd like to write a short story about the incredible saga of researching specifics for this chapter. My memorabilia for the ECA/Panther flights must have been spirited away by poltergeists or devoured by gremlins lurking in the shadows since WW II. I had some documentation, of course, but needed to find a copy of one official report. Suffice it to say that, after fourteen months of work, hundreds of phone calls, scores of letters and faxes, the contractor's report of this dive demonstration remains hidden away in the catacombs of government files.

Dozens of wonderful people have tried to help, but Bill and Carolyn Rymer went far beyond the proverbial extra mile by doing a personal search, on a Saturday, in the Suitland Branch of the National Archives and excavated enough facts to make this chapter much more accurate for you, and easier for me. I am so grateful!

If any reader can locate a copy of

the report identified as TKD NO PTR DE-215, "Flight Demonstration of Model F9F-2 Airplane with Magnesium Outer Wing Panels," I'd sure like to have it!]

The electrical system repairs were completed at Pax in a couple of days and, once again, the plane was ready for final instrument calibration. The instrumentation initially had been done by the Navy at Philadelphia, but upon delivery of the plane NATC had assumed that responsibility. The dive contract (No. NOAS 51-218) was supplemented by an instrumentation memo that required, as a part of the total of fourteen measurements, time vs altitude, airspeed, acceleration (Gs) and speed-brake position. The information obtained from these would verify that I had met the conditions of the contract. The Navy and ECA had agreed that additional instrumentation, while possibly desirable, would be redundant since this was a structural demonstration and not an aerodynamic investigation.

The original contract included several less important dives, the conditions of which, it was agreed, could easily be met. This was a standard procedure and acceptable to me. Each of them would serve as a build-up dive, thus enabling me to become more familiar with the plane and to improve my technique before the "big one." They would also provide the ECA engineers with an opportunity to analyze the effects that speed, Gs and torsion might have on their wing panels or the attachment points. Additionally, it gave the Navy time to work out any minor bugs in the instrumentation. The dives went smoothly, and there were no problems other than the fact that I felt it took too long for the speed-reduction brakes to deploy.

None of my dives had to go beyond the limiting tactical Mach number of .79 or to get outside of any curve of the performance envelope (Exhibit 14b), because ECA only had to prove the structural integrity of the wing panels. But, the contract specifications on one of the more critical dives required me to attain a speed of 470 knots (540 mph) at 7,000 feet, and then activate the speed-reduction brakes until the speed

had reduced to 400 knots (460 mph), at which time I was to pull out at a load factor of 7.5 Gs.

Although it sounded pretty much cut and dried during the planning stages, like the best laid plans of mice and men, it just didn't work. During build-up dives I had documented that the speed-reduction brakes (more frequently referred to as "dive brakes" during our discussions) took at least *six seconds* to become fully deployed. At 7,000 feet, heading downhill at over 500 mph, six seconds is a significantly long time - especially when the arc of pullout is factored in! This had caused some concerns and we had a meeting which resulted in a few changes. A report about that meeting, submitted on February 20, 1952 by Mr. L. B. Hutchinson, the cognizant engineer stated:

This change was subject of discussion among DE22 and ECA (including pilot) on 2/19/52. Original requirements involved diving at 470 K to 7,000'; activating dive brakes and waiting (about six seconds in this particular airplane) for brakes to fully open; when speed reduced to 400 K to make pullout. [This] meant the pilot would be dodging the tree tops at the bottom of pullout. Dive brakes are on the fuselage - do not cause outer-panel loads - and the only reason for making the test is to determine if unusual turbulence or other undesirable conditions occur. By diving to 400 K with dive brakes open and then pulling out, the purpose of the test is fulfilled and safety of plane and pilot is not endangered.

This was another example of common sense! It resulted in a Naval Speed Letter on February 21, 1952, which modified the requirements as follows:

Perform with empty wingtip tanks. With the speed-reduction device at full displacement, there shall be executed a pullout to a load factor of 7.5 and an equivalent airspeed of not less than

425 K [488 mph].

Perform with empty wingtip fuel tanks, and six (6) 250-pound bombs. With the speed-reduction device at full displacement, there shall be executed a pullout to a load factor of 6.5 at an equivalent airspeed of not less than 400 K.

Not exactly what Mr. Hutchinson had recommended, but we all felt it to be reasonable and agreed to continue the tests.

At this point there was a feeling of confidence that we could move ahead rapidly. But we had forgotten that, although a few years older, the monster still had an insatiable appetite for men and machines, especially when everything appears to be going better than expected. On the next dive we were reminded; it huffed and puffed, shook its fist and twisted *my* tail.

Oddly enough, the only thing I can recall about that particular dive was that there were six 250-pound bombs hung below the wings. Whatever the exact circumstances, after I landed the crew found some popped rivets in the tail section. This caused enough worry that a service engineer from Grumman was called in. He did a very thorough inspection, supervised the replacement of the rivets, and asked me to repeat the dive "to make certain it didn't happen again." I did so and everyone breathed a collective sigh of relief when all went well. The incident was filed away under "one-time thing, unlikely to reoccur." And the monster had to be content with lurking in the clouds for the balance of the tests.

During the repairs I made another commute to Florida and found that I had another, very serious, problem to face. LaVerne was extremely upset about my work and wouldn't, or couldn't, even talk to me about her feelings. Such distractions, important in their own right, can seriously and adversely affect a pilot's attitude and performance - and endanger his life.

Thankfully, the next dive on my return to Pax would prove to be the final one. It was as close to perfect as anyone dared expect. I had hit the specs right on the money and the Navy observer certified compliance with the contract. Once again, before leaving the base to celebrate with the crew at a local seafood restaurant, I shook hands with and said farewell to many wonderful people at Pax. I also felt profoundly grateful that I had been able to do my job successfully - and safely.

Later that year "my" plane (No. 123057) successfully completed carrier suitability tests and, as far as I was concerned, that was the end of the trail. The result of these tests was that the Navy placed an initial order for ten sets of the magnesium wing panels from East Coast Aeronautics. However, there is no record that these panels were ever installed on any Panthers, and I never heard if similar panels were developed for other aircraft.

[Historical note: From 1949 until 1953 a total of 1,385 Panthers were constructed, 564 of which were designated as F9F-2s and regarded by many as the best of the new generation of naval jet fighters. In the Korean War Lieutenant Commander W. T. Amen, flying a Panther, became the first Navy jet pilot to shoot down an enemy jet, a Russian-built MiG-15 (November 9, 1950). Ensign Neil A. Armstrong and Major John H. Glenn (two of our first seven astronauts) and Lieutenant Ted Williams (of Boston Red Sox fame) also flew Panthers during that conflict. Twenty years later, the last dash-2 retired - from the Argentine Navy.]

On my trip home, I remember thinking that I had added one more notch to my gun. I had never been, in the truest sense of the word, a "free-

lance" or "contract" test pilot before the ECA F9F-2 tests. In this case, that had been my exact role. Hopefully, Dad, Mr. Bill and my "giants" were sharing my sense of fulfillment. At the same time, they were probably telling me not to go shopping for a larger hat!

Then, out of the blue, my thoughts went back into my past. One of my childhood heroes was Jimmy Collins, an early contract test pilot whose final project/flight had been in a Grumman fighter. (When I was in Canada I had flown a biplane similar to the one in which he was killed.) I never imagined then that I also would end my test-flying career as a contract pilot, in a Grumman fighter - but I had survived. It was a sobering thought; and it started me thinking about many things.

My confidence, right from the start, in my ability to handle this project in spite of a five-year hiatus was now, in fact, justified. Probably because I had made an extraordinary effort to concentrate, my test results were as accurate as they had ever been. The technique and skills were in no way diminished.

This was all very comforting to me but, in truth, I wasn't surprised. If I hadn't felt a deep sense of certainty, I would not have undertaken the job. There had been a subtle, underlying difference within me, however.

In all my previous test flying - once I was airborne and ready to dive, or spin, or take whatever risk was forthcoming - I never, and I do mean never, had any mental hesitation, reservation or feeling of doubt about what I was going to do. There had been no need to force myself to concentrate. My entire focus was on the test at hand. Deep in the recesses of my brain there was almost an impatience, an eagerness, to see what would happen. It was as though a part of my mind was detached, floating around somewhere above me, waiting for the results. It was the antithesis of apprehension: a "high," a "rush" experienced by risk takers and, perhaps, beyond the perception of less

adventuresome individuals.

Like any normal, honest-to-himself human, before the flight I was not without moments of apprehension, trepidation and, sometimes, fear. But nagging thoughts never entered my mind during those last few moments prior to entering the test itself.

Herein was the key to my self-analysis. A door had opened to the awareness that I was no longer the person I had been five years earlier. True, I still retained the skills, the knowledge, the wherewithal for the job. But the *addiction*, the need to feel that adrenalin kick, to be an "extra-special" pilot, had been replaced. I no longer had to prove myself, to myself; or prove myself to anyone else, anywhere. I now realized that I already had done so. I had attained my goals. I was content with my achievements as a test pilot.

Subconsciously, this was an underlying thought that had come to me several times during the Panther tests. They were fun, and each dive was satisfying to my ego. It had been another challenge, and I always enjoyed facing them. However, and this was the bottom line, I simply didn't need it anymore. I was completely satisfied without it. Only after the tests were over was I aware that I had asked myself, not once, but several times, "What in the world are you doing this for?" And I had been unable to give myself a satisfactory answer.

Then a little light came on. I understood. I had moved beyond that stage of my life. I had made my last flight as a test pilot.

There was a sadness but, moreover, a feeling of having arrived at a new threshold, a door to be opened into a world of new opportunities. And I, like many of my "giants" had been, was content and looking ahead to far horizons. I was wonderfully happy.

CHAPTER 15

A TIME TO DANCE

The truest expression of a people is in its dances and its music. Bodies never lie.

Agnes DeMille in New York Time Magazine

To tell my story without including more than just an occasional reference to folk dancing or square dancing did not seem apropos, since dancing always coexisted with my flying. Chronologically, I was flying before starting to dance. But, from my teens until today, forty years after retiring as a test pilot, there never has been a prolonged period that I was not dancing or teaching/calling dances on a professional basis.

How could these two widely-divergent activities be fused into one life and each be so supportive of the other? Square or folk dancing provided me with two things which I desperately needed. First, I was able to "turn off my brain" - completely disassociate myself from the problems of the current series of flight tests. Almost equally important, I enjoyed and benefited from the physical exercise of two or three hours of dancing.

There were also fringe benefits. Socially, it was wonderful because I was "holding hands" with an entirely different circle - people to whom flying was not the primary conversational theme. After an evening of fun, fellowship and exercise I'd sleep like a baby and wake up physically rested, emotionally refreshed and ready to fly. Those hours could have been, quite literally, life savers. They were - and have remained - fun!

But, how did being a test pilot benefit my dancing and, later, my professional teaching/calling career? My dancing opportunities were so much greater than the average person's since my test work entailed a great deal of travel, which allowed me to dance or call in many different areas of the country. I danced with or called for people from many ethnic backgrounds, enjoyed a wide variety of music and dances. Everywhere I went I made new friends, m a n y o f whom are close friends today.

As a dance professional, the fact that I was fairly well-known as a test pilot - and made a special effort to cultivate this association for promotional purposes - didn't hurt at all! Media

interviewers quickly picked up the "test-pilot connection," used photos of me in my checkerboard crash helmet - sometimes with a second photo showing my checkered shirts - and, to my chagrin, a few blatantly conjured up some pretty far-fetched stories about me! Occasionally there was also an added bonus, an extra honorarium, earned when I could arrange to give a "We Flew Them First" talk at a school or service club.

Test flying and dancing went hand-in-hand, and both had an enhancing effect upon my life and the person I have become. To delve into detail about dancing, while sharing my flying experiences, would have been disruptive for the reader, so I've partially dissected one from the other.

By the same token, since flying threaded its way throughout the fabric of my dancing, this chapter could not have been written without the inclusion of a flying vignette now and then. Remember, the following events overlap the times and places you have, and will, read about. But always keep in mind that each contributed to the other. What comes next will give you a peek into my

131 Maule M-4, Jetasen (name coined from "Jet Ascent"); four-seat, cabin, high-wing, monoplane; Continental 0-300-A, 145-hp opposed.
Mr. B. D. Maule and his family deserve special mention here. It has been said of them, "They have become something of a symbol for entrepreneurial tenacity and adherence to the old engineering axiom - KISS: Keep It Simple, Stupid." Maule is probably the only family-owned U.S. aircraft manufacturer who has continuously built single-engine aircraft since the early 1960s. The versatile Maule aircraft, certificated and available on wheels/floats/skis, are truly easy-to-maintain workhorses and inexpensive by today's standards. Their short takeoff/landing capabilities are legendary. Many readers will enjoy the video tape, *Maule - the Belford D. Maule Story* (available from Maule Air, Inc., Rt. 5, Box 319, Moultrie GA 31768). It will reinforce your faith in family enterprise and in the American Dream! (Courtesy of Maule Air, Inc.)

"other life." So now... it's time to dance!

Throughout the United States in the 1950s, square dancing was growing at an almost unbelievable rate. Traditional square dances (perennial in the northeast and other areas) had moved west, combined with cowboy dances and transformed into a new "western square dance." The result virtually exploded into a hobby activity enjoyed by untold thousands.

I was one of the first "traveling callers," in demand for one-night stands, workshops, seminars and festivals throughout the "lower forty-eight" states and Canada. Later, I became one of the first nationally-known callers to make records (many with my own band), and they sold like hot dogs at a ball game! In addition to my recordings, I also wrote and produced several books and manuals for teachers and callers, which were snatched up almost before the ink was dry. Realizing that my involvement had become far more than a casual one, once again I made the checkerboard a part of my image - tailoring all of my western shirts and the band's costumes from checked gingham. I was as busy as a squirrel burying acorns in the fall and, just as I had throughout my life, was thoroughly enjoying every minute of it. I had a new, full-time and very lucrative profession.

What little flying I did in the early 1950s, mostly around Florida, was relaxed and laid back. That is, until the fall of 1951, when I returned to test flying and did the dive demonstrations on a Grumman F9F-2 Panther jet fighter. This reinvolvement prompted Dick Bothwell, a feature writer for *The St. Petersburg Times*, to do a half-page story (February 18, 1952) about my dual roles, and the complicated logistics of my simultaneously being a test pilot and square-dance caller.

When negotiating my F9F test contract with Don Garges of East Coast Aeronautics, one of my stipulations was that the company had to cover all of my expenses in Washington, D.C., or Patuxent, and also to provide the means for me

15b Chester "Chet" Boltz, good friend and fellow pilot, with one of his Maules. (C. Boltz collection)

to commute by air between Tampa and Washington - every weekend. This second condition would allow me to call my very remunerative square dances at St. Petersburg's Gulfport Casino on Saturday nights. Admittedly, this was an unusual contractual arrangement. But East Coast had no choice. It was the only way I would accept the job.

It all boiled down to this: I'd fly to Washington each Sunday and be available for test flights at Pax from Monday through Thursday. On Fridays I'd fly back home to prepare for and conduct the big Saturday night dance. Then, on Sunday, the process repeated itself - week after week - until after the final dive.

On paper, it looked great. But the only predictable thing about east coast, mid-winter weather is its unpredictability! This affected not only the test flights, but also made a mess of my commuting schedules. One weekend I was weathered in at Pax until Saturday, and finally got out by flying the right-hand seat in a Navy flight to Orlando. Another weekend I couldn't get there at all, so Don, Junior - then only thirteen years old - called the entire program in my place!

[Author's note: My son, even at this early age, was a great little caller and a fine musician who often played drums or

bass in the band. A few years later he also played accordion, guitar, mandolin and saxophone, had become an excellent caller and teacher and easily could have had a successful career in either music or calling, had he chosen to do so.]

Whenever I was in Florida, even though I devoted a good portion of my life to my dance career, I took time to fish, hunt and raise and train Brittanys for bird hunting. Had my "giants" told me to stop and smell the roses?

Because my calling career took me all over the U.S. and Canada, many people questioned why I didn't own and fly an airplane on my tours. I was very tempted by the idea, especially after a long, hard drive to my next engagement but, after a considerable amount of thought I decided against it. In order to adhere to a fairly tight schedule during the winter months, I would undoubtedly have been faced with many flights in marginal weather. There would frequently have been the need for one of those nasty, "I-think-I-can-make-it" decisions - the kind that require a pilot to be rested and alert enough to cope with adverse weather and the complex system. After an emotionally-draining one-night stand or a long weekend workshop, I might not have been able to do so in a competent, confident manner. Under less-pressured circumstances it would have been pleasant, and perhaps even cost-effective but, in fairness to myself and others in the system, it was not the smart thing to do.

In order to understand how popular square dancing was at that time, consider the following: I was asked to make a two-month long, 12,000-mile trip - "The City of St. Petersburg Square Dance Good-Will Tour" - primarily to entice square dancers to visit Florida's west coast. LaVerne and Don came along, and at each of my engagements we passed out Chamber of Commerce literature to publicize the dance opportunities in the St. Pete area.

During the Good-Will Tour, I made a special effort to meet Dr. Lloyd Shaw of Colorado Springs, Colorado. Dr. Shaw was an innovative teacher, superintendent of the Cheyenne Mountain School District,

the man primarily responsible for the growing interest in western square dancing and the author of two texts that have contributed immeasurably to American dance, *Cowboy Dances* and *The Round Dance Book*. "Pappy," as he was affectionately called by his many friends, was a joy to be around and I am proud that I was among his colleagues.

This was a busy time. In September 1952 I was appointed social recreation consultant for the Recreation Department of the City of Tampa and served for several years. In this capacity I was responsible for dance activities for all age levels and conducted the majority of in-service seminars for their staff.

In December I became a recording artist and signed a contract with Windsor Records. A number of these recordings are still in use all over the world, and on some of the records I am the caller as well as the drummer in the band. Looking back, I have recorded

15e "Boy wonder" - Don, Junior, calling a dance for me. He was not more than sixteen years old at the time his mother took this picture. (D. Armstrong collection)

Emory University in Atlanta. Little did I realize that I would continue to do similar seminars, year after year, at universities throughout the entire United States.

By the beginning of the winter season that year I had opened my own square - and folk-dance hall in Largo, which quickly became *the* dance center for Florida's west coast.

Sadly, however, in the next few months, it became evident that LaVerne had become the victim of my test flying: there simply had been too many days of living with the terrors - the danger and uncertainties of my job - that were a part of being a test-pilot's wife. I realize that during the F9F dives I'd gone to the well once too often. It was as though a rubber band had snapped - she was never quite herself following these tests, and our marriage ended. (Tom Wolfe, in his book *The Right Stuff*, graphically describes this situation.) It was an amicable separation, with no messy recriminations, and I was able to retain custody of my children - thanks, entirely, to the unfailing support and assistance that my mother offered.

LaVerne returned "home" to live with her mother and happily, after

15a Yours truly, with his band, The Quadrilles. From left to right - ladies, Althea Beck and Kay White; men, Jack Beck and Evan White. Note the "checkerboard" pattern of the shirts and skirts! (D. Armstrong collection)

over 300 records for seven U.S. companies, am on one Canadian label and now, under special arrangement, on German and Belgian labels as well.

In July 1953 I entered yet another area of the dance field by serving on the staff of a week-long institute at moving back to Texas, was able to put her life back together, remarried and had two more fine daughters, one of whom works at the NASA Space Center in Houston, and the other who is a stage actress in Dallas. When attempting to locate material for this book, our daughter Terry and I visited LaVerne in Dallas. She cheerfully gave me lots of help - and old photos - and I am grateful for what she contributed.

Flying had taken a back seat for a while but I did take an occasional trip within Florida: fishing in the panhandle or the Keys. Luckily, I had a square-dance friend in Clearwater who owned a Cessna 180 and invited me to use it almost any time. All I had to do was leave it with a clean windshield and full of fuel and oil. One day, when I landed at Captiva Island, I was asked if I would help in an offshore search for a pleasure boat that had not been heard from in several days. Although the search proved unsuccessful, I met a pilot who was also flying a 180 and, a couple of weeks later, over coffee, made a new friend.

He and his wife were planning a long flying/camping trip in his 180 after he put it on floats. Their itinerary took them up to Maine, across Quebec and Ontario, down through Minnesota and along the Mississippi on the way back to Florida. They planned to tent-camp, enjoy fishing and photography and, perhaps, write a series of magazine articles about the trip.

It sounded great to me, but they were beginning to have second thoughts about the whole thing because he had never flown a floatplane. They subsequently asked me to spend a week or so with them at their camp on Lake Apopka, while giving him the necessary instruction and added that I would be able to enjoy lots of bass fishing between flights. I considered it - for about two seconds - and agreed.

It was a truly delightful and pleasurable week for me, associating with a couple who knew how to enjoy their retirement - who knew how to stop and pick daisies. Their trip lasted over three months with no more than

minor problems and, although I never saw any of the proposed magazine stories, they had such a good time that they went back to northern Ontario on a similar trip the next summer.

A young lady named Marie Lowrey attended the Emory University Institute in July 1954. She was an aspiring caller with dancing experience both around her home in North Carolina and in Alaska. (She had been the personal secretary of the commanding officer of the Air Force cold weather test unit in Fairbanks for several years.) In brief, two months later she helped out at my weekend "Dancetitute" in Clearwater, and on Halloween Day that fall became Mrs. Don Armstrong. For the past thirty-nine years I've told friends that "she came to Emory for a short-course, and hasn't finished the long-course with me yet."

Over the next few years we called and taught dancing as a team, at home and in at least twenty states and four Canadian provinces. Then in June 1959 - after having walked away unscathed from crashes, fires and belly landings and suffering only a broken ankle when I bailed out of the Curtiss fighter - I broke my back. I fell off a ladder while trimming a tree with a chain saw! It was hard to believe... and harder to accept.

I declined fusion surgery in favor of a long rehabilitation program, recovered fully and resumed calling locally about six months later. My "giants" must have been hanging around, just to make sure I was going to be O.K.!

Abroad, my books and records were in wide use, not only at American military establishments, but anywhere that square dancing had spread. It was, therefore, not unexpected that I'd be invited overseas. With help from the State Department and the Air Force, Terry, Marie and I made a ten-week trip throughout Europe, calling dances for Americans and their local guests and doing programs for English, German, French and Spanish square-dance groups.

While in Spain I arranged for the use of a U.S. military flying club's

Cessna and flew to Morocco for a weekend. We departed from the U.S. base without clearing Spanish Immigration and, because we landed at a U.S. base in Morocco, we had no problems. It was our intention to fly back to the same base in Spain on our return but, unexpectedly, I was instructed by radio to land at a local airport and to clear with the Spanish Customs office. That's where all the fun began!

Their English, and our Spanish, was practically nonexistent. To sum it all up, after thirty minutes of gestures and phone calls, they conveniently figured out that "we could not be arriving, because we had not departed!" The problem was finally solved by their simply waving us away, telling us to "Vayase, vayase... (Go, go...)." And that's exactly what we did. Sometimes it pays to smile a lot - and appear confused, helpless or slightly stupid.

An old friend and long-time private pilot, Chester "Chet" Boltz, and I had purchased a Piper PA-12 Super Cruiser together, and once again I was enjoying "boring holes in the sky," flying for the pure joy of it. Over the next few years Chet and I jointly owned the Super Cruiser, a Stinson Station Wagon and a Maule.

The little four-place Maule quickly became a real favorite of mine. It got off the ground almost before I had the throttle open, was a soft, fuzzy Teddy Bear to fly and got me where I wanted to go in a "reasonable hurry," without spending a fortune on fuel. Being a "taildragger" (not a tricycle landing-gear), it was easy to handle on "off-airport" landings, even in sand. If I were to purchase a plane for my personal use tomorrow, especially in view of the fact that I live in the mountains of Colorado, the Maule would be an odds-on favorite.

Thinking back about the Maule brought to mind a story which depicts the more casual, friendly system in which we flew during those years: I took the Maule to Canada to go on a fishing trip. After one of the refueling stops I took off and filed my flight plan by radio. The "N" number of the plane

15c One of Maule's newest planes, the MXT-420. The turbine engine certainly mates well with their tried-and-true airframe. I wonder if I could get one, on floats, down in Spring Creek? (Courtesy of Maule Air, Inc.)

ed by his lovely widow, Mrs. Dorothy Stott Shaw. In 1964, Bob Osgood and I proposed that this core group form a not-for-profit foundation "to recall, restore and teach the folk rhythms of the American people." In memory of Dr. Shaw, it was called the Lloyd Shaw Foundation, and I had the honor of being the first president. In order that Dr. Don Obee (Dr. Shaw's son-in-law) could assume this office, the following year I resigned the presidency, but have continued to serve on the board of directors and, for the past thirty years, have been the head of the Recordings Division. Today Dr. Shaw's granddaughter, Mrs. Lew (Enid) Cocke, holds the office, fittingly keeping the presidency in the Shaw family.

In the meantime, my daughter Terry was considering her college options, and she and I spent the better part of the summer of 1965 on a long camping and fishing trip, while visiting schools throughout the New England states. It was a great adventure, and an opportunity that few fathers are privileged to have - even though she did catch more trout than I did, in Baxter State Park in Maine. During our trip, I didn't miss dancing, or flying, at all.

Square dancing continued to be very kind to me during the next few years. I traveled three times to Europe, twice to Australia/New Zealand and around the South Pacific, twice to Japan and the Orient, all over Central and South Africa, and enjoyed an extended trip in South America.

While in Argentina I had a wonderful, serendipitous experience. I was strolling down a side street one evening, near our hotel district, and heard *my voice* on a square dance record coming from a second-story window! I quickly went upstairs and found a small group of people, two

was 12021 and, after I had given all of the usual information, the radio operator called me back to confirm the details. His transmission normally would have started, "Maule 12021, this is the center..." Instead, he called, "The *palindrome* Maule, this is the center..." ("Palindrome" - a word or phrase which reads the same backwards as it does forward.)

I knew what he meant and wrote down my confirmation, but a few moments later some local pilot piped up, "What the hell is a palindrome Maule?" I answered him, wished him a safe trip and continued my flight. Now I ask you - would this happen today? I'm afraid not - everyone seems too busy, and that's sad!

Chet and I still laugh about the Stinson "Station Wagon" that we bought. Unbelievably, after Chet and

his son Mickey spent untold hours rebuilding and beautifully refinishing it, inside and out, *neither* Chet *nor* Mickey ever had the opportunity to fly it. We got "an offer we couldn't refuse" and sold the plane before I could check either of them out in it.

Later on we thought we might be interested in buying an Ultralight, so each of us "test-flew" a Hummingbird. It was powered by two chainsaw motors and really flew quite well. We didn't get too excited about it, however, primarily because of the damn engines - it seemed that just about the time one was running smoothly, the other wasn't. (Today they're powered with much more reliable engines.)

Dr. Lloyd "Pappy" Shaw had passed away in 1958, but his friends and associates continued to meet in Colorado Springs every summer, host-

15d My daughter Terry Stanley and I sharing a special moment while performing an exhibition folk dance. (T. Stanley collection)

"squares," dancing to my recording of *Trail of the Lonesome Pine*. Language was a mutual problem, but I showed them my passport photo, pointed to my name on the record, and all of us were astounded. Sadly, I left the city without being able to see them again, but I did send them more of my records and corresponded, with difficulty, for a couple of years! It's such a small world.

For several years I had been planning to write a book, actually a teacher's manual, on how to teach and call "Contra dances" - a traditional form of dancing in facing lines, more familiar at that time in New England. With the help of Dr. William "Bill" Litchman, a friend and dance leader I knew through the Lloyd Shaw Foundation, I was given a three-quarter-time associate professorship at the University of New Mexico in Albuquerque. I found a small apartment near the campus; taught folk-, square - and ballroom dancing four days each week and wrote *The Caller/Teacher Manual for Contras*, a text which was published by the American Square Dance Society in 1973, and is still in worldwide use today.

My travels resumed immediately following my year at UNM, and I returned to the South Pacific and Japan. Marie joined me in 1974 when we took a group of dancers completely around the world. Can you imagine calling dances on the long, narrow porch of the U.S. embassy in Peshawar, Pakistan, near the Khyber Pass, to the music of a hand-held cassette player? Or to the music of an accordion in Egypt when the musician knew only a few "sort-of-American tunes?"

Following others trips - to Russia, Scandinavia and the British Isles - and completing an hour-long documentary on American dancing for Scottish television in Glasgow, I went into China in September 1979, long before "American groups" visited the country.

Those years provided one wondrous experience after another which, all in all, took me to forty-six countries, six Canadian provinces, all fifty States and every continent except Antarctica. Terry persistently teases me and asks, "Daddy, when are you going to teach the penguins to dance?"

My overseas calling/teaching trips continued, and I made several other trips to Europe. In 1985, after calling and teaching almost every other night or weekend (in Germany, Denmark, England and Belgium) for six weeks, I suddenly felt "different." I had learned to "listen to my body" while test flying and wanted to see a doctor. Gerhard Kamm, a German caller in whose home I was staying, knew a physician who not only spoke English, but was a flight surgeon as well! After a stress test he advised me to finish the tour, but to get more rest, not over-exert myself physically - and see a physician immediately upon my arrival home. I followed his prescription, of course, and wound up having a quadruple bypass operation.

Thanks to a long-ingrained habit of daily exercise (dating back to the RCAF routines I'd started in 1940) my recovery was uneventful; I actually was on staff at a dance workshop five weeks later. And though the cardiac surgeon prohibited my use of a rifle, because of the recoil, I still went hunting ten weeks after surgery, and harvested a nice antelope... with a pistol... at ninety yards!

That fall we moved to Colorado and my calendar continued to be filled with dance camps, workshops and calling dates, now more frequently scheduled around the time I spent in the mountains - hunting, fishing and camping.

Then, in 1989, while I was on another calling tour in Europe, my son Don died from a heart attack at forty-nine. He had had a previous coronary, while visiting with us, en route to Arizona. Because his recovery had been uncomplicated he was offered, and scheduled, cardiac bypass surgery.

Two days before his operation, he told me that he had decided against the surgery. As we talked, I realized he had done a lot of soul searching, and admitted to himself that, while I had maintained or lost weight, exercised daily and watched my diet very carefully, he was overweight, smoked, intensely disliked exercise and couldn't accept the idea of a lifelong low-fat, low-salt diet.

In view of these recommended changes and certain, beyond a doubt, he did not want to alter his lifestyle, he concluded that he was not a candidate for the surgery.

Although his decision absolutely devastated me, I realized, deep inside, that what he said was probably true. I told him how much I loved him, how I wished he felt differently - but the ultimate decision was his - and that I would support him, no matter what my feelings were. He stood by his choice and the following morning went on to Arizona to live. Ninety-one days later, on May 23, his body was found near Sedona - under a tree, in the mountains he loved so dearly.

The past five years can be summed up easily. I have continued to dance and maintain a fairly active calling and teaching career; I've been back to Europe; had a second bypass in 1991; hunted in Colorado, Wyoming, Missouri, Alberta, British Columbia and Alaska and, for at least a month every summer, fly-fished with my daughter, her husband and mutual friends. Most of all, I have loved every minute of each day.

My second career – dance – still stimulates me. Even though I'm now seventy-four years old, I have six seminars, from California to the east coast, scheduled for the remainder of 1994. In addition, I have frequent calling dates within Colorado and I'll be teaching several workshops in Germany and the Czech Republic.

I know that this sounds ridiculously busy, and that you're probably asking yourself, "Why doesn't the ol' geezer sit back and retire?" My only answer is - when I no longer feel capable, no longer can thoroughly enjoy what I'm doing, I'll quit! But until then, every day is the first day of the rest of my life, and I'm not going to waste a single second of it! And who knows, perhaps I'll start another book.

CHAPTER 16

THE LURE OF THE ISLANDS
Fall 1962 - Fall 1977

Don, Junior, had been successfully working in broadcasting for several years and now insisted that the New Port Richey (Florida) area would financially support a radio station. His exact words were, "Dad, it's ripe and ready - let's do it!"

Neither of us was aware that a local group, spearheaded by my long-time friend and attorney, Sam Y. Allgood, Jr., had already applied to the FCC for a license to build an AM station in town. When I discussed Don's idea with Sam he, in turn, revealed their plans and asked me if I would like to join the group and manage the station, if the license was awarded. (Sam's main interest was to have a station that could serve the region. Neither he, nor any of his associates, was even remotely interested in the day-to-day management of a station.) They offered to let my son and me become shareholders, and I agreed to become manager while Don became the program director. Utilizing his knowledge and experience enabled us to do many things in advance, such as getting some of the equipment lined up and tentatively arranging for a very limited staff.

By an interesting coincidence, Marie's brother, Thad Lowrey, had recently graduated from the Carolina School of Broadcasting after obtaining a degree in Political Science and History from High Point University. We discussed our venture with him; he was eager to join us and, when I suggested that he be included in the group, all of the founders agreed. The FCC application was amended to reflect the new partners and the waiting - for the granting of the construction permit - began.

A few months later, the FCC license was granted and we put our plans into high gear - acquiring and renovating a building on US Hwy 19 that had been owned by one of the

original investors. In a surprisingly short time, with Don's help and contacts, we prepared, equipped and tested a small, local AM broadcasting facility - WGUL - which went on the air on October 31, 1963.

Right from the start my philosophy, and the policy I insisted upon, was to provide family entertainment with great emphasis on local news and events. WGUL, the "Golden Gull," was an instant success. Even our first month of broadcasting showed a profit! I remain convinced that, because we dedicated ourselves to serving our community, we never failed to show a profit - and we kept the station for twenty years!

On November 22, 1963, President John F. Kennedy was assassinated and I, just by happenstance, was looking at the Associated Press teletype machine at the precise moment the initial "FLASH" came over the wire. Almost in shock, I instantly asked Don, in the control room, for a microphone and stood right there, in front of the machine, reading over the air each bulletin as it came in. Amazingly, WGUL was the *only* station within a fifty-mile radius to broadcast the news of the tragedy for at least ten or fifteen minutes! For some unknown reason, perhaps because Tampa, St. Petersburg and Clearwater television and radio stations were "on network," or maybe they simply failed to notice the AP or UPI "FLASH," they were very slow to react.

In any event, WGUL was broadcasting the news - and other stations were not. It's easy to understand that my announcements generated many angry phone calls, and most of the irate callers insisted we were perpetrating a criminal hoax far worse than Orson Wells' *War of the Worlds!* Of course, within a few minutes, it became clear that the bulletins were all devastatingly true. Needless to say, I will forever remember my sad and shocking introduction to instant broadcast journalism.

[Author's note: Several people volunteered their services to us at WGUL in those early years. Most

prominent was a young lady who acted as a receptionist and "gofer" for many months - Elizabeth H. "Libba" Grey. She and her son Jim (now with a lovely family of his own) have remained very close to my immediate family, and Libba has been my personal researcher and assistant throughout the writing of this book.]

Since I was so busy at the new radio station, when my mother suggested a family trip to the Caribbean, I agreed to go if she selected our destination and made the arrangements. She did - we had a delightful trip - and it was our introduction to the wonderful Cayman Islands. (I hadn't even known they existed - much less where they were!) We all found ourselves absolutely enchanted with the gorgeous seven-mile beach, the always-summer weather and the island's greatest treasure, its people.

For the next few months my mother kept insisting that I should go back to Cayman and buy some property on Seven Mile Beach, and Marie and I agreed. However, I had just invested most of my available cash in the radio station and didn't want to become overextended. Although the following year my mother died, we kept her dream alive by visiting Grand Cayman at every opportunity. Then, in 1967, we bought some property on the beach, right next to the place we had stayed when my mother was with us four years earlier.

I turned the day-to-day operation of the radio station over to Don, Junior, and Thad and built a cottage. My mother would have loved it! For the next several years, we enjoyed a story-book life on the "Island that Time Forgot," and still return for frequent visits.

In the following poem, Rachel Field unquestionably echoes our sentiments about the lure of the islands:

If once you have slept on an island,

you'll never be quite the same;

you may look as you looked before -

and go by the same old name.

You may hustle about in street and shop,

you may sit at home and sew,

but you'll see blue water and wheeling gulls

wherever your feet may go.

You may chat with the neighbors of this and that

and close to the fire keep,

but you'll hear ship whistle and lighthouse bell

and tides beat through your sleep.

And you won't know why and you can't say how

such change upon you came,

but once you have slept on an island

you'll never be quite the same!

The Cayman Islands - Grand Cayman, Cayman Brac and Little Cayman - are a crown colony of Great Britain, situated about 200 miles south of Playa Giron, Cuba, and 250 miles west of the Ayr Hill omni in the center of Jamaica. When we built our cottage the population was about 10,000 - of which eighty percent was "of some degree of color" - a handsome and happy people descended from predominately Scottish and English immigrants intermixed with Jamaican, Barbadian and other islanders. At that time, the beach was relatively unspoiled and the lifestyle of the people was laid-back and easygoing. Because of their unusual political status there was, except import duty, no taxation - no income tax, no death duties/inheritance tax, no property tax and no sales tax. Even though many of the residents earned very little money, all of what they made was theirs to use or keep; and they enjoyed a health and happiness not

found in many places in our so-called "civilized" world.

In those years, several times a week, LACSA Airlines (the flag-carrier of Costa Rica) and BWIA (British West Indian Airways) provided service to the big island, Grand Cayman (twenty-three miles long and eight miles across), but the smaller, sister islands (one hundred miles away) sorely needed a reliable air-charter service.

About the same time, I was beginning to want to do something other than dance, swim, water-ski, scuba-dive, snorkel and spear-fish; and Godfrey Paul, M.D., flew down from Vancouver, British Columbia, in his Cessna 310 and eventually built a condominium complex a couple of miles north of us on Seven Mile Beach. We each kindled in the other a desire to do something about the absolutely virgin territory for a flying school, and equally obvious needs for an air ambulance, a search-and-rescue aircraft and charter service to the other islands. The Cayman Island Government acknowledged the need for, and was enthusiastic about the prospect of, local air services and gave us their almost unqualified permission to proceed.

It was a fun-filled and fruitful three-way partnership. Godfrey already had the six-place twin for charter flights and immediately purchased and delivered a brand-new two-place Cessna 150 for the flying school. I was a very experienced and licensed commercial pilot and instructor and quickly accumulated the materials to use in teaching ground school. And the Cayman Island Government bent over backwards to assist and cooperate.

Cayman Flying Service was welcomed with open arms, successful almost beyond belief. It was the first time these folks had the opportunity to learn how to "pilot an airplane," and they ate it up. What a thrill it was to share with them the experience and exhilaration of learning to fly!

The beautiful airport and absolutely ideal, totally unpolluted

weather, combined with the verdant island and the clear-as-crystal water, made almost every flight a hymn of beauty and joy. The little 150 was in the air almost every available day, sometimes for several hours. Originally, I was the only instructor and seldom wearied of it - logging over 800 hours in the right-hand seat in less than two years! I conducted an exceptionally tough ground school with never a complaint and very, very few absences. The flight and operational discipline was as good as, maybe better than, any throughout the United Kingdom or the States. We earned, and kept, the respect and cooperation of the Director of Civil Aviation, members of the Legislative Assembly and the local business community.

The student pilots represented practically every founding family on the island and many expatriates, mostly from Great Britain. Since most of the pupils had family members in the United States (and/or could visit there far more frequently than they could travel to England), Cayman's Director of Civil Aviation agreed to grant Caymanian pilot's licenses based on U.S. FAA pilot-certification methods, regulations and tests - amended slightly to suit local needs. This prudent decision enabled several of my students, Caymanians and "expats," to obtain Cayman Island and/or U.S., British or Australian pilots' licenses. To my knowledge none of the students, who had earned a Caymanian pilot's license, failed to pass a similar test in the United States, Canada, Great Britain or Australia.

Soon after the Cessna 150 arrived on the island, Sands Sherwood came to see me with a very determined gleam in his eye. He was an Englishman who had lived all over the world but finally put down his roots in Grand Cayman and who owned and operated the Cayman Arms - the most popular pub in Georgetown, the principal city of the islands. No longer a young man, his only flying experience "left-over" from the *first* World War, Sands fervently wanted the distinction of obtaining Cayman Island's Private Pilot's License (Flying Machines), Number One. Frankly, I was dubious. Would he make the commitment? Would he attend the ground school regularly and study hard enough to pass the five difficult written tests? Could he take the time away from his lucrative business? And, would he strictly adhere to my "no-drinking-for-twelve-hours-before-flying" policy? Everyone knew I considered this policy inviolate, and I wondered if he could abide by it, especially in his particular situation.

His commitment was absolute. He never missed a class and studied, many times in his pub with other students, diligently and effectively enough to set a fine example to the younger students and pass all of the written tests with way-above-average grades. Although he was a slow starter, his coordination and confidence built with almost every flight, and it soon became obvious to everyone who knew him, that he had seriously dedicated himself to learning to fly, all over again, in a safe and compe-

tent manner.

His wife, however, had mixed emotions about all of this. She didn't think he'd stick to it, and that it might even be detrimental to their business. Not surprisingly to me, the exact opposite occurred. The Cayman Arms became the place for the flyboys to congregate after dark and compare notes, as well as the locale for the "first solo," ground-school graduation and "got my license" parties. Most noteworthy, and to his great credit, he honored his promise to me: he never took a drink from the day before his first flight with me, until the night we all offered him a toast, as we celebrated the attainment of his dream! Sands Sherwood, then in his fading sixties, was granted Cayman's first Private Pilot's License; and I was happy and proud to have been his instructor and friend!

Learning to fly was a family affair in Cayman. Spouses, siblings and lots of cousins were enrolled in ground school at the same time. The Adam family probably took the prize, however, when brothers Timmy, Billy and Mike all joined in the fun. Just as I had polished Mr. Bill's airplanes thirty years

before, young Timmy Adam cleaned and polished our planes in exchange for instruction and flying time. Seeing him at work brought back many fond memories for me. He was a considerate and trustworthy youngster, a promising young flyer and I think he could have made a career in aviation, had he wished to do so.

I designated a practice area for instruction and for student solo flying which was out of the airport traffic pattern, over the north-south road crossing the interior of the island. The green-and-white Cessna soon became very familiar to the people living in Boddentown and Northside. Whenever Marie went to the grocery store or post office, someone inevitably stopped her to say that they had seen "Mr. Don and his flying machine."

Not long ago when Marie was

---

142 Cessna 336/337, Skymaster; six-seat, cabin, high-wing, monoplane; two Continental IO-360-A, 210-hp opposed, in pusher/tractor (push/pull) position. (C. Boltz collection)

147 Britten-Norman BN-2, Islander; up to ten-seat, cabin, high-wing, monoplane; two Lycoming 0-540, 260-hp opposed. (Courtesy of San Diego Aerospace Museum)

visiting the island, our friend Crosby Ebanks reminded her that I had taken his son Daniel for a ride on his eleventh birthday (twenty-three years previously). There are dozens of memories similar to this that I still enjoy.

Most of the students were young men, but some of the island's well-known young ladies surprised their friends and families by learning to fly. One of the earliest was Iva Johnson Good (then a familiar face in the hospital X-ray department who, in 1993, became International President of the Girls Brigade). Another was Zoe Bodden, now Airport Manager of Cayman's Owen Roberts Airport, the same airport from which she made her first solo flight.

Most of the students were content to know that they could - and did - fly a plane. Many moved on to other parts of the world and there are folks presently living in Australia, New Zealand, Africa, England, Switzerland, Canada and the U.S.

who learned to fly with me in Cayman. Still others went on to become proficient in larger aircraft. Harrison Bothwell, for example, became a captain on Cayman Airways when the newly-formed Cayman Island flag-carrier started operating its jet airliners.

After a year or so, Godfrey became so involved in his condominium project that the only logical thing for me to do was to buy out his portion of the business. Since this meant I would no longer have the twin Cessna 310 available for charter or air-ambulance flights, I took a short leave from instructing and returned to the States to try to locate a suitable, substitute aircraft.

I traveled around the Southeast and evaluated a few planes, including the Piper Aztec, Apache and Cherokee Six. Although it was a low-wing plane, I liked the six-place Cherokee; but the Cayman Islands Civil Aviation Department would not approve a single-engine aircraft for commercial over-water flights.

The Britten-Norman Islander was simply too expensive, and the DC-3 too big and too costly to operate and maintain. I liked the push-pull Cessna 337 very much and was exceptionally pleased when I found a Cessna 336 in Fort Myers, Florida - essentially the same plane as the 337 but with a non-retractable landing gear. (Retractable wheels meant

more costly maintenance problems since frequent flights to the sister islands and Swan Island, all of which had rough, shell and sand landing strips, would exact a toll on retracting mechanisms.)

I bought the 336 and headed for St. Petersburg to have some carpeting and cosmetic work done in the interior, before ferrying it to Cayman. As I flew up the Gulf coast, crossed Tampa Bay and headed over St. Pete toward the airport, the cockpit suddenly filled with smoke. It seemed to emanate from behind the instrument panel. Although it seemed much longer, in just a few seconds the smoke thinned out and I determined that the navigation radios (ADF and omni) and some of the electrically-operated instruments were not functioning. I notified St. Pete tower of a possible emergency, but landed without incident. I remember thinking to myself how fortunate I was that the fire did not spread because, unlike during my test-pilot years, I was not wearing a parachute.

Inspection revealed that some stupid - and I use that word deliberately - mechanic had replaced a "hot" wire running directly from the battery to the instrument panel. It was much too large, improperly tied down - and had *bypassed* the circuit breaker!

Normal vibration had worn off the insulation, grounding the circuit. The ensuing fire burned the wire completely through, though doing very little damage. However, it damn sure disturbed my peace of mind and stimulated my adrenal glands. It also cost me several days of inspection time to make absolutely certain there were no other surprises hidden in the electrical system. I scrupulously detailed the incident in writing, took photos, enclosed copies of the logbook and sent it all to the FAA in hopes they might be able to track down the fool who did the work. Other than a form letter acknowledging my correspondence, I received no reply.

The direct flight route from south Florida to Grand Cayman involved flying through Cuban airspace. Because of the tension between the two countries, special permission had to be granted, in advance, to overfly Cuba through a narrow, north-south corridor not far from the Bay of Pigs. This saved about 500 miles of over-water flying en route to Cayman. When I flew the push-pull through "Castro's Alley" I looked down on Cuba and thought how fortunate I was to be a citizen in a free society. What a beautiful place Cuba must have been to live in - before Batista and Castro - compared to what it had become!

The Cessna 336 could have been designed specifically for me and my air-charter business, especially on the frequent flights to Cayman Brac or Little Cayman. It got off the ground quickly, landed comfortably short, and the centerline thrust of the push-pull engines eliminated the main worry about a faltering engine on takeoff. It also filled the bill, because of the unobstructed downward view from the cabin (under its high wing), when showing real estate parcels from the air during the Cayman "land boom." In addition, it had a huge, low-entry door and rear seats that could be quickly removed for cargo or a litter patient and, over time, proved economical to

operate and maintain. The Skymaster was not a "fast" plane but I was, for example, able to transport a patient (with a doctor or nurse) from Cayman to Jamaica in less than two hours. Translated into reality: including ground-transport time, from hospital to hospital in under three and a half hours! That elapsed time was more than doubled if a plane had to be arranged for and flown over from Kingston. Cayman Flying Service was, literally, a life-saver - several times!

Among the air-ambulance flights is one that will always stick in my mind. Early one morning I received a phone call from Swan Island asking if I could take off immediately and evacuate an injured U.S. merchant seaman. They thought he had a broken neck from a shipboard fall, and his vital signs were not good. A U.S. Coast Guard aircraft responded to the call - only to become bogged down in the mud about one-third of the way up the Swan Island sand and crushed-shell runway. My Skymaster was the only plane within hundreds of miles that the mired-down Coast Guard pilot believed could land and take off on the remaining, treacherous, muddy runway.

As soon as I could get the seats out of the back of the plane, I was in the air!

Swan Island is a mere flyspeck on the map, about 200 miles from Cayman, and at that time the only inhabitants were the U.S. Weather Service personnel. Direct radio communication was impossible that morning, so a northbound Brazilian airliner offered to relay messages between me and the grounded Coast Guard plane! As the Brazilian pilot got nearly out of range, he set up yet another communication relay with a southbound airliner. Remarkably, before landing at Swan - thanks to the invaluable assistance freely offered by pilots I never saw or met - I had been fully informed about the runway obstruction, where the soft areas were and the condition of the patient. It was a memorable experience and a wonderful example of how people spontaneously help each other when the need arises.

When I landed, it was as though a carrier arresting gear grabbed my

plane, so I never let the Skymaster stop until I reached the far end of the runway. I had it almost turned around when a Land Rover drove up with my patient and a Coast Guard medic who had volunteered to fly to Jamaica with the injured seaman. I was down... but, could I get it back up in the air again - with two more people on board?

After I repaired some slight damage, they loaded the litter, strapped the patient down as thoroughly as possible, the medic climbed in - and then my work began in earnest! The rear (pusher) engine is higher above ground than the front one, and gave more propeller clearance from the mud, sand, shells and standing water, so I attempted to taxi with the rear engine alone. The plane wouldn't even budge, with almost full power on the rear engine! If I added very much power with the front (puller) engine I could easily have damaged the propeller with pieces of shell or sod and we'd be stuck there, with the runway now effectively blocked at both ends. Also, don't forget, we had a critically-injured man on board.

U.S. Coast Guard aircrews are acutely aware of the danger of a spinning aircraft propeller, but this group of very special guys offered to try to push the plane - with both engines running and the rear prop spinning dangerously close to their heads - until the 336 was aimed down the runway. They offered to continue pushing until I could get up a little speed, add front-engine power and attempt a takeoff. Only "plane people" can visualize how hazardous this would be! One slip in the muddy footing could throw a man into the prop, killing him instantly. I explicitly pointed this out to them, and their pilot asked them to think about it very seriously. They did, and with no hesitation again asked me to let them take a crack at it. I was scared stiff!

To everyone's relief, it worked. Those gutsy men got me moving. I gave the front engine full-power as soon as I dared - no one fell or got hurt

- and somehow I got into the air and headed for Jamaica! You'll never convince me that the gods and my "giants" weren't right there, pushing, too!

But it wasn't quite over yet. It was 450 miles or so to Kingston, the weather there was lousy and the patient was causing the medic a lot of concern. As I neared Jamaica I was informed that air traffic was badly stacked up, but when I explained our situation and the condition of the patient, once again everyone jumped in to help. Traffic was diverted and I was granted immediate landing clearance and priority taxiing. On the ground an ambulance was standing by to transport the patient to the hospital, as the Jamaicans say, "Post haste, Mon!"

[Author's note: The patient not only survived, but within a year was back at sea and able to work normally. On the next trip that the Coast Guard crew made to Cayman, Sands Sherwood and I celebrated by treating them to a nice dinner at the Cayman Arms.]

Search flights, for overdue fishermen or yachtsmen, were not common, but I was able to help out a few times. Again, the unobstructed view from the cabin made it much easier to see and the extended range at slow speeds was a great asset. All in all, the "push-pull" was an ideal island charter aircraft, and mine served me, and the islands, well.

[Historical note: The Cessna 336 Skymaster was first flown in 1961, production started in 1963 and, in two years, 197 were built. In 1965, the factory switched over to the 337 model (with retractable landing gear), and by the end of 1978 production had reached 1,889 aircraft, including 84 built in France. In confirmation of its versatility, the reader should realize that over 540 military versions were delivered to the U.S. and Iranian air forces, designated as O-2A or O-2B. In 1989, twenty-eight years after its first flight, five air forces were still using the aircraft. A remarkable history, for an aircraft originally designed basically for civilian use.]

The Cessna Aircraft Company took note of my activity in Cayman and invited me to tour, along with a company ferry pilot, some of the other Caribbean Islands and demonstrate their new Cardinal and Aerobat models to prospective customers. The Cardinal was a four-place, single-engine plane designed as an improvement upon the 172. The Aerobat was essentially a beefed-up 150 trainer, suitable for elementary aerobatic flying.

The trip was lots of fun. We started visiting flying schools and charter services in the U.S. Virgin Islands and, from there, went to Guadalupe, Martinique and right on down the island chain to my dad's birthplace, Barbados. We spent no less than a couple of days at each stop and invited local pilots to fly both aircraft (free) for evaluation purposes. None were permitted to fly solo because of insurance restrictions, and because I had an instructor's rating I rode the right-hand seat. I had two parachutes with me, so I gave several flying-club instructors an aerobatic flight and/or some aerobatic instruction in the Aerobat. This was a real selling point for Cessna since there were very few planes, suitable and certified for aerobatics, anywhere in the Carribean at that time.

On Martinique, the local flying club reciprocated by graciously inviting me to fly its single-place Fournier powered sailplane. It was my first experience in such a plane and was one pleasant surprise after another. To begin with, it was "functional but graceful," with a slender fuselage, high-aspect-ratio wings, a canopy and, lo and behold, a Volkswagen Beetle engine up front. The single main-wheel landing gear was assisted by wingtip skids that kept the wings from touching the ground.

Inside the cockpit were two landing-gear levers - one to lock/unlock the gear and the other to retract/extend it - and a third lever which operated the spoilers. Additionally, a T-shaped handle protruded from the panel – to move the prop to the horizontal (lowest drag) position when flying power-off and to assist in engine air starts.

The Fournier sailplane was originally designed by a Frenchman, Rene Fournier, initially financed by a Belgian count, and first built in an Alpine town named Gap. Later models were manufactured in West Germany. Now, here I was - an American, operating out of a British Crown Colony, flying the plane on a French island, in the Caribbean!

Takeoff seemed practically instantaneous and the climb with the little 1,100-cc engine was satisfactory. Following the climb I shut off the engine, got the prop stopped and horizontal, quickly became used to the feel of the slightly-heavy ailerons, and soared and flew through slow and stately aerobatics until I'd bled off the altitude. Then I simply dove to pick up a little speed, yanked on the starter and did it again... and again. The plane was so aerodynamically clean that it picked up speed startlingly fast, especially coming out of a loop, but a touch of the spoilers kept things easily within safe operating speeds. Approach and landing were as easy as apple pie. Did I have a good time? I posi-damn-tively had a ball!

I've often wished I could have had one for myself - just to bore holes in sky when I felt like it. A "Homesick Angel" It was not; but it seemed, especially in the convection currents that day, like a bird enjoying itself - reluctant to return to land.

After the tour, I returned to Cayman and almost immediately went to the States again. This time I ferried a twin Beech down from Texas, and used it for charter business on an hourly-lease basis from the owner. Later, while flying this plane on a charter flight, Carleton Bodden (one of the fine local young men I had trained who had gotten his U.S. commercial license), never arrived in Miami. He is still listed as "missing on a flight over Cuba."

Soon, because business continued to grow, I hired an assistant instructor, Harry Ison, which gave me more time to become involved in some real-estate ventures with an acquaintance who was to become one of my very best friends, Clyde Daniels.

Clyde was from Oklahoma City, retired from the FAA, a competent engineer and former private pilot. He was also a perceptive investor and entrepreneur who recognized the need for some innovative real-estate development.

Traditionally, in the Cayman Islands, there were almost no mortgages, installment plans, automobile financing or credit cards used by the majority of the local people. Property was purchased for cash, and building done when money was on hand to pay for it. Automobiles, purchased in Miami, were paid for on the spot and shipped to the island by freighter.

Clyde and I were among the first to purchase a relatively large bit of land, survey and divide it into small house lots for subsequent sale to the local people on a small monthly-payment basis. The Caymanian compulsion to "own a small piece of land" was attainable, at last - because we had put in roads and were selling parcels of land they could get to and afford. Our subdivisions prospered.

I continued to fly - having a second instructor, more charter work than teaching - and increased my trips to the other islands, Cayman Brac and Little Cayman. They both had airstrips but no radio-navigation aids. Even though only about 100 miles from Grand Cayman, being small and low, they were sometimes difficult to locate in bad weather. This was also the case when the sky was filled with low, puffy clouds whose shadows on the water resembled islands, until you got near them.

Through Clyde's influence and contacts in the FAA, we were able to obtain an ADF transmitter as a "permanent loan" from the U.S. Government to the Cayman Islands. Clyde installed, tested and put it into service. My contribution consisted of flying it (and him) over to the Brac and handing him the tools he needed. Now all pilots could more easily locate the little

islands, and flying to either the Brac or Little Cayman was a pleasure instead of a chore.

As in the past, when the challenge of my work was lessening, I became restless and was looking for something new to keep me busy. LACSA Airlines ran very low-cost, round-trip flights between Grand Cayman and Costa Rica and, after visiting several times and enjoying every minute of each trip, the Daniels and the Armstrongs decided to relocate there and build an "urbanization" (housing development). I sold the Cayman Flying Service to a group of local pilots - most of whom I had trained - rented our beach house, started to learn Spanish (not very successfully, although I never went hungry) and moved.

Costa Rica was, and is, a beautiful country with absolutely charming people. Its illiteracy rate is far lower than in the States, many speak English and the democratic government (patterned after the U.S., with executive, judicial and legislative branches) serves the people very well. Voter turnout in every election is more than *double* that in our country. Welfare rolls, at that time, were low and the government gave wonderful incentives to *pensionados* (foreign retirees) who wanted to live there.

Clyde and I scouted the countryside with borrowed Cessnas. We finally found a well-situated farm, bought it, created *Colonia del Prado* and built homes for ourselves and our clients in a small country-club atmosphere. For three years we had a wonderful time. We rammed all over the country in our big Land Rover; I also did some folk dancing and taught American squares and contras in San Jose. We both enjoyed lots of fabulous fishing (rainbow and German brown trout are plentiful in a few of the rivers and streams) and did some great bird hunting. Most importantly, however, we were privileged to meet and make friends with many wonderful people.

Even though Marie had gone to school, becoming fluent in Spanish and involved in the local community, once

again, I had itchy feet. WGUL was growing by leaps and bounds - we had added an FM station - and I felt a need to hold the reins again. With mixed emotions, we sold our lovely home, said *adios* to our friends and returned to Florida.

When I first arrived in the States, I realized I would be facing an extremely difficult and momentous decision. Flying had been a major factor in my life since I was thirteen years old. I had undeniably been an excellent pilot because I worked hard at doing it properly, kept myself in good condition, maintained my aircraft well, and tried my very best to refrain from doing stupid things.

Now I was returning from the hinterlands into an air-traffic system that had grown and changed almost beyond belief, into a smothering morass of regulations and restrictions. I fully understood the obvious necessity for all of this while, at the same time, I was infinitely saddened by it.

The freedom of flying that I had enjoyed during my formative years was gone forever. The challenges of my test-flying career had been faced, conquered and comfortably relegated to cubby-holes in the corners of my mind. The unfettered flying throughout the Caribbean and teaching in a non-competitive atmosphere joined many other wonderful memories.

It all seemed that, maybe, this would be a good time to step aside. So I decided not to renew my medical certificate. I could always "bore holes in the sky" with a friend, or paddle around in an ultralight now and then. And, if I quit flying now, most of my recollections would be good ones.

I had done something very few had ever been privileged to do - *I HAD A DREAM, AND I LIVED IT.* Now, it was time to say thanks, once again, to my "giants" and move on.

CHAPTER 17

FLIGHT TESTING - THEN AND NOW

Fifty years have flown into history since I made the structural dive demonstration flights on the Curtiss XP-60D. One of the objectives of this book is to give readers an accurate understanding of the test flights of the 1940s: to visualize how the tests were conducted; what it felt like to be the test pilot; how and what information was collected and, most of all, to be aware of the almost unbelievable risks quietly assumed by the pilots.

The purpose of this chapter is to call attention to the changes in the methods and equipment used to garner test data, to the fantastic differences in the amount of information gathered and to the incredible improvement in the realm of flight-test safety. Risks, willingly assumed five decades ago, and the horrifying attrition of aircraft and pilots that accompanied them, would be totally unacceptable today.

In addition, this chapter will probably amaze and enlighten those of my peers who are still with us. They will be able to compare a half-century of progress, and a few may be surprised by the differences in preparation and pilot training. Some may have difficulty in comprehending, for example, the methods and equipment used today, especially how much data is obtainable in each microsecond of every flight. But one thing is certain, they'll all be delighted to learn some of the reasons that so few aircraft or test pilots are lost in contemporary developmental programs, as well as more about how the pilots are warned before a failure in equipment or judgment occurs. We, the "old-timers," can continue to be proud of the contributions we made and, at the same time, be pleased for the test pilots who are carrying the torch today.

In order to compare effectively the programs of the 1940s to those of fifty years later, it was obviously necessary for me to refer to incidents in previous chapters - tests that I flew personally - and then try to relate them to the methods and equipment in use today. To portray events from my era was relatively easy, but I needed an accurate and authoritative source for comparative procedures in the 1990s. I found it, and made a friend, when I met Mr. J. W. "Bill" Rymer, the head of the Telemetry Data Systems Department at the Naval Air Warfare Center Aircraft Division in Maryland.

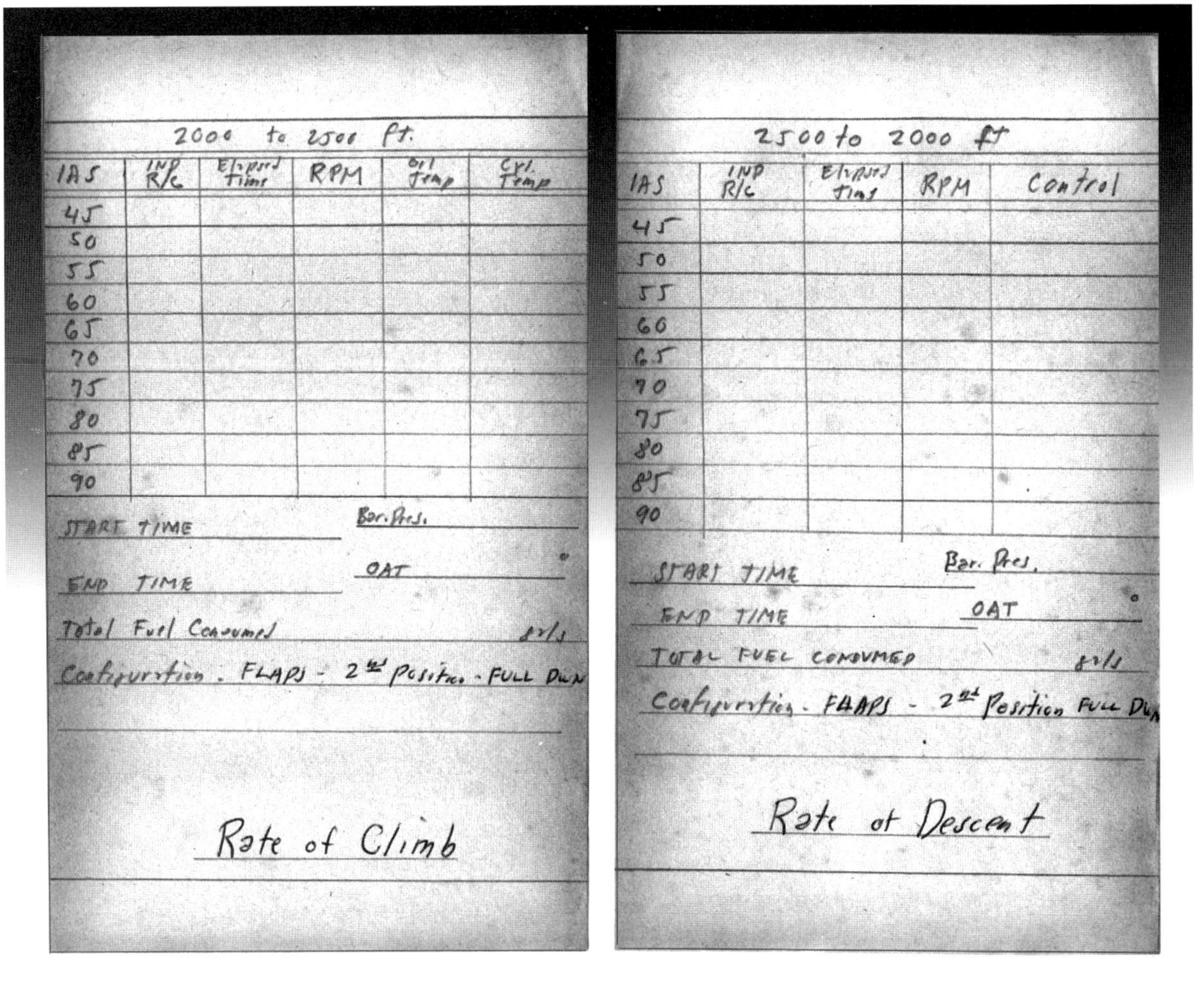

17a Kneepad performance charts - two examples. The earlier handmade one shows how elementary data-gathering once was: only two or three objectives, obtained in small increments, could be tabulated on an ascent and decent...

2000 to 2500 ft.					
IAS	IND R/C	Elapsed time	RPM	Oil Temp	Cyl. Temp
45					
50					
55					
60					
65					
70					
75					
80					
85					
90					

START TIME _____ Bar. Pres. _____

END TIME _____ OAT _____ °

Total Fuel Consumed _____ l/s

Configuration - FLAPS - 2nd Position - FULL DWN

Rate of Climb

2500 to 2000 ft				
IAS	IND R/C	Elapsed time	RPM	Control
45				
50				
55				
60				
65				
70				
75				
80				
85				
90				

START TIME _____ Bar. Pres. _____

END TIME _____ OAT _____ °

TOTAL FUEL CONSUMED _____ l/s

Configuration - FLAPS - 2nd Position FULL DWN

Rate of Descent

There'll be much more about - and from - him later. But for now, let me take you back again to 1943 and recall the events to which I shall refer. Then, I hope, you'll be better able to see them in their proper perspective and compare them with the "now" portion of this chapter.

To keep in the correct time frame I refer you to the events in Chapter 8. You might wish to glance at it again, as we proceed. It is devoted to the final stages of the developmental and demonstration flights of the XP-60D (AAF serial 41-19508).

For flight No. 211 (the last test flight) the test requirements were two-fold: could the airplane be controlled at the contractually specified design speeds and would it stay together if it did? No "multi-discipline" items of infor-mation were requested, nor could any have been obtained. We had our hands full without adding anything extra!

Ground facilities were minimal, consisting primarily of a company radio station (in my case, call-letters 53-Y) enabling me to communicate dur-ing the dive. Once the dive was started, the ground never interrupted by trying to communicate with me. My trans-missions were recorded on every dive and I still have a ten-inch record of my voice during that last dive - you can actually hear the aircraft breaking up! In any event, intervention from the ground was totally impractical - ground observers might be able to watch the aircraft through binoculars or a theodo-lite, but they could not even hope to see anything that was significant enough to assist the pilot.

"Instrumentation," the very best available at that time, was all *on-board* and included the following:

1) An oscillograph to record graphically the readings from four strain gauges on the wings (two on each side), one on a main beam in the fuselage between the wings and one on the elevator arm - a total of only six. (A good photo of an oscillograph is in Exhibit 17e, a pick-up for the unit is shown in Exhibit 17f and an excellent graph obtained from an actual dive test may be examined in Exhibit 17c. The photo in Exhibit 17g shows an aileron position transmitter whose readings were also recorded on Exhibit 17c.)

2) A photo observer (actually a 35mm camera and a separate small instrument panel in a box) was posi-tioned in the fuselage behind the pilot. During the dive, this continuously photographed the faces of an altime-

On the printed (production test) card there was space where more pieces of information could be recorded. In both cases, however, all of this had to be done by the pilot. (D. Armstrong collection)

139

ter, outside air temperature gauge, sensitive airspeed indicator, accelerometer (Gs), and elevator deflection and elevator balance-tab position instruments. Again, only six items - a total, now, of twelve!

3) A V-G recorder, like the one shown in Exhibit 17d, which kept a record, created by a stylus scratching a line on a small piece of smoked glass, of speed vs G-load. (See the result in Exhibit 17b.) This instrument, specified in the contract, was really only a "confirmation instrument" and added no extra data.

4) A pilot's kneepad on which I was to notate any comments after a successful dive. I didn't write a damn thing during that final dive, or after the tail came off! But, I didn't drop or lose it either. My daughter Terry still has that same old kneepad!

Take a few seconds to fix this fact in your mind: the total number of information items collected was only twelve, none of which was available to the engineers on the ground during the flight! Fortunately, although the aircraft crashed, the majority of the on-board test data was recovered, since the wreckage did not burn. But, as in all fighter-plane dive tests of that era, the data could be analyzed only *after* the flight. Had the information not been recovered, because there was nothing transmitted to the ground at that time, no material could

have been studied and very little determined about the cause of the failure.

"Safety of the flight" was then, and remains now, the prime concern. However, fifty years ago, the concern for safety could be addressed only *before* the flight. The ground crew prepared the aircraft to the very best of their ability. The engineers tried in every possible way to *predict* what might happen and inform the pilot of all known contingencies.

During the dive itself the chase pilot couldn't help much, except to confirm visually something that already had happened. After the flight, all the data was analyzed, new guesstimates arrived at and the whole process repeated itself. In the event that after-flight inspection revealed no structural damage, but there was still a suspicion that the airframe had been bent or twisted, the usual way to check it was to measure distances between extremities of the plane, thereby ascertaining if any permanent deflection had occurred. Primitive, you say - but it's all we could do. Later, Bill will share with you what a far cry this is from the "early warning" of testing today.

The only real-time information came from the pilot's radioed observations, or from something visually noticed by a chase pilot. By the time I could notify the ground about severe

buffeting or porpoising, I was already attempting a recovery. So, even in this circumstance, the term "real-time" was not truly applicable - it was actually after-the-fact reporting.

"Tracking" was only what could be "eye-balled" from the ground and was so poor that some "X" planes crashed and could be found only after a farmer or passer-by reported having seen them.

Today, information is collected so fast that it routinely enables engineers on the ground to call for, if necessary, the repeat of a portion of a test. Sometimes in a simple performance test, thanks to Doc Gerhardt, I was able to work up data and find a particular point, or run, that needed repeating, but only a few pilots could do so. This was the exception rather than the rule.

Today, as Bill Rymer will tell you a little later, a simulator not only familiarizes a pilot with a test aircraft, but it actually enables him or her to "fly" the test without leaving the ground. My first simulator experience was in a Link Trainer - to practice instrument flying and radio navigation. Again, years later, before flying the F9F-2 jet fighter, I went to the Naval Air Station at Jacksonville, Florida, and "flew" the F9F simulator, until I felt comfortable about strapping myself into the real thing for the ferry flight and subsequent dive tests. In 1951 I could get to know the plane in advance but I couldn't simulate on the ground, for any practical, evaluative or comparative purpose, the tests I was about to conduct in the aircraft itself.

It is also nearly impossible to visualize the phenomenal differences between the number, and availability, of items of information obtained from flight tests "then, and now." Equally amazing is how, and in what manner and form, the informa-

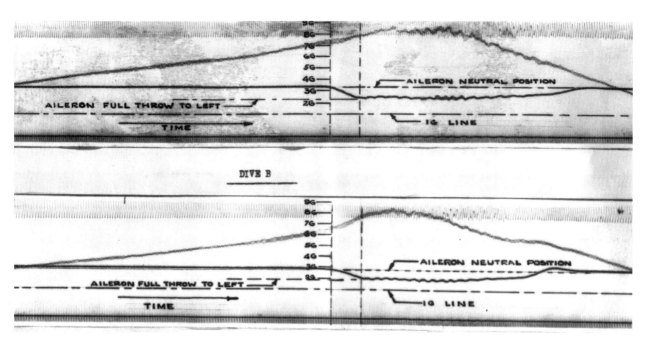

AILERON NEUTRAL POSITION

AILERON FULL THROW TO LEFT

TIME

IG LINE

DIVE B

AILERON NEUTRAL POSITION

AILERON FULL THROW TO LEFT

TIME

IG LINE

17c An example of a rolling-pullout oscillograph record, recording aileron position vs time. (D. Armstrong collection)

tion is made accessible for the decision makers. During WW II all of the data from an entire test (without any accompanying charts, photos and graphs) might average less than twenty-five printed pages. On top of this, it might have taken weeks to reduce (adjust, correct, plot) the information to presentable form. Today, in contrast, there are millions of data samples to glean from - available on disk, already reduced and, on demand, immediately available for print-out!

Bill Rymer may astonish you as he shares some of the wondrous flight test methods, and results, at Pax today. Moreover, when you are reading his "now" part of this chapter, try to remember how it was "way back then."

How did this come to pass? How did Bill Rymer become involved in my look into the past?

In April 1993, I was an invited guest at the 50th Anniversary celebration of the Patuxent River Naval Air Station. One week later I had the privilege of being shown through the Telemetry Data Systems Department at the Naval Air Warfare Center Aircraft Division. It was a memorable visit for several reasons. First, of course, was seeing the facility and, once again, being absolutely astounded by its capabilities. A unit like this, with its information-gathering potential, was far beyond the wildest imagination of the test engineers when I was

actively testing aircraft. Yet, in fifty years, what would have been construed "then" as pure science fiction was "now" a fully functioning reality.

After recovering from sensory overload, my next conscious reaction was one of unmitigated pleasure, and a deep sense of gratitude, in response to the staff, and the courtesies they extended to me. They freely gave of themselves, not simply showing me around, and but took extra time and made a sincere effort to answer my questions in terms that I could understand. It was truly something special. Here I was, a test pilot who had last flown at Pax forty-two years previously, being given a gracious reception worthy of someone far more important than I. There'll always be a warm spot in my heart - for what those kind, and keenly perceptive, people did for me that day.

But, there was more! The highlight of the day was meeting and chatting with the head of the department, Bill Rymer. By the time our conversation got around to my book, I had already realized that I was totally unqualified to write the "now" portion of this chapter. In short, I asked Bill to help, eventually asking him to actually write it. To my great pleasure, he agreed, and provided what appears in this chapter. I feel greatly privileged and honored by his contribution!

Now let me introduce you to Bill, then he'll take over from here.

J. W. "Bill" Rymer (BSEE, West Virginia University, 1966; MSEE, Purdue, 1967) began work at Patuxent River, Maryland, in 1962, in the Data Systems Lab of Flight Test Instrumentation. He did electronics interface work for Purdue's Lab for Applications of Remote Sensing in 1967 and did acceptance testing on Grumman's Automated Telemetry System in 1969. He wrote the specifications and procured the Real-time Telemetry Processing System (RTPS)

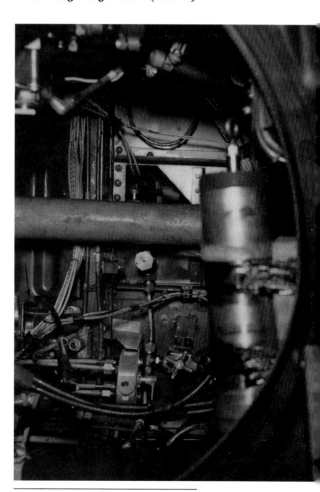

17g) Aileron Position Transmitter. (D. Armstrong collection)

17h) Project engineer station room at the Telemetry Data Center, Patuxent River Naval Air Test Center, Patuxent, Maryland. (Photo by Vernon Pugh)

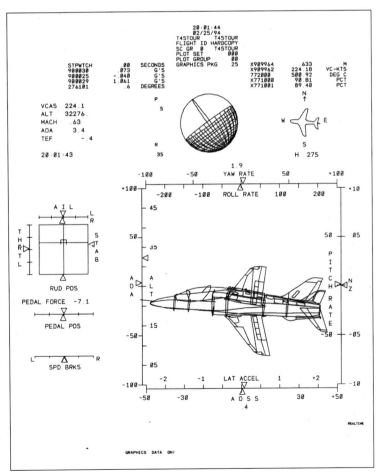

17i) "Hard copy" of a computer-driven picture of the aircraft being tested, along with corresponding data (graphs) "coming down from the aircraft... even though there [are] no optics or cameras around." (Courtesy of NATC Patuxent River, Maryland)

installed by Xerox at the Naval Air Test Center, Patuxent River Naval Air Station in 1973. This was the first successful system of its kind in DoD, handling over 20,000 test flights between 1973 and 1989.

He was chairman of the RCC "IRIG" Telemetry Group in 1990-1991 and remains chairman of its Data Multiplex Committee, producing standards in the telemetry field. He has guest-lectured on data systems at the Navy's Test Pilot School for twelve years. He is currently head of Patuxent's Telemetry Data Systems Department.

Mr. Rymer's father Hubert was a Marine, killed on Iwo Jima in WW II. Bill has two daughters - Ann and Amy - and resides with Carolyn, his patient wife of over twenty-five years, in Lexington Park, Maryland.

Ingenuity Is The Most Important Thing

by J. W. "Bill" Rymer

What if a Naval aircraft dive demonstration were conducted today? Since the WW II era, with a short pause in the late 1940s, data demands have grown at an exponential pace. Test requirements, instrumentation and ground facilities have evolved with steadily increasing complexity and sophistication. Telemetry - wherein thousands of measurements are radioed to the ground - has become a major player. Multi-discipline testing has become common, where the flight-control systems, propulsion, flying qualities and weapons release people are all likely to be involved in a single test. As a result, this hypotheti-cal dive demo in the 1990s includes a wide array of high-tech gizmos, real-time (e.g., immediately as it happens) computer facilities, laser tracking devices, pull-up cues radioed to the pilot, safety-of-flight limit checking and project engineers driven to extract the last ounce of data from the event.

In many ways the basics have not changed. The test objectives have to be clear. The test plan has to be approved and the instrumentation must work or we get only qualitative (read that informed but speculative) answers. The priorities are still the same. Safety of flight has to come first. Second is getting the most possible out of the flight. Third is getting the report written and the answers to the decision makers.

The basic "measureands" or "parameters" (one "measureand" is altitude, another is airspeed or acceleration or temperature or pressure) sought by the project engineers are still the same. While today's data customer may be picking from over 2,000 measureands, a cursory glance at the measureands on the 1940s dive demo shows gross weight, center of gravity, altitude, airspeed, Mach number, acceleration, lift and drag coefficients, engine rpm, stick force and dive angle on the list of tabulated dive data.

The exact measureands are of interest in 1994. Now, more are directly measured and are looked at in real time. Now they are corrected to standard temperatures and pressures, processed to minimize instrumentation imperfections and scaled to engineering units in *less than five microseconds per sample* for easy reading. ("Scaling to engineering units" or "engineering unit conversion" is conversion from the internal terms of instrumentation to the terms directly appreciated by the user of the data. For example, in your car the engine temperature is routed around under the dash as a voltage on a wire and the gauge on your dash converts that voltage to degrees Fahrenheit which are your engineering units.) Today, most data handling is digital instead of analog, meaning that the data consists of samples, each in a pattern of discrete ones and zeros, rather than continuously changing voltages.

Measureands may be fed to many different equations, and many different "derived measurements" may be made out of those directly measured. They may be alongside hundreds, or even thousands, of other measureands - but the physics did not change - the basic measureands are still the same ones. In general, the transducers (the "sensors") are much more stable, deliver greater precision and "drift" less than in 1973 and much less than in 1943. Impressive strides were made during NASA's boom years with the space program in terms of miniature transducers, lightweight instrumentation, types of direct measureands, packaging, power consumption, reliability, etc. This continues to improve and

make possible many of the things which are invisible until the "bits" of data reach the ground station.

Don't forget i n g e n u i t y . Rudimentary temperature and pressure corrections were already being done with instrumentation in the mid-1940s according to author Don Armstrong. Considering what they had to work with, I am convinced that more ingenuity was exercised then than now, especially per capita!

How does that telemetry ("TM") data get to the ground? The earliest known Navy telemetry was a very few parameters using frequency modulation (FM) near the end of WW II. Yes, FM means the same thing here that it does for station KDKA. Your FM stereo has two parameters it "demultiplexes" from the received signal - namely left and right sound. The basic TM mechanism is to combine several measureands in the test vehicle into a single signal (a process called "multiplexing") and transmit that signal to the ground antennas' receivers and processing equipment over a radio link. On the ground, the measureands are separated back to their original identity ("demultiplexing"). The data gets to the ground

17k) MMSC-800 encoder. A 1990s state-of-the-art airborne instrument "capable of handling as many as 8,196 measurands in simple format and several times that number in more complex, expanded configurations... with a data rate capability up to ten-million bits per second." (Courtesy of Aydin-Vector Corporation)

just the same way that your TV or radio signal gets to your home set.

Why or how radio transmission works is not known. It is fascinating to see crowds of highly-educated doctoral degree people clamor over that one. Endless descriptive material explains terms, quantifies characteristics, describes what is happening (but not how or why) and sounds official. If you pin them down with ever-more incisive questions, the truth is no one *really* knows how or why radio works - even at the most fundamental level. We do know that it works.

Ingenuity is always the ingredient that separates the winners from the also-rans. There is a very strong case for the idea that it took more ingenuity to pull off this dive demo in 1943 than in 1994. The engineers needed to see a cross-plot of acceleration vs airspeed to document the maneuver and the "envelope," or the extremes. Don Armstrong shows how, in 1943, a stylus was used to scratch off the carbon on smoked glass, on a background grid of numbers, to produce a cross-plot in the aircraft.

In 1968 I was plotting such cross-

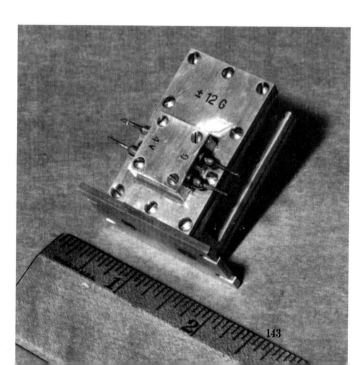

17f Acceleration pickup for oscillograph. In the mid-1940s this instrument electronically gathered and fed acceleration measurements into the oscillograph unit - essentially a single item of information. For comparison, see the Encoder in Exhibit 17k. (D. Armstrong collection)

17d Installation of the V-G, G-A (speed vs G load, G load vs altitude) recorders and airspeed balancing cans. (D. Armstrong collection)

plots on a pen-and-ink plotter driven by analog voltages in a ground station at the Naval Air Test Center, Pax River, Maryland. The paper was held down by a vacuum pump and the signals came from instrumentation that allowed up to forty-five measureands twenty times per second or, as a tradeoff, ninety measureands ten times a second.

In 1994, my data customers, who are project engineers, merely type in the name of any measurements they wish to cross-plot against any other named measurement on a computer screen - and it happens! (This feature has been available since 1973.) The data may be displayed by computer-driven graphics, tabular displays, time-history traces on graph paper, printers and various other devices. Data is normally being plotted in a "ground station" as much

as two hundred miles from the test aircraft. If they want it for their report, a special interface zips the signals to a laser printer and a report-quality hardcopy emerges for the notebook.

On one current project-instrumentation, these measurements would be selected from among *1,931* available, from a telemetry signal at *two million bits of data per second* and from a wide selection of possible

sampling rates. This example project is not stretching the state of the art nor is it the highest data rate in use today.

Because of the exponential increase in the number of measureands, number of samples per second and large number of instrumented test aircraft, a strong argument can be made that ninety-five percent of all samples - of aircraft and aircraft weapons system test data gathered by mankind - have been gathered since 1970. Progression from 60 measureands on A-7A testing, to 160 on F-4B and 400 on F-14A testing was documented in 1972 ["What Real-time Testing Should Offer," AIAA paper 72-783, J. W. Rymer, 8/8/72].

The "mux bus" (a standardized digital means of sharing and routing thousands of samples and commands around an aircraft on a single cable) which became commonplace in the late 1970s has radically accelerated that data explosion. According to Air Force officials, more data was collected on the first six flights of the B-2 program than on the entire duration of the F-16 testing at Edwards AFB, California. As many as ten thousand measureands are telemetered from the B-2 [*Aviation Week*, 5/10/93, p. 58]. If you are wondering how the humans absorb all that, they don't! If you are wondering whether they sometimes get bewildered by what is available and lose sight of the point, you are right - they do! Fortunately, the machines do a much better job, today, of assisting and allowing the humans to "manage by exception."

17j) Range control room at the Chesapeake Test Range, Patuxent River Naval Air Test Center, Patuxent, Maryland. (Photo by Vernon Pugh)

In the modern data display room, about one hundred measurements are being concurrently displayed, for viewing by about fifteen to twenty project engineers. They change which ones they wish to look at, or concentrate upon, many times during the flight. An audible alarm warns them when a limit has been reached. A bar chart turns yellow when close to limits and red when over limits. Figures blink at the customers when needing attention. The system may check as many as 2,000 potential limits concurrently. A half-dozen different disciplines, two or three companies and two or three organizations may well be in the room simultaneously monitoring the test data.

While this test proceeds in 1994 (or any time since the early 1980s) a computer-driven figure of the aircraft moves in step with the data coming down from the aircraft. When the pilot performs the roll-out at the end of the hypothetical dive demo, a project engineer is "watching" the aircraft via a computer-driven picture that responds to the data even though there may be no optics or cameras around. If there were proper instrumentation, the user might view the actions of parts of the aircraft or subsystems or even a flow chart of valves and fluid paths within the aircraft, much as the operator of a nuclear power plant monitors the conditions of valves, fuel, fluids and safety mechanisms. One might watch control surfaces, structural flexing, vibratory limits or any of a wide variety of phenomenon limited primarily by human ingenuity (and money, and taxes). The test director may also save considerable money and time in the test schedule by knowing the answers in real time; by sorting good data from bad; by telling whether the objective was met before landing; by avoiding unnecessary repeats and by effectively extracting so much from each test flight.

Meanwhile, where is it? What path or "track" did the aircraft take? What is the exact trajectory of the weapon released during that dive? What was its exact impact point? Test Range devices such as the laser tracker or instrumentation radar are sensing the track information and it is being plotted - in real time - on a wall-sized, computer-driven screen, against a precise background map of the test area. The range controller has directed the aircraft to a push over point and given a verbal go-ahead, by voice link, to the pilot for the dive. Special software begins to execute, watching that the pilot does not get into too steep a dive, at too great a speed, with too little ability to pull up. The specific characteristics of the aircraft, of the air density, of the weapon being carried, of the weight of the fuel remaining, of the limits of the airframe structure - and a myriad of other factors - can all be taken into account. The most apparent result of all this is preservation of life and of the multi-million dollar aircraft. A "pull-up cue" is radioed to the pilot in case he gets too aggressively headed for the ground. In the rare event of a problem (or the thankfully very rare event of a crash) one hundred percent of the data is usually recorded on the ground via telemetry and by range instrumentation.

In 1994, the project engineer/test pilot team may "fly" that dive many times on the simulator before actually committing aircraft or life. (During the test flight they will also compare, in real time, the simulator results alongside the actual results. They can also compare against fixed boundaries such as wind-tunnel data.) The Manned Flight Simulator at Patuxent River is a full-scale, man-in-the-loop facility, using fully-configured aircraft cockpits to test scenarios and to train personnel. The visual aids include "view from the cockpit" as well as "six degrees of freedom" motion base for realistic feel. This means that the person in the simulator both sees (a computer-drawn image) what one would see out the windows of the test aircraft and feels many of the motions in each axis. The cockpits are modules that are changed (in fact, made locally) to be realistic for each type of aircraft simulated. The effectiveness of a flight test is greatly enhanced by having done practice runs in the simulator. Though we do not have accurate statistics, we know clearly that "making the test point" is far more likely after the practice runs, especially for the more difficult cases.

In 1994, the new element is being able to analyze and digest both actual and simulated data side-by-side during the flight. The economics of the "plan, simulate, fly and plan again" cycle are impressive. Test flights can cost in the tens of thousands of dollars each. The simulate-and-fly cycle is a very effective tool for major cost savings, for reducing

17e The Heiland Oscillograph. (D. Armstrong collection)

the number of flights needed for a given test objective and for getting more out of each actual test flight.

What if the aircraft manufacturer wants to optimize the use of engineers and specialists at the home plant and it is impractical, or uneconomical, to have all of these people at the test site? In the fall of 1982 sixteen flights (involving three different aircraft types at Edwards Air Force Flight Test Center) were monitored, in real time, at Patuxent River via satellite. Soon afterward Grumman and the X-29 used "satcom" for routine coast-to-coast telemetry transmission. In 1994, multiple Navy test aircraft concurrently send their TM signals "back to the factory" in real time via satellite from Pax River.

The dive demo is over. The customer leaves the ground station for the office in the hangar. What's that in her hands? Optical disks containing the data from the flight which will be studied in greater detail, and her own personal computing favorites applied, back at the office. *About 160 million samples of data are on each disk, but that is only today! Tomorrow there is always more.*

In the next five to ten years I expect Pax River to be the center for consolidation of testing Naval aircraft and related systems. There are likely to be more prototypes to be tested and fewer production aircraft than over the past decade. This will place more emphasis on quantitative and complex testing - not less. The airframe manufacturers are more likely to do their test work at government centers and less likely to invest many millions of scarce dollars per program on test facilities at their plants. I expect to see "purple suit" tests (e.g., those involving tri-service or multi-service projects) become a greater fraction of our workload. This will mean increased "interoperability of testing" where the geographic test location needs to be nearly transparent to the customer.

Standards for these test methods will have to be developed. Communications of all sorts, including expansion of our existing satellite earth station utilization, will become a dominant tool. The battle for frequency spectrum (FCC assignments and channels to transmit on) has already been rough over the last three years, just to minimize encroachment on our existing telemetry bands. Higher data rates which require more frequency space are a fact of life. Over the next decade this is certain to intensify, and Congress may well be deciding tradeoffs between our nation's ability to test aircraft versus mass-market personal communications and pop music by satellite.

[Author's note: I fully realize that it is impossible for anyone not of my generation, nor with test flying experiences during those years, to thoroughly appreciate the monumental changes that have occurred in fifty years of aircraft testing. For me, not having done any experimental flying in over forty years, to return to Pax and see the things that Bill has shared with us, was similar to taking part in a successful cryonic experience. It was like awakening in a new world, surrounded by new machines, and finding people who resembled friends from the past - who spoke the same language, but now with different buzzwords and a brand-new vocabulary. Thank you, Bill - for enlightening us!]

The camaraderie we shared that April afternoon will remain, for the rest of my life, among my most treasured memories. It was almost as though we had known each other for years and each was "transported," for a brief moment in time, into the other's world.

As incredible as some of Bill's technology and experiences sounded to me so, to Bill, were some of the methods, devices and instruments that I used in the 1940s. For example, when I explained to him that we determined take-off distance by rigging up a shotgun-like device that automatically fired a "load" of ordinary baking flour onto the runway when the wheels lifted off the ground, he chuckled. And he laughed out loud with me when I told him I measured landing roll in a Fleet biplane (fitted with experimental brakes) by hand-firing a sawed-off, small-bore shotgun - similarly loaded - downward from the cockpit as I touched down, then simply measured the distance on the runway from the "white spot" to where the plane stopped.

Today's "equipment," Bill pointed out, was just a little (?) more expensive. They determine takeoff or landing distances with a laser tracker!

Were both of our methods accurate? Of course. But from a practical standpoint, we agreed that one method was just as good as the other.

It was a fun afternoon. Two different generations and two different viewpoints. I had been the one in the cockpit. He was the man on the ground. Our quests, though, remained the same - good test results, safely obtained. Then... and now...

CHAPTER 18

WHAT IT ALL MEANT TO ME

It's been warm and comfortable sitting around the fireplace and chatting... and staring into the glowing embers with you has been a great deal like finding long forgotten photo albums and scrapbooks in the attic at the old family place.

For my part, it's brought back many memories and, thankfully, the passing of years has dulled the pain of the sad ones, while multiplying the joys of the good ones. For you, who knows? Most of all, I sincerely hope that you're glad you dropped in for a visit - and that you've enjoyed the listening as much as I've enjoyed the telling.

We've added quite a few logs to the fire since I first welcomed you at my hearth and invited you to pull off your shoes, put up your feet and relax and listen to some stories. I've shared my life with you, not just because it was "my" life, but because it gave me an opportunity to take you back in time. I wanted you to walk hand-in-hand with me and see, through my eyes, an era of aviation which only someone who had lived it - like myself - could hope to portray.

The advances made during the first fifty years of aviation were achieved primarily because of the indomitable spirit of men and women who were willing and eager to accept the risks of the unknown in order to conquer their last frontier - flight. Now - and I say this without recrimination or sadness - technology is replacing much of that human spirit. We have to accept this - it is an inevitable, natural phase of our evolution. But, as we continue into the future, it also behooves us to think back to our beginnings and remember those years, those methods, those machines. And, most important of all, those men and women who "flew them first."

As my story unfolded, I've shared only what I could recall, pieced together from incomplete memorabilia or squeezed from old friends, faded files and dog-eared reports. As I mentioned in the preface, this is neither an aviation treatise nor an authoritative

text. To a nit-picking historian, it may not always be precisely accurate. But, after all, it was intended solely to be a narrative about my life, my friends and associates and the wonderful years in which we lived and flew, and told as I remember it!

So, let's put one more log on the fire and share a few more moments together. I hope that by now you have greater insight into that era and pilots like myself - what we did; how and why we did it; how we lived; and how some of us died. Perhaps also, now that we've become friends, you'd like to know what it all meant to me.

Thinking first about my formative years, I realize how extremely fortunate I was to have grown up in a time when my parents took the time to be with me, made me feel loved and wanted, and imbued me with confidence in myself and with the career I had chosen so early in my life. Osmosis helped, to be sure; much of what became a part of me I had absorbed from my family environment. But as I matured, I realized more and more just how much time and effort my mother and father unselfishly devoted to preparing me for my future. Without this legacy, so lovingly bestowed upon me by my parents, I cannot imagine what turn my life would have taken.

From childhood into my teens, no one can possibly comprehend the extent of the positive influence Dad's friends - my "giants" - had upon my life. Unfortunately today, Americans don't seem to create many heroes for themselves (except athletes or entertainers) and, to me, this is very sad. Back then many of my aviation heroes were internationally - known household names - and I knew them personally, grew up in their aura and was almost like a nephew to them! How could I not have been inspired by these people? I cannot express how much it meant for me to know, beyond a shadow of a doubt that, as the years went by, neither my dad nor I ever "used," or imposed upon, their friendship to further my career.

It was their acceptance, understanding and support that I drew upon.

Initially, they helped me to believe in myself, and then, as I grew a little older, I began to learn from them. Memories remain vivid today - I see them easily in my mind. I still feel their presence.

When I first went to Texas two separate events had a lifelong effect on me. First, the wonderful, awesome flight when I suddenly realized that flying a plane had become an instinctive act, surfacing from somewhere deep within me - far greater than an acquired skill - and somehow I was destined to be, from that moment on, totally at home in the sky. The second was a gradual recognition that, in order to achieve my goal, I needed to have much more than a pilot's license, because almost anyone can learn to fly! This awakened my career-long pursuit of knowledge and excellence.

Also, as you know, two *other* very special people exerted, each in his own way, a profound influence upon my life. They were, of course, Mr. Bill and Doc Gerhardt. With widely-divergent skills, and from totally different backgrounds, they shared much the same philosophy of life, which they passed along to me. And, they shepherded me through two memorable milestones - one early in my Life, the other early in my Career.

Mr. Bill was the man who carefully and caringly gave me the know-how and confidence to make my first solo flight and, not unlike my own father, painstakingly showed me how to fix things, while always taking time to "just talk."

A decade or so later, Doc took a young, eager-to-learn pilot and patiently, thoroughly and unselfishly molded me into a confident, competent test pilot. In so doing he not only taught me how but, step-by-step, showed me why.

Among my "giants," these two men were unquestionably my severest critics and disciplinarians. Neither could have claimed that they knew me better, and both (one like a father, the other like a teacher) must have loved me. The lift I got from their wings undoubtedly made me a better pilot... and a better person.

Some of the things I did in my career meant a great deal to me professionally while personally they had little, or no, positive effect. My military service gave me an absolutely priceless, unparalleled opportunity to fly an unbelievable variety of high-performance aircraft. In a span of only two years I flew thirty-three different military planes: trainers, bombers, fighters, cargo planes, flying boats; single- and multi-engined; on wheels, floats and skis - some of which were among the best military aircraft in the world. The icing on the cake was the invaluable, *personalized* test-pilot training I was given by Doc Gerhardt! All the applicable adjectives in the dictionary could not embellish the word "opportunity" enough to describe this situation. Yet, military chores (although necessary) were, to me, exactly that - chores: boring, time-consuming and restrictive. Thankfully, because we definitely need them, many people enjoy military life. I did not.

I found myself in almost the same boat while with the CAA, except that the aircraft were mostly civilian planes modified for trainers or liaison use. Admittedly, I honed my testing skills on a couple of performance testing projects and enhanced my experience by flying twenty different types of planes in the nine months I was in Civil Service. But it was even less appealing than the military. Once again, the flying part of my job was fine, and the accompanying paperwork proved interesting when related to specific flights or tests. But the "busy work" - the inane, justify-your-existence reports and the unacceptable wartime waste of time and money - boggled my mind! Bureaucracy is like quicksand: it sucks in and consumes all initiative. The more you fight it, the faster you

are destroyed and, like bacteria in a Petri dish, it grows... and Grows... and GROWS. I honestly don't know how my creative, goal-oriented friends tolerated it. I couldn't!

How can I convey to you how much it meant to me to test the Curtiss, Douglas and Goodyear experimental military planes and, later, the Grumman jet fighter? Put yourself in my place and think about it. I was not even a teenager when I knew I wanted to be a test pilot. I didn't want to be a doctor or a lawyer; I didn't want to be a hero, a hockey player, or even rich or famous. All I wanted to be was a test pilot. And, I was!

Additionally, I must share something special with you. The following comments, written by a fifth-grader from Williamsburg, Virginia, are displayed in the Marine Corps Air/Ground Museum at Quantico:

When I grow up I want to be a test pilot because it's a fun job and easy to do. That's why there are so many pilots flying around.

Pilots don't need much school. They just have to read numbers so they can read their instruments. I guess they should be able to read road maps too so they can find their way if they get lost.

Pilots should be brave so they won't get scared if it's foggy and they can't see or if a wing or motor falls off. They should always stay calm so they will know what to do.

Pilots have to have good eyes to see through the clouds and they can't be afraid of thunder and lightning because they are so much closer to them than we are.

The salary pilots make is another thing I like. They make more money than they know what to do with. This is because most people think that plane flying is dangerous, except pilots don't because they know how easy it is.

I hope I don't get air sick because I get car sick and if I get air sick I couldn't be a pilot and then I would have to go to work.

Every time I read that, I chuckle, and my day is brighter.

To help you understand more of what being a test pilot meant to me I'd like to point out some of the little things, the lagniappe, that came right along with my job and made it more satisfying - especially to my ego. Being at the pinnacle of one's profession - an experimental/demonstration test pilot is at the "top of the heap" - puts a person in a unique position with the company, the community, the industry and throughout the aviation world. If the pilot earned and maintained the respect of the people with whom he worked, that reputation spread and opened doors and avenues that normally might have remained closed to him.

In my case, for example, an insignificant item illustrates the situation quite well. At Goodyear, the executive dining room was reserved for certain department heads, vice-presidents and their guests. I was included on that list early in my first month with the company. All of the other usual "perks" afforded to this level of executive were also mine.

Within the community, I was extended similar courtesies and privileges at athletic, golf and men's clubs, and received invitations to countless social events.

Industry-wide, I could fly almost any plane, at any company. All I had to do was ask. When test flying for four companies, I flew forty-three different military aircraft! (This does not include those flown in the RCAF and the CAA.)

To have flown all of these planes may not be significant to the readers who are not pilots and, if that is the case, may I suggest asking some of your pilot friends how they would like to have had the opportunity to do the same!

To be accepted into the offices, clubs and homes of people who were, in many cases, highly regarded throughout the industry was more than merely a status symbol. It meant new faces, new ideas and stimulating conversations. These were not the also-rans. They were highly-educated, informed, interesting people; they were the achievers. It was always a pleasure to associate with this type of people.

Surprisingly, my "fringe benefits" extend to this day. Here are three that come to mind: fifteen years after my Grumman Panther tests, while living in Grand Cayman, I was asked to travel to Canada (with all expenses paid, plus a reasonable fee) in order to testify in Quebec, as an expert witness, in a highly-technical aviation legal dispute. Upon examination of my credentials, I was permitted to testify without challenge, and was treated with utmost respect and courtesy by both sides of the case. And I certainly enjoyed the Chateau Frontenac and the fine food in Quebec City once again!

Then, in April 1993, while researching this book and visiting the National Archives of Canada and the National Aviation Museum in Ottawa, at the moment the persons in charge realized I was a former experimental test pilot, it was like being given the keys to the city! Were these courtesies really important? Not particularly. Did they mean something to me? Of course. It's very gratifying to be recognized and respected - after all these years.

The third is much more meaningful. After winding up my research in Canada, I went back to Pax to try to ferret out some additional facts about my F9F-2 tests, and improve my very limited knowledge of contemporary test procedures for the "Now" portion of the previous chapter. (Fortunately, Bill Rymer offered to handle that for me!) But, while there, I had an experience that proved to be one of the most gratifying "fringe benefits" of my flying career.

Bill described the Manned Flight Simulator: how valuable it is for test-pilot training and simulating tests before risking pilot or machine. He also pointed out that it has become routine to make side-by-side comparisons between the simulator flight and the "live" test flight - while the flight is actually in progress.

No one but a test pilot from my era could imagine how much I wanted to get into that marvelous machine!

But there's even more. Many of you have seen photos of, or read about, the amazing Bell Boeing V-22, with its wingtip-mounted engines that can be tipped-up for vertical takeoff and landing and leveled for horizontal flight.

Now, picture this: here I was - a seventy-plus year old former test pilot who had learned to fly sixty years earlier, who had last tested an aircraft at Pax in 1952... and who had very little rotary-wing experience. To my great pleasure and honor, I was invited to "fly" the V-22 Manned Flight Simulator! What a rare privilege! Had my reputation opened yet another door after

nearly fifty years?

I could probably write several thousand words about that hour, how it was to be at the controls and how the sensations were amazingly like the real thing; but that's not the subject of this chapter. Instead, I will reflect upon how thoughtfully and considerately Joe Carbonaro and Joe Kleponis first explained the unit, then familiarized me with the controls and handled my "flight" - and how much it meant to me! Was I impressed with the unit? Absolutely, to the extent that I had tears in my eyes when I thought of the loss of so many of my friends, whose deaths could have been avoided with such a simulator, combined with the test methods and equipment described by Bill.

Did I get it in the air and back down again without crashing? You bet I did - several times; but I sure did overcontrol a lot. And, even though I probably gave them cause to, nobody laughed - at least not out loud!

Yes, there is a point to all of this: I hope you can understand how

18a) Bell Boeing V-22, Osprey. No, I didn't fly this amazing machine; I "flew" the simulator. An impressive bird, isn't it? The world's first tilt-rotor convertiplane to enter service. Its wingtip 6,150-shp Allison turboshafts give it a level-flight speed of over 300 knots. I'd sure like to take a crack at the real thing! (Courtesy of NATC Patuxent River, Maryland)

much it meant to me to be treated so courteously and respectfully by these two fine young men. Therefore, to Joe Carbonaro and Joe Kleponis, I say again, from the bottom of my heart, "Thanks, it was a privilege to meet - and `fly' - with you!"

Now, let's dig a little deeper. I'd like to talk about my peers, my test-pilot friends, and what knowing and associating with them meant to me. Even after all these years, it's still a very bitter-sweet subject. I realize that today it must be difficult for someone to fathom the type of relationship that existed between many of the test pilots in the 1940s. We respected and held each other in the highest esteem, cooperated fully with one another, were friends - and yet, as it was among many combat pilots, there was a "holding back," an unwillingness to become close - because we knew that the odds of a lasting friendship were low, to say the least.

I speak now, only for myself, when I say that I resisted closeness more and more, every time one of my peers lost his life. Here were wonderful, vibrant and talented people that I yearned to be closer to but, at the same time, I was afraid to let myself do so. It pains me right now, as I'm writing, to remember the dozens of my friends, my fellow test pilots, who lost their lives. Take a minute, think back, to those I told you about in earlier chapters. So few survived.

On the other side of the coin, however, it's wonderful to remember the pride we shared in our profession, how much we learned from each other, our individual and mutual achievements, the seemingly little things that so many of us did to make our planes safer or better-suited to fulfill their purpose and the fun we had when we got together. It was not a closely-knit fraternity, but there was a bond between us that was wonderful to experience. I am honored to have been one of them.

Test pilots could rightfully be known as "explorers of the air." From early Greek mythology, through the fifteenth century, to the pilots of today's latest experimental aircraft - all have ventured into the unknown.

Long before the Wright Brothers actually flew, men were trying to fly. Did it all, perhaps, start in Crete, with young Icarus, in 1700 B.C.? And what about Leonardo da Vinci (1485), Thomas Walker (1810), Sir George Cayley (1853), Otto Lilienthal (1893), Sir Hiram Maxim (1894), Samuel Pierpont Langley (1896), Alberto Santos-Dumont (1901) - to name but a few? All were visionaries of flight, but were they not also would-be "test pilots?"

Following Orville's flight, along came men and women such as Alessandro Anzani, Louis Bleriot, Octave Chanute, Henry Farman, Lawrence Hargrave, Blanche Scott (credited by many as being the first female aviator), Gabriel Voisin and Edna Gardner Whyte. Of course, there were many others, little known, who "flew them first."

Even while in my teens, I had the privilege to see behind the public facade of many of my friends and "giants." Like my dad and myself, quite a few were rather private people who savored and nurtured their personal lives and family time. Some were voracious readers, others had hobbies that included music, model building or gun or stamp collecting. One of the Curtiss pilots knitted beautiful afghans; two whom I recall did wood working; and, like myself, quite a few enjoyed fishing and hunting. It surprised me to learn that there is, in the archives of the Society of Experimental Test Pilots, a fairly large, unpublished collection of poems by Lloyd Child. (Lloyd was instrumental in getting me my first civilian test-pilot job, at Curtiss.) In all the years I knew him, he kept this facet of his life to himself. By the same token, very few people, even within my family, have ever seen any of my verse.

There's a few embers softly glowing in the fireplace; but I don't think we'll put on another log - my story's almost told.

Having shared so much of my life, you're now aware of the wonderful years that I have enjoyed as a pilot and of how beautifully my dance avocation blended in, became a larger part of my world and, subsequently, developed into a vocation. Initially, of course, flying dominated everything in the unremitting pursuit of my childhood dream - and I

achieved it! Then, unlike many less-favored, my new career also has given me tremendous personal satisfaction.

Do I have regrets? Of course I do. I've made many, and will probably make other, mistakes. When they have hurt someone else, they also hurt me - perhaps even more. And I mourn the loss of my son. I so would have enjoyed sitting around a fire with him as he read this book. But, at a campfire like the ones he loved, perhaps my daughter and I will feel his presence as the moon comes up along Spring Creek. I am sure we'll both cry a little, and remember when...

Now, already past the usual "three-score and ten," I consider myself to be one of the most fortunate people in the world. I was able to earn the means whereby I could choose my lifestyle and have been given the time in which to enjoy it. During most of my life I have been surrounded with people - family and friends - who, although they did not always agree with me, faithfully or lovingly supported most of my endeavors and have been understanding of my whims and tolerant of my faults. I faced danger many, many times, but early on learned to accept fear as part of being human. At the same time, I have never permitted fear to conquer my mind. And, most wonderful of all, after I entrusted my dream to my "giants" as a child, I saw it fulfilled! Who could ask for more?

My "giants" - they all are gone now, but I choose to believe I can reach them still; can thank them one more time.

Looking back in his old age... Isaac Newton wrote, "If I have seen farther than [others] it is because I stood on the shoulders of giants."

Crash Landing

Tangled in metal suddenly alien and heavy,
　　He rushes out of the sky.
There is no chart for this.　Words are no good now -
　　Only the hand, the eye,

Only the brain (half terror and half cunning)
　　Only the dying mind
That will live again if the rudder be responsive
　　If the aileron be kind,

If earth he loves will rise and take him gently.
　　He sees white faces stare
Safely on the lovely land, firm and immortal,
　　And he in the rocking air.

His fingers grow lost in a world of levers and dials -
　　He has forgotten their names -
There is a scream of iron.　He bounces... drops...
　　　And twists and skids forever and tilts... and stops...
　　There are no flames.

And he is again a part of the hills and the flowers,
　　A part of the fields again;
And laughing, he clambers out of the cockpit, eager
　　To grip the hands of men.

(Following my F2G belly landing, 1946)

151

The Goodyear F2G "Super Corsair" was a natural choice for air racing in the Unlimited Class because of its proven structural integrity and the huge Pratt and Whitney R-4360 engine. The Wasp Major was the largest piston engine used in production aircraft and, because they had been used in B-36s, B-50s, C-124s and KC-97s, many were available on the postwar market.

To review, the R-4360 radial engine looked like a corncob with four staggered rows of seven cylinders per row. Each of the twenty-eight cylinders displaced 155.8 cubic inches. To put this into sharp focus for the average private pilot, each cylinder had over three-fourths the displacement of an entire Continental 0-200 engine! The unmodified Wasp Major engine was rated at 3,500 hp (with water injection) at 2,700 rpm. It was awesome, raw power.

Although races were held in Cleveland in 1946, no F2Gs were yet available. (Cook Cleland finished sixth in a Goodyear FG-lD.)

The 1947 National (Cleveland) Air Race was among the most spectacular air races ever witnessed: the wildest, fastest and, sadly, among the most destructive. Although twelve others qualified, my friend Skip Ziegler (a self-designated "alternate starter") took off when Ron Puckett could not get the engine of his F2G started. From that moment on, things became more frantic with each lap. By the end of the first lap Jack Hardwick had bellied in his Mustang with a sick engine and Ron Puckett was now in the air. The second lap saw Charles Walling's P-38 return to the field with engine trouble. Paul Penrose dropped out in his P-51 with similar engine problems in the sixth lap.

Then tragedy struck. In the seventh lap, Tony Janazzo flew into the ground at approximately 400 mph in Cook Cleland's F2G, No. 88457-last flown by me on September 28, 1945.

Only one-third into the race and four planes are already out! In lap eleven Woody Edmundson's Merlin engine literally exploded but he survived. Next out on lap fourteen was Skip in the XP-40Q, last of the three experimental "Q planes" I had flown at Curtiss. Fortunately,

when Skip bailed out at low altitude he got away with only a broken leg.

Now in fourth place, even after starting one lap late, Ron Puckett's F2G Wasp Major engine gave up the ghost in the last lap but he landed without incident. I had last flown this plane - No. 14694 - on September 19, 1945.

By remarkable coincidence, three types of planes in which I had done experimental testing were among those in the air races in 1947. In addition to the F2Gs and the XP-40Q, James DeSanto had entered the Curtiss one-of-a-kind YP-60E but was forced to bail out during the qualifying rounds. Now there were two of us in the Caterpillar Club because of tail failures in the P-60s!

After forty-five minutes of competitive no-holds-barred racing - brutal on pilots and their machines - six pilots remained in contention for the trophy. Cook Cleland, in F2G No. 88463 and owner of three of the four Super Corsairs entered, flew on above wrecked and burning airplanes and was six miles in the lead at the checkered flag. Finishing in second place was Dick Becker in the fourth F2G of the race, No. 14693. I had last flown the winning aircraft on January 22, 1946, and Becker's on July 5, 1945.

Unbelievably, four planes were lost, three others disabled... and one pilot was dead.

1947 Thompson Trophy Race
Cleveland, Ohio - 20 laps, 15 mile course
1st place, F2G, # 74, Cook Cleland.......396.131 mph
2nd place, F2G, # 94, Dick Becker........390.133 mph
--- F2G, # 18, Ron Puckett.........DNF lap 19
--- F2G, # 84, Tony Janazzo.....crashed lap 7

I was greatly pleased, not only that "my" F2Gs had taken first and second place, but because the winning aircraft was emblazoned with a checkerboard nose - it seemed to belong there! Also, I think it's quite interesting that, after collecting his purse, Cookie was quoted as saying, "I had to win since I had mortgaged myself to the gills buying and modifying three F2Gs." For all that was at stake, just how much did the pilots win? First place - $16,000 plus $2,000 (the Allegheny-Ludlum

Award) and $100 for each fastest lap. Second place - $8,000. Third place - $4,500. And Ron Puckett ended up with a $500 consolation prize! In view of the astronomical salaries paid to athletes these days, readers must find it difficult to believe just how little these skilled and daring pilots actually earned!

1948 Thompson Trophy Race
Cleveland, Ohio - 20 laps, 15 miles course
-- F2G, # 74, Dick Becker...........DNF lap 3
-- F2G, # 94, Cook Cleland..........DNF lap 5
(On laps three and four, Cookie bested 410 mph!)

1948 Tinnerman Trophy Race
(The engine size was restricted to 2,850 cubic inches to keep the big Wasp Major Corsairs out!)

1949 Thompson Trophy Race
Cleveland, Ohio - 15 laps, 15 mile course
1st place, F2G, # 94, Cook Cleland.......397.071 mph
2nd place, F2G, # 18, Ron Puckett........393.527 mph
3rd place, F2G, # 57, Ben McKillen.......387.589 mph
------ F2G, # 74, Dick Becker................DNS

1949 Tinnerman Trophy Race
Cleveland, Ohio - 7 laps, 15 mile course
1st place, F2G, # 57, Ben McKillen.......386.069 mph

1949 Sohio Trophy Race
Cleveland, Ohio - 7 laps, 15 mile course
2nd place, F2G, # 18, Ron Puckett........384.866 mph

As the checkered flag went down, pilots and fans alike had absolutely no inkling that an era was ending with the conclusion of the 1949 air races. The public outcry created by Bill Odom's crash, in which he and two others were unfortunately killed, resulted in the withdrawal of corporate sponsorship. That, and the onset of the Korean War, combined to cancel the 1950 Cleveland Air Races and they never resumed. Many of the big, beautiful racing planes were literally "left outside to rot."

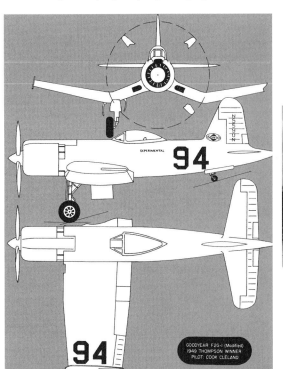

Ib Photograph of same plane mentioned on this page. Note the end plate. (Courtesy of Western Reserve Historical Society)

Ia Schematic of F2G - # 94 (No. 14693) purchased for air racing by Cookie Cleland, showing the "clipped" wings. In 1948, Cleland took eighteen inches off the wing tips, and the following year he whacked off another twenty-nine inches. Because this resulted in a greatly reduced roll rate he placed "plates" into the open ends, the first time that this had ever been done. (D. Armstrong collection)

APPENDIX I – THE F2G IN POSTWAR AIR RACING
1947 - 1993

Although racing resumed over Bill Stead's Reno ranch in 1964, the unmistakable roar of the Wasp Major rounding a pylon would not be heard again for thirty-three years. By that time, however, no original F2Gs were available for competition.

The amazing story of how another "F2G" got back into air racing is related in Chino's (California) Planes of Fame Museum brochure. In 1982 Ed Maloney, with his crew of Fighter Rebuilders, created a "new" airplane that, as closely as possible, resembled the F2Gs of the Thompson, Tinnerman and Sohio races. The crew started with the empty fuselage of an F4U-l, added a wing from an F4U-4, another from an F4U-5 and clipped just under four feet from each tip. The propeller was off a Douglas A-1H Skyraider, the cowling from a Douglas A-26 Invader and the spinner lifted from a Vickers Varsity. The Wasp Major came out of a Douglas C-124 Globemaster and the oil coolers were taken from a Grumman S-2 Tracker. This conglomeration was named, appropriately (although not technically correct, of course), "The Super Corsair." That thousands of hours of volunteer labor accomplished the near-impossible is dramatically demonstrated in how well it still performs, upholding the reputation of the "real thing."

In 1982 at Reno, Nevada
8 laps - 9.187 mile course
4th place, F2G, # 1, Steve Hinton.........362.50 mph

In 1984 at Reno, Nevada
8 laps - 9.187 mile course
3rd place, F2G, # 1, Steve Hinton........413.686 mph

In 1985 at Reno, Nevada
8 laps - 9.222 mile course
1st place, F2G, # 1, Steve Hinton........438.186 mph

In 1987 at Reno, Nevada
8 laps - 9.222 mile course
4th place, F2G, # 1, John Maloney........416.905 mph

In 1988 at Reno, Nevada
8 laps - 9.171 mile course
6th place, F2G, # 1, John Maloney........368.126 mph

In 1989 at Reno, Nevada
8 laps - 9.171 mile course
3rd place, F2G, # 1, John Maloney........406.265 mph

In 1990 at Sherman, Texas
8 laps - 8.507 mile course
4th place, F2G, # 1, John Maloney........376.479 mph

In 1990 at Denver, Colorado
8 laps - 8.82 mile course
3rd place, F2G, # 1, John Maloney........398.332 mph

In 1990 at Reno, Nevada
8 laps - 9.128 mile course
5th place, F2G, # 1, John Maloney........410.786 mph

In 1991 at Reno, Nevada
8 laps - 9.128 mile course
7th place, F2G, # 1, John Maloney........406.420 mph

In 1992 at Reno, Nevada
8 laps - 9.128 mile course
6th place, F2G, # 1, Kevin Eldridge......420.800 mph

In 1993 at Reno, Nevada
8 laps - 9.128 mile course
5th place, F2G, # 1, Kevin Eldridge......418.656 mph

Special note: the majority of the information (from 1946 through 1949) in this Appendix was researched and compiled in Cleveland by my very close friend and associate, Henry "Hank" Caruso, of Middleburg Heights, Ohio.

APPENDIX II – LIST OF AIRCRAFT I HAVE FLOWN

(* - see photo)

Chapter 1

* 1) Travel Air 2000, "Old Elephant Ears"; tandem, two-cockpit (open), biplane; Curtiss OX-5, 90-hp liquid-cooled.

Chapter 2

2) Fleet, originally known as Consolidated Husky Junior; tandem, two-cockpit (open), biplane; Warner Scarab, 110-hp radial or Kinner, 125-hp radial.

3) Stearman C3B; tandem, two-cockpit (open), biplane; Wright J-5, 225-hp radial or Pratt and Whitney Wasp Junior, 330-hp radial.

* 4) Bellanca Pacemaker; six-seat, cabin, high-wing, monoplane; Wright Whirlwind, 300-hp radial.

* 5) Waco YKS-7; five-seat, cabin, biplane; Jacobs L-4, 225-hp radial.

* 6) Curtiss JN-4, "Jenny," known in Canada as the Canuck; tandem, two-cockpit (open), biplane; Curtiss OX-5, 90-hp liquid-cooled. The only American mass-produced aircraft to have played a major role during WW I. Ninety-five percent of all American and Canadian aircrews were trained in the Jenny.

* 7) Swallow, a refined Laird Swallow; tandem, two-cockpit (open), three-seat, biplane; Curtiss OX-5, 90-hp liquid-cooled.

Chapter 3

8) Piper Cub, "The Model T of Aviation"; tandem, two-seat, cabin, high-wing, monoplane; Continental A-40-4, 40-hp opposed. Successor to the Taylor E-2, used extensively in WW II as a primary trainer.

* 9) Monocoupe; side-by-side, two-seat, cabin, high-wing, monoplane; Velie, 55-hp radial.

* 10) Curtiss Robin; three-seat, cabin, high-wing, monoplane; Curtiss OX-5, 90-hp liquid-cooled.

11) Curtiss Robin; three-or four-seat, cabin, high-wing, monoplane; Curtiss Challenger, 180-hp radial.

* 12) Curtiss Junior; tandem, two-cockpit (open), parasol-wing, monoplane; Szekely, pusher, 45-hp radial.

* 13) Ford Trimotor, "The Tin Goose"; multi-seat, cabin, high-wing, monoplane; two Wright J6, 300-hp (wings)/one Pratt and Whitney Wasp, 450-hp (nose) radials. Fuselage was corrugated metal.

* 14) Great Lakes 2T-1A; sport trainer; tandem, two-cockpit (open), biplane; Cirrus, 85-hp in-line.

* 15) Spartan C-3; tandem, two-cockpit (open), biplane; Wright J6-5, 175-hp radial.

Chapter 4

16) Luscombe Silvaire; side-by-side, two-seat, cabin, high-wing, monoplane, Edo floats; Continental A-65-8, 65-hp opposed.

* 17) Fairchild 24; four-seat, cabin, high-wing, monoplane, Edo floats; Warner Super Scarab, 145-hp radial.

18) Stearman - Chapter 2, Number 3.

Chapter 5

* 19) Fleet - Chapter 2, Number 2. Known in Canada as the Finch; most Canadian versions were equipped with canopies.

* 20) North American BT-9, known in Canada as the Yale; basic trainer; tandem, two-seat, canopied, low-wing, monoplane, nonretractable gear; Wright Whirlwind, 450-hp radial.

* 21) North American AT-6, "Texan," known in Canada as the Harvard; advanced trainer; tandem, two-seat, canopied, low-wing, monoplane, retractable gear; Pratt and Whitney Wasp, R-1340, 550-hp radial.

* 22) Avro Anson, "Faithful Annie"; navigational trainer; multi-seated, low-wing, monoplane, retractable gear; two Armstrong Siddeley Cheetah, 325-hp radials.

* 23) Lockheed 10, Electra; ten-seat or cargo, low-wing, monoplane, retractable gear; two Pratt and Whitney Wasp Junior, R-985, 450-hp radials. Used by early airlines.

24) Lockheed 12, Electra Junior; smaller and faster version of the Lockheed 10, six-seat or cargo.

* 25) Lockheed 212; a modified Lockheed 12. Ordered by the Netherlands with both turret and forward-firing guns.

* 26) Boeing 247; civil transport; ten-seat, low-wing, monoplane, retractable gear but no flaps; two Pratt and Whitney Wasp, 550-hp radials.

* 27) Noorduyn Norseman; eight-seat or freight, high-wing, monoplane, wheels/floats/skis; Pratt and Whitney Wasp, R-1340-AN-1, 550-hp radial. Most famous "bush plane" in Canada and Alaska.

* 28) DeHavilland Moth - Gipsy; basic trainer; tandem, two-seat, some with canopies, biplane; Gipsy I, 100-hp in-line. - Tiger; same as Gipsy; Gipsy Major, 130-hp in-line.

* 29) Northrop A-17A, known in Canada as the Nomad; tandem, two-seat, canopied, low-wing, monoplane, retractable gear; Pratt and Whitney (twin-row) Wasp, R-1535, 750-hp radial. Designed as an attack/dive bomber but used in Canada primarily for target towing.

* 30) Supermarine Stranraer, "Stranny"; flying boat, long-range coastal patrol; crew of seven, biplane; two Bristol Pegasus X, 1,060-hp radials.

* 31) Consolidated PBY, Catalina, known in Canada as the Canso; flying boat; two Pratt and Whitney, R-1830, 1,200-hp radials.

* 32) Bolingbroke IV (Bristol Blenheim manufactured by Fairchild of Canada); two Bristol Mercury VIII, 920-hp radials. Experimental, the only Bolingbroke ever fitted with floats.

* 33) Grumman FF-1, known in Canada as the Goblin; tandem, two-seat, canopied, biplane, retractable gear; Wright, R-1820, 750-hp radial. Built by Canadian Car and Foundry.

Chapter 6

34) Avro Anson - Chapter 5, Number 22.

* 35) Blackburn B-6 Shark; carrier-born torpedo bomber; biplane, nonretractable gear; Armstrong Siddeley Tiger, 700-hp radial. Built by Boeing Aircraft of Canada.

* 36) Fairey Swordfish, "Stringbag"; early torpedo bomber; biplane, nonretractable gear; Bristol Pegasus, 690-hp radial.

* 37) Northrop Delta; transport; nine-seat, low-wing, monoplane, nonretractable gear; Wright Cyclone, SR-1820-73, 690-hp radial. Built by Canadian Vickers.

* 38) Handley Page Hampden, "Flying Panhandle," "Tadpole"; light bomber; monoplane; two Bristol Pegasus XVII, 980-hp radials.

* 39) Douglas DB-18, Bolo, known in Canada as the Digby; bomber; low-wing, monoplane; two Wright R-1820-53, 1,000-hp radials. Adaptation of the Douglas DC-3.

* 40) Hawker Hurricane; fighter; single-seat, low-wing, monoplane; Rolls-Royce Merlin, 1,185-hp V-in-line.

* 41) Supermarine Spitfire; fighter; single-seat, low-wing, monoplane; wide range of single Rolls-Royce Merlin, 1,030- to 1,185-hp V-in-lines. Probably the most famous Allied fighter of WW II. Earlier models easily recognized by their elliptical wing. Evolved from the early Supermarine racer on floats.

* 42) Lockheed 14, Super Electra, known in Canada as the Hudson; bomber/transport; two Wright GR-1829, 1,000-hp radials. Originally built for the British as a military conversion.

43) DeHavilland Tiger Moth - Chapter 5, Number 28.

44) Noorduyn Norseman - Chapter 5, Number 27.

* 45) Fairey Battle; target towing; three-seat, low-wing, monoplane; Rolls-Royce Merlin, 1,030-hp V-in-line. Best remembered as the first RAF aircraft to shoot down a German aircraft early in WW II.

46) Cessna AT-17 Bobcat, "Bamboo Bomber," known in Canada as the Crane; trainer; cabin, low-wing, monoplane, wheels/skis; two Jacobs R-775-9, 245-hp radials.

* 47) Airspeed Oxford, "Ox-box"; advanced trainer; low-wing, monoplane, wheels/skis; two Armstrong Siddeley Cheetah, 355-hp radials or Pratt and Whitney Wasp, 450-hp radials.

* 48) Bristol Blenheim (Bolingbroke), "Boley"; wheels/skis; two Bristol Mercury, 1,000-hp radials. This series originated with the design of the 1935 commercial Bristol, Type 142. Initial tests revealed it to already be 50-mph faster than Britain's newest fighter. The versatile aircraft saw service as a light bomber, as the testbed for pioneering British airborne radar and remained fully operational until the end of 1943. Over 6,000 were produced.

* 49) Westland Lysander, "Lizzie"; observation/ liaison; tandem seating, high-wing, monoplane, wheels/skis; Bristol Perseus XII, 905-hp radial. Short takeoff/landing capabilities. Was also used for covert operations.

* 50) Fleet Fort; trainer; tandem, two-seat, canopied, low-wing, monoplane, nonretractable gear; Jacobs L-6MB, 285-hp radial. Rear seat was elevated for excellent visibility. Only ninety were built.

* 51) Fleet Fawn - Chapter 2, Number 2. Also known as the Civet; Armstrong Siddeley Civet, 165-hp radial.

52) Douglas DC-3, "Gooney Bird" (known in the U.S. military as the C-47/R4D); transport; twenty-one to twenty-eight seat/cargo; wide range of twin Wright Cyclones or Pratt and Whitney Twin Wasps, 1,000- to 1,200-hp radials. General Eisenhower considered the C-47 one of the most significant weapons of WW II. The surplus planes formed the backbone of most postwar airline fleets.

* 53) Curtiss P-40 Warhawk, known in RAF and Flying Tigers as the Tomahawk; fighter; single-seat, low-wing, monoplane; Allison V-1710-19, 1,160-hp V-in-line. Famous for the "shark tooth" paint job on the nose. P-40Ds and P-40Es were improved models known as Kittyhawks with the RAF, RCAF and the Soviet Union.

* 54) DeHavilland Mosquito, "Wooden Wonder"; photo reconnaissance/bomber; two Rolls-Royce Merlin 76, 1,710-hp V-in-lines.

* 55) Stinson 105; trainer; cabin, high-wing, monoplane; Continental, 75-hp opposed. Classified as "non-spinnable."

Chapter 7

56) Curtiss P-40, Models F, K, M and S; see Chapter 6, Number 53. These were succeeding models of the P-40 utilizing different engines (Allison or Merlin), armament and mechanical changes to increase proficiency.

57) Curtiss XP-40N; same basic plane as Chapter 6, Number 53, with revised seat, bomb racks, fuel tanks and wheels; Allison V-1710-81, 1,200-hp V-in-line.

* 58) Curtiss XP-40Q; same basic plane as Chapter 6, Number 53, with the addition of a bubble canopy. When the wings were later clipped, the speed increased to 422 mph at 20,500 feet, making it the fastest of the P-40s.

59) Republic P-47, Thunderbolt, "Jug"; fighter/bomber; Pratt and Whitney R-2800-21, 2,000-hp radial. Many built under contract by Curtiss.

60) Bell P-39, Airacobra; fighter; tricycle gear; Allison V-1710-85, 1,200-hp V-in-line. The engine was behind and below the pilot. More than half the production of P-39s went to Russia to act as close-support planes. The second most successful Soviet Ace of WWII, Alexander Pokryskin, chalked up twenty of his fifty-nine kills in a P-39.

* 61) Curtiss C-46, Commando; troop carrier/cargo; two Pratt and Whitney R-2800-51, 2,000-hp radials. Several hundred survived the war and served in a commercial capacity for many years.

Chapter 8

62) Curtiss XP-60, all models. Detailed descriptions can be found in the text.

63) Chance-Vought F4U-1, Corsair; fighter; inverted gull-wing; Pratt and Whitney R-2800, 2,000-hp radial.

64) Grumman TBF, Avenger; torpedo bomber; crew of three; Wright R-2600-8, 1,700-hp radial. The designation TBM indicated those built by Eastern Aircraft Division of General Motors.

65) Grumman F4F, Wildcat; fighter; Pratt and Whitney R-1830-86, 1,200-hp radial.

66) Grumman F6F, Hellcat; fighter; Pratt and Whitney R-2800-10W, 2,000-hp radial. Along with the Corsair, one of the most significant Navy fighters, achieving many major victories and producing many Aces.

* 67) Martin B-26, Marauder, "Widow Maker"; medium bomber; two Pratt and Whitney R-2800-5, 1,850-hp radials.

68) Vultee BT-13, Valiant; basic trainer; tandem, two-seat, low-wing, monoplane, nonretractable gear; Pratt and Whitney R-985, 450-hp radial.

Chapter 9

69) Fairchild PT-19; primary trainer; tandem, two-seat, usually open-cockpit, low-wing, monoplane; Ranger L-440-1, 175-hp in-line.

70) Fairchild PT-23; same as Number 69; Continental R-670, 220-hp radial.

71) Fairchild PT-26, known as the Cornell; same as Number 69; Ranger L-440-7, 200-hp in-line. This plane was adopted by the RCAF as their primary trainer.

In addition to being built by Fairchild, Numbers 69, 70 and 71 were built by various other manufacturers. Some Fairchilds were designated as AT-19s and should not be confused with the British designation of AT-19 given to the Stinson SR Reliant.

72) Stinson SR Reliant; four or five-seat, high-wing, monoplane; Lycoming R-680-13, 290-hp radial.

73) Stinson AT-19; navigation/communication; three-seat, high-wing, monoplane; Lycoming R-680-13, 290-hp radial. Manufactured for the Royal Navy under lend-lease; a modification of the SR Reliant.

74) Stinson L-5, Sentinel; communication/short-range liaison; tandem, two-seat, high-wing, monoplane; Lycoming O-435-1, 190-hp opposed. General George Patton chose this plane for his personal use.

75) Aeronca L-3B, "Grasshopper"; trainer; tandem, two-seat, high-wing, monoplane; Continental O-170-3, 75-hp opposed. Also used as a liaison and observation aircraft.

* 76) Curtiss SB2C-1, Helldiver; dive bomber; tandem, two-seat; Wright R-2600-8, 1,700-hp radial.

77) Culver LCA; side-by-side, two-seat, cabin, low-wing, monoplane, retractable gear; Continental O-170, 75-hp opposed.

* 78) Meyers OTW 160; trainer; tandem, two-seat, open-cockpit, biplane; Kinner R-56, 160-hp radial.

79) Waco UPF-7; two-cockpit, biplane; Continental, 225-hp radial.

* 80) Funk 65; side-by-side, two-seat, cabin, high-wing, monoplane; Lycoming, 75-hp opposed.

81) Culver YPQ-14A; pilot-ferryable/radio-controlled target-drone; single-seat, low-wing, monoplane; Franklin, 80-hp opposed.

82) Aeronca Chief; side-by-side, two-seat, cabin, high-wing, monoplane; Continental, 65-hp opposed.

83) Piper J-5, Cruiser; three-seat, cabin, high-wing, monoplane; Continental A-75-8, 75-hp opposed.

* 84) Driggs 3-95, Skylark; tandem, two-seat, open-cockpit, biplane; Cirrus Hi-Drive, 95-hp in-line. Only twenty were built.

85) General G1-80, Skyfarer; side-by-side, two-seat, cabin, high-wing, monoplane, tricycle gear; Continental, 75-hp opposed. Twin fins with no rudders, placarded by the CAA as spin-proof.

⅃ 86) Howard DGA-15A, "Damn Good Airplane" (known in the U.S. military as the GH-1/NH-1, Nightingale); four-or five-seat, cabin, high-wing, monoplane; Pratt and Whitney Wasp Junior, 450-hp radial. The DGA nickname is currently being used by Doug and Dave Shillen, Texas, fabricators of custom firearms and components, to describe their excellent - Damn Good Actions - bolt-action design. They custom-built a 7mm Rem. Magnum rifle for me, with which I've hunted for nearly ten years. Maybe they knew fellow-Texan, Benny Howard?

87) Beech 18, Twin Beech, known in Canada as the JRB Expeditor; crew of two, plus six passengers/cargo; low-wing, monoplane, retractable gear; two Wright R-760, 320-hp radials.

88) Naval Aircraft Factory N3N-3, "Yellow Peril"; trainer; tandem, two-seat, open-cockpit, biplane; Wright R-760-2, 235-hp radial.

Chapter 10

* 89) Douglas A-20, when converted to night fighter known as the Havoc, known in Canada as the Boston; bomber - Models C and G, two Wright R-2600-11, 1,600-hp radials - Model H, two Wright R-2600-29, 1,700-hp radials.

* 90) Douglas SBD/A-24, Dauntless, "Slow But Deadly," "The Clunk"; dive bomber/scout - SBD-3; Wright R-1820-52, 1,000-hp radial - SBD-5; Wright R-1820-60, 1,200-hp radial.

* 91) Douglas XBTD-2; torpedo bomber; single-seat, inverted gull-wing; mixed propulsion: Wright R-3350-14, 2,300-hp radial (nose); Westinghouse 1,000 s.t., jet (tail).

* 92) Douglas BTD-1; torpedo bomber; single-seat, inverted gull-wing; Wright R-3350-14, 2,300-hp radial.

* 93) Douglas DC-4/C-54, Skymaster; civilian/ military transport; four Pratt and Whitney Twin Wasp, 1,100-to 1,450-hp radials.

* 94) Douglas XSB2D-1; bomber; two-seat, laminar-flow, inverted gull-wing; Wright R-3350-14, 2,300-hp radial.

95) Bell P-63, Kingcobra; fighter/bomber; tricycle gear; Allison V-1710-93, 1,325-hp V-in-line. "Big brother" of the P-39 - Chapter 7, Number 60. The engine was behind and below the pilot. Most of those produced were delivered to Russia under lend-lease.

96) Grumman F6F, Hellcat - Chapter 8, Number 66.

* 97) North American B-25, Mitchell; bomber; shoulder-high wing (passing above the bomb bay), tricycle landing gear; two Wright Cyclone R-2600-9, 1,350-hp radials. Used for the famous "Doolittle raid" on Japan.

* 98) Douglas A-26/B-26, Invader; bomber; two Pratt and Whitney R-2800-27, 2,000-hp radials.

* 99) Lockheed P-38, Lightning, "Forked-tail Devil"; fighter/escort/bomber; tricycle gear, twin-boom; two Allison V-1710, 1,475-hp V-in-lines.

Chapter 11

100) Goodyear FG-1, Corsair; fighter; single-seat, inverted gull-wing; Pratt and Whitney R-2800, 2,000-hp radial. Same aircraft as the Chance-Vought F4U-1 - Chapter 8, Number 63.

* 101) Goodyear XF2G-1, Super Corsair; fighter; single-seat, bubble canopy, inverted gull-wing; Pratt and Whitney R-4360 Wasp Major, 3,500-hp radial. Land-based version with manually folding wings.

102) Brewster SB2A, "Buccaneer," also known as the "Bermuda"; scout bomber; mid-wing, monoplane, dive-flaps; Wright R-2600, 1,700-hp radial.

103) Supermarine Spitfire - Chapter 6, Number 41. When modified for carrier use known as the Seafire.

* 104) Fairey Firefly; fighter; Rolls-Royce Griffon, 1,990-hp V-in-line.

105) DeHavilland Mosquito - Chapter 6, Number 54.

* 106) Mitsubishi A6M, Zeke/Zero; Japanese fighter/bomber; Nakajima Sakae 21, 1,330-hp radial.

107) North American P-51, Mustang; fighter; Packard V-1650-3, 1,520-hp V-in-line.

* 108) Grumman F7F, Tigercat; fighter/bomber; two Pratt and Whitney R-2800, 2,100-hp radials.

* 109) Bell P-59, Airacomet; fighter; General Electric J-31-GE-3, 2,000 s.t., jet. First American-designed and built turbojet fighter.

110) Bell P-63 - Chapter 10, Number 95.

111) Lockheed P-38 - Chapter 10, Number 99.

Chapter 12

112) Goodyear XF2G-2; see Chapter 11, Number 101. Carrier version with hydraulically folding wings and arresting gear.

113) Goodyear FG-1 - Chapter 11, Number 100.

114) Beech 18 - Chapter 9, Number 87.

115) Martin B-26, Marauder - Chapter 8, Number 67.

116) Chance-Vought F4U-4; same basic aircraft as Chapter 8, Number 63; four-bladed propeller, redesigned cockpit and chin scoop.

117) Curtiss SB2C-3 - Chapter 9, Number 76. Wright R-2600-20, 1,900-hp radial.

* 118) Goodyear GA-2, Duck; amphibian; three-seat, high-wing, monoplane; Franklin, pusher, 145-hp opposed.

119) Cessna AT-17 (UC-78 - Twin) - Chapter 6, Number 46.

120) North American P-51, Mustang - Chapter 11, Number 107.

* 121) Lockheed P-80, Shooting Star; fighter; two Allison J33-A-9, 3,850 s.t., jets.

* 122) Messerschmitt Bf 109; German fighter; Daimler-Benz, 1,475-hp in-line.

* 123) Focke-Wulf Fw 190; German fighter; BMW 801C, 1,600-hp radial. Looked amazingly like a Curtiss P-36, Hawk 75.

124) Lockheed Ventura; medium bomber/transport; two Pratt and Whitney R-2800, 1,850-hp radials. A military version of the Lodestar.

Chapter 13

125) Meyers OTW 160 - Chapter 9, Number 78.

126) Stearman PT-17/PT-13, "Kaydet," "Yellow Peril"; primary trainer; tandem, two-seat, open-cockpit, biplane; Continental R-670-5, 220-hp radial. This was the military version of the venerable Stearman (Boeing) trainer. I wonder just how many WW II pilots learned to fly in one of these?

127) Piper Tri-Pacer; four-seat, cabin, high-wing, monoplane, tricycle gear; Lycoming, 125-hp opposed.

Chapter 14

* 128) Grumman F9F-2 Panther; fighter; Pratt and Whitney J42-P-8, 5,750 s.t., jet. Test aircraft No. 123057 was equipped with experimental magnesium outer-wing panels.

Chapter 15

129) Cessna 180, Skywagon; four-seat, cabin, high-wing, monoplane, wheels/floats; Continental 0-470-U, 230-hp opposed.

130) Piper PA-12, Super Cruiser; three-seat, cabin, high-wing, monoplane, wheels/floats; Lycoming, 100-hp opposed.

* 131) Maule M-4, Jetasen (name coined from "Jet Ascent"); four-seat, cabin, high-wing, monoplane; Continental 0-300-A, 145-hp opposed.

Mr. B. D. Maule and his family deserve special mention here. It has been said of them, "They have become something of a symbol for entrepreneurial tenacity and adherence to the old engineering axiom - KISS: Keep It Simple, Stupid." Maule is probably the only family-owned U.S. aircraft manufacturer who has continuously built single-engine aircraft since the early 1960s. The versatile Maule aircraft, certificated and available on wheels/floats/skis, are truly easy-to-maintain workhorses and inexpensive by today's standards. Their short takeoff/landing capabilities are legendary. Many readers will enjoy the video tape, *Maule - the Belford D. Maule Story* (available from Maule Air, Inc., Rt. 5, Box 319, Moultrie GA 31768). It will reinforce your faith in family enterprise and in the American Dream!

132) Stinson, "Station Wagon"; four-place, cabin, high-wing, monoplane; Franklin, 150-hp opposed.

133) Hummingbird; ultralight; two chain-saw engines.

Chapter 16

134) Cessna 150; two-seat, cabin, high-wing, monoplane; Continental 0-200-A, 100-hp opposed.

135) Cessna 152, Aerobat; same basic aircraft as Number 134, with aerobatic capability; Lycoming 0-235, 110-hp opposed.

136) Cessna 170; four-seat, cabin, high-wing, monoplane; Continental C-145-2, 145-hp opposed.

137) Cessna 172; same basic aircraft as Number 136, with tricycle gear.

138) Cessna 177, Cardinal; four-seat, cabin, high-wing (cantilever), monoplane; Lycoming, 150- to 180-hp opposed.

139) Cessna 180 - Chapter 15, Number 129.

140) Cessna 182, Skylane; same basic aircraft as Number 139, with tricycle gear.

141) Cessna 310; five or six-seat; low-wing, monoplane; two Continental IO-520-M, 285-hp opposed.

* 142) Cessna 336/337, Skymaster; six-seat, cabin, high-wing, monoplane; two Continental IO-360-A, 210-hp opposed, in pusher/tractor (push/pull) position.

143) Piper Apache; four-seat, cabin, low-wing, monoplane; two Lycoming 0-320, 150-hp opposed.

144) Piper Aztec; six-seat, cabin, low-wing, monoplane; two Lycoming IO-540-C4B5, 250-hp opposed.

145) Piper Cherokee Six; six-seat, cabin, low-wing, monoplane; Lycoming 0-540-E, 260-hp opposed.

146) Piper Comanche; four-seat, cabin, low-wing, monoplane; Lycoming 0-360-A1A, 180-hp opposed.

* 147) Britten-Norman BN-2, Islander; up to ten-seat, cabin, high-wing, monoplane; two Lycoming 0-540, 260-hp opposed.

148) Douglas DC-3 - Chapter 6, Number 52.

149) Fournier Glider; sailplane; single-seat; powered by a Volkswagen engine.

150) Beech 18 - Chapter 9, Number 87.

SUPPLEMENTAL PLANE LIST

(The following planes are not included in the text.)

My insatiable curiosity about an aircraft I'd never seen or flown before (an inherent characteristic first encouraged by my father, and my "giants," and later fostered by Dr. William F. Gerhardt), led me to try, whenever possible, to finagle at least one familiarization flight in the aircraft. Some of those planes are unusual - or old - enough that I felt they should be mentioned.

* 151) Aeronca C-3, "Flying Bathtub"; two-seat, high-wing, monoplane; Aeronca E-113C, two-cylinder, 40-hp opposed.

152) Alexander OX-5 Eaglerock (A-2); three-place, open-cockpit, biplane; Curtiss (surplus) OX-5, 90-hp liquid-cooled. One of the first - if not the first - airplanes made available to the public on time-payments, as early as 1928-1929.

153) American Eagle, A-129, "Ant-eater"; three-place, open-cockpit, biplane; Kinner K-5, 90-hp radial. Really odd looking, but nice to fly.

* 154) Arrow F (Sport); single-seat, open-cockpit, monoplane; converted Ford engine. Designed to use cheap, mass-produced motorcar engines. In my opinion, the high weight-to-power ratio made this "female dog" miserable to fly.

155) Beech 17, Staggerwing; four-passenger, cabin, biplane; Wright, 420- to 450-hp radial.

156) Beechcraft, Bonanza; four-place, cabin, low-wing, monoplane, V-tail; Continental, 285-hp opposed. A very popular aircraft that, for some odd reason, seemed just ordinary to me.

157) Berliner, CM-4, "Parasol"; three-place, open-cockpit, high-wing (parasol), monoplane; Curtiss OX-5, 90-hp liquid-cooled. I liked this airplane!

158) Bristol Beaufighter; night interceptor/long-range fighter/torpedo carrier, "Torbeaus"/anti-shipping striker; two Bristol Hercules XVII, 1,725-hp radials. It is highly probable that the rotating radar antenna and AI system that I flight tested at MIT was later incorporated into some of these aircraft. A large number of the Beaufighters were manufactured in Australia, with the combined production exceeding 5,500.

159) Cessna 188, AGwagon; agricultural; single-seat, canopy, low-wing, monoplane; Continental O-470-R, 230-hp opposed.

160) Curtiss XP-62; fighter; single-seat; Wright, 2,300-hp radial. The only prototype built, it was huge and looked remarkably similar to the SB2C dive bomber. Like the XP-60C before it (on which I also had made engineering/evaluation tests) this plane had con-tra-rotating propellers. The XP-62 was the last pro-peller-driven fighter plane built by Curtiss and, sadly, performed in a manner that could, at best, be described as marginal.

161) Erco Ercoupe 415; two-seat, cabin, low-wing, monoplane, twin fins and rudders; Continental, 65-hp opposed. FAA certificated "unspinnable." I flew both two and three control models, much preferring the latter.

162) Fisher XP-75; fighter. Not unlike the General Motors "psychobilly" Cadillac described in "One Piece at a Time" (Wayne Kemp's Country and Western ballad sung by my friend Johnny Cash), this plane was a collection of "spare" parts and designs. It included Corsair (F4U) landing gear; Mustang (P-51) wings, subse-quently replaced with Warhawk (P-40) wings; Dauntless (SBD/A-24) tail; Airacobra (P-39) engine placement (centrally located Allison); and Warhawk (P-40) wind-shield and canopy. Of the few that were built five flew and three crashed, losing two pilots. Designed by Don Berlin (whom I had known at Curtiss) for the Fisher Division of General Motors, his concept of using already available parts looked good on paper. My comment was that it could best be described as a "Turkey buzzard."

163) Grumman AGcat; agricultural; single-seat, biplane; Pratt and Whitney R-985, 450-hp radial.

164) Grumman G-21, "Goose"; amphibian; eight-seat, high-wing, monoplane; two Pratt and Whitney R-985, 450-hp radials.

165) Meyers MAC 125; two-seat, cabin, mono-plane; Continental, 125-hp opposed.

166) Meyers OTW 145 - Chapter 9, Number 78. Warner, 145-hp radial.

167) Mooney, M-20A; four-seat, cabin, low-wing, monoplane, retractable gear; Lycoming O-360-A1; 180-hp opposed.

168) Northrop P-61, "Black Widow"; night fighter; three-place; two Pratt and Whitney, 2,000-hp radials.

169) Parks - P-1; three-place, open-cockpit, biplane; Curtiss OX-5, 90-hp liquid-cooled. - P-2; same basic airplane as P-1; Wright J6-5, 175-hp radial. Built by the students of Parks Air College.

170) Piper P-18, Super Cub; tandem, two-seat, cabin, high-wing, monoplane, floats; Lycoming 0-320, 150-hp opposed.

171) Piper PA-36, Pawnee; agricultural; single-seat, low-wing, monoplane; Continental, 285-hp opposed.

172) Pitts Special; single-seat, sport/aerobatic biplane; Lycoming, 200-hp opposed. A good friend and aerobatic flyer, Eric Huddleston (Florida) was killed in his - the same one that I flew.

173) Porterfield; two-seat, cabin, high-wing, monoplane; Continental, 50-hp opposed.

174) Rearwin Sportster; two-seat, cabin, mono-plane; Warner Scarab, 90-hp radial.

175) Taylorcraft; two-seat, cabin, high-wing, monoplane; Continental, 40-hp opposed. I always thought that this plane would be fun to fly on floats, and for a long time tried to find one.

APPENDIX III – SUGGESTED READING

Allen, Hugh. *Goodyear Aircraft.* Cleveland: Corday, 1947.

Angelucci, Enzo, with Peter Bowers. *The American Fighter.* New York: Orion Books, 1985.

Aymar, Brandt, editor. *Men in the Air.* New York: Crown, 1990.

Berliner, Don. *Unlimited Air Racers.* Osceola, Wisconsin: Motorbooks International Publishers, 1992.

Bowers, Peter M. *Curtiss Aircraft 1907-1947.* London: Putnam, 1979.

-----, and Gordon Swanborough. *United States Navy Aircraft since 1911.* London: Putnam, 1990.

Boyne, Walter J. *The Smithsonian Book of Flight.* Washington, D.C.: Smithsonian Press - New York: Orion Books, 1987.

Caidin, Martin Strasser. *Test Pilots: Riding the Dragon.* New York: Bantam Books, 1992. (Bantam Air & Space Series. Number 21.)

The Champlin Fighter Museum. Mesa, Arizona: Champlin Press, 1991.

Dade, George C., and Frank Strand. *Picture History of Aviation on Long Island, 1908-1938.* New York: Dover Publications, Inc., 1989.

The Epic of Flight. 23 Vols. Melvin B. Zisfein, Dr. Hidemasa Kimura, Charles Harvard Gibbs-Smith, consultants. Alexandria, Virginia: Time-Life Books, 1982-1984.

Francillon, Rene J. *Grumman Aircraft since 1929.* London: Putnam, 1989.

Gunston, Bill, ed. *Chronicle of Aviation.* Liberty, Missouri: JL International Publishing, 1993.

-----, ed. *The Encyclopedia of World Air Power.* New York: Cresent Books, 1980.

Gurney, Gene, ed. *Test Pilots.* New York: Franklin Watts, 1962.

Guyton, Boone T. *This Exciting Air: the Experiences of a Test Pilot.* New York: McGraw-Hill Book Company, 1943.

-----. *Whistling Death: The Test Pilot's Story of the F4U Corsair.* New York: Orion Books, 1990.

Hallion, Richard P. *Test Pilots: The Frontiersmen of Flight.* Washington, D.C.: Smithsonian Institution Press, 1988.

Leary, William M., ed. *Aviation's Golden Age: Portraits from the 1920s and 1930s.* Iowa City, Iowa: University of Iowa Press, 1989.

LeVier, Tony, with John Guenther. *Pilot.* New York: Harper & Row, 1954. (Reprinted - New York: Bantam Books, 1990. Bantam Air & Space Series. Number 7.)

Lindbergh, Charles A. *Autobiography of Values.* New York: Harcourt Brace Jovanovich, 1976.

-----. *The Spirit of St. Louis.* New York: Charles Scribner's Sons, 1953.

-----. *We.* New York: Putman, 1927.

Maule - The Belford D. Maule Story (video). Produced and distributed by Maule Air, Inc., Moultrie, Georgia, 1992.

Milberry, Larry, and Hugh A. Halliday. *The Royal Canadian Air Force at War 1939 - 1945.* Toronto: CANAV Books,1990.

Morlan, Michael. *Kitty Hawk to NASA: A Guide to U.S. Air & Space Museums and Exhibits.* Shawnee, Kansas: BON A TIRER Publishing,1991.

Shaw, Lloyd. *Cowboy Dances.* Macks Creek, Missouri. Lloyd Shaw Foundation, 1994.

-----. *The Round Dance Book.* Caldwell, Idaho: Caxton Printers, Ltd., 1948.

Smith, Gene. "Tinker, Soldier, Airplane Maker - Belford D. Maule's Life..." *Air Progress* (June, 1988), pp. 48 ff.

Thomas, Lowell, with Edward Jablonski. *Doolittle: A Biography.* Garden City: Doubleday & Co., 1976.

Thruelsen, Richard. *The Grumman Story.* New York: Praeger Publishers, 1976.

Tillman, Barrett. *Corsair: The F4U in World War II and Korea.* Annapolis: Naval Institute Press, 1987.

-----. *Dauntless - A Novel of Midway and Guadalcanal.* New York: Bantam Books, 1992.

-----. *The Dauntless Dive Bomber of World War II.* Annapolis: Naval Institute Press, 1976.

-----. *Hellcat: The F6F in World War II,* 2nd edition. Annapolis: Naval Institute Press, 1986.

-----. *Wildcat: The F4F in World War II,* 2nd edition. Annapolis: Naval Institute Press, 1990.

Wagner, Ray. *American Combat Planes,* 3rd edition. Garden City: Doubleday & Co., 1982.

Veronico, Nicholas A., with John M. and Donna Campbell. *F4U Corsair.* Stillwater, Minnesota: Motorbooks International Publishers, 1994.

Wolfe, Tom. *The Right Stuff.* New York: Farrar, Straus & Giroux, 1979.